MW00559753

Praise for
THE ANTI-ABLEIST MANIFESTO

"Tiffany Yu guides readers through a cross-disability exploration of ableism in a warm, easy-to-read style. Her book is a precious gift for new allies and experienced advocates alike."

—**Haben Girma, bestselling author of**
Haben: The Deafblind Woman Who Conquered Harvard Law

"Tiffany Yu's *The Anti-Ableist Manifesto* is a powerful journey, merging personal narratives with collective insights to confront and dismantle ableism. As someone deeply immersed in the study of prejudice, including the often overlooked discrimination faced by people with disabilities, I find that Yu delivers a timely and indispensable guide for our times."

—**Amy Cuddy,** *New York Times*
bestselling author of *Presence*

"It can be difficult to know how to respond to ableism when one encounters it in the wild, but Tiffany Yu's *The Anti-Ableist Manifesto* offers a timely, practical, and generous field guide. It's a clear, comprehensive, and accessible instruction manual for anyone who cares about disability (and, even more crucially, for those who don't)."

—**Andrew Leland, author of the Pulitzer Prize-finalist**
The Country of the Blind

"Tiffany Yu has been a wonderful resource for me over the years and for so many who are looking to understand and end ableism in order to contribute to a more inclusive and equitable world. This book is a must-read!"

—**Amy Purdy,** *New York Times* **bestselling author of**
On My Own Two Feet **and three-time Paralympic medalist**

"Tiffany Yu's *The Anti-Ableist Manifesto* is brilliantly written and very well researched! It provides a much-needed framework for any discussion of ableism and methods for defeating this deeply harmful practice of supremacism. Credibility comes from Yu's lived experience with disability and her powerful way of expressing its harm and how to stop it."

—**John D. Kemp, cofounder of the American Association of People with Disabilities and author of** *Disability Friendly: How to Move from Clueless to Inclusive*

"Tiffany Yu's approach to dismantling ableist structures and advocating for comprehensive accessibility in both personal and professional spaces is a crucial addition to our collective efforts. *The Anti-Ableist Manifesto* does more than just challenge the status quo; it offers a blueprint for genuine allyship. Yu's work is a clarion call to broaden our understanding and embrace the full potential of all individuals. This book is a must-read for anyone committed to building more equitable workplaces and a more just world. Yu has not only provided us with the context and vocabulary to confront ableism but also the inspiration to forge a path forward together. *The Anti-Ableist Manifesto* will serve as a seminal guide for generations to come, propelling us toward a disability-inclusive future."

—**Jennifer Brown, bestselling author of** *How to Be an Inclusive Leader* **and host of the** *Will to Change* **podcast**

"Tiffany Yu just made my life a lot easier with this thorough, yet approachable, guide to disability and ableism. From now on, when someone asks me how to become a better disability ally, I'm simply going to hand them this book. Our world has needed a book like this for a long time."

—**Shane Burcaw, author of** *Laughing at My Nightmare*

"For the first time, we have a comprehensive guide outlining the steps to transform a world entrenched in ableism. Tiffany Yu has given us that gift."

—**Sasha Hamdani, MD, board-certified psychiatrist and author of** *Self-Care for People with ADHD*

"*The Anti-Ableist Manifesto* is a vital resource that will shape how we understand and confront ableism. This book is essential reading for anyone committed to equity, inclusion, and meaningful allyship. I'll be using it as a reference for years to come."

—**Liz Plank, international bestselling author of**
For the Love of Men

"Tiffany Yu has created an essential field guide to help people learn about ableism, how to navigate the ways it permeates everyday life, and what to do about it. *The Anti-Ableist Manifesto* will help those unfamiliar with ableism—and those outraged by it—learn how to combat it. *The Anti-Ableist Manifesto* will be required reading for decades to come."

—**Eric Garcia, author of *We're Not Broken:***
Changing the Autism Conversation

"*The Anti-Ableist Manifesto* is a guide for everyone. Tiffany Yu has a way of mapping out ableism and bias that is digestible and eye-opening. This book will help the disabled community create extraordinary progress!"

—**Ali Stroker, Tony Award-winning actress**
and coauthor of *The Chance to Fly*

"An insightful guide.... Interweaving her own disability experience into the account—a car accident at age nine paralyzed the author's arm and led to a PTSD diagnosis many years later—Yu overviews many different aspects of ableism.... While Yu carefully untangles the ways in which ableism insidiously shapes everything from language and the economy to TV, her most valuable contributions are concrete tips for approaching others' disabilities with awareness and sensitivity, including scripts for asking people if their access needs are being met without demanding they explain their limitations. Readers will find this to be a sensitive and helpful resource."

—***Publishers Weekly***

THE ANTI-ABLEIST MANIFESTO

Smashing Stereotypes,
Forging Change, and Building
a Disability-Inclusive World

TIFFANY YU

hachette
BOOKS

NEW YORK

Hachette Go, an imprint of Hachette Books
Hachette Book Group
1290 Avenue of the Americas
New York, NY 10104
HachetteGo.com
Facebook.com/HachetteGo
Instagram.com/HachetteGo

First Edition: October 2024

Published by Hachette Go, an imprint of Hachette Book Group, Inc. The Hachette Go name and logo are trademarks of the Hachette Book Group. The Hachette Speakers Bureau provides a wide range of authors for speaking events. To find out more, visit HachetteSpeakersBureau.com or email HachetteSpeakers@hbgusa.com.

Hachette Go books may be purchased in bulk for business, educational, or promotional use. For information, please contact your local bookseller or email the Hachette Book Group Special Markets Department at Special .Markets@hbgusa.com.

Print book interior design by Sheryl Kober.

Library of Congress Cataloging-in-Publication Data

Name: Yu, Tiffany, author.
Title: The anti-ableist manifesto: smashing stereotypes, forging change, and building a disability-inclusive world / Tiffany Yu.
Description: First edition. | New York: Hachette Go, [2024] | Includes bibliographical references.
Identifiers: LCCN 2024012575 | ISBN 9780306833663 (hardcover) | ISBN 9780306833670 (trade paperback) | ISBN 9780306833687 (ebook)
Subjects: LCSH: People with disabilities. | Discrimination against people with disabilities. | Sociology of disability.
Classification: LCC HV6158 .Y82 2024 | DDC 305.9/08—dc23/eng/20240516
LC record available at https://lccn.loc.gov/2024012575

ISBNs: 978-0-306-83366-3 (hardcover), 978-0-306-83368-7 (ebook)

Printed in the United States of America

LSC-H

Printing 2, 2024

To nine-year-old Tiffany:
I can't wait for you to see who you become.

To my dad, Stanley (1948–1997):
May your memory live on in these pages and beyond.

CONTENTS

Contents

PART 3 ANTI-ABLEISM AND SOCIETAL CHANGE

THE ANTI-ABLEIST MANIFESTO

INTRODUCTION

L et's start from the beginning.

I'm the youngest daughter of a Taiwanese immigrant and a refugee from the Vietnam War. I was born in Washington, DC, and grew up nearby in Maryland, with short stints in Barbados and Taiwan, both when I was too young to remember.

On November 29, 1997, I was in fourth grade. It was a Sunday, and I was getting ready to go back to school after the Thanksgiving break. I had not only celebrated Thanksgiving with my mom, dad, and three siblings, but my dad's forty-ninth birthday had been the day before, on November 28.

My mom had a business trip to Taiwan planned the next day, so my dad, one of my brothers, my sister, and I piled into our Toyota Camry to see her off to the airport.

When we were on our way home, my dad lost control of the car, which flew across the empty lanes of the highway. The last thing I remember was some greenery on the side of the road. Luckily, no other cars were involved.

When I regained consciousness, I was in a helicopter on my way to Children's National Hospital in Washington, DC. I had broken my femur and tibia in my left leg and had acquired a severe nerve injury in my right arm, known as a traumatic brachial plexus injury (TBPI), a type of paralysis.

My dad passed away as a result of the accident. At nine years old, I was mostly in shock and didn't know how to process everything. No one really offered me guidance, either. I lived at the hospital for three weeks, with a cast that covered almost the entirety of my left leg, and moved about in a manual wheelchair, my right arm limp in a sling.

I spent a long time after his death feeling angry. No one else I knew at the time had lost a parent. My mom also didn't really want me to talk about him, perhaps influenced by her own cultural upbringing and views around death. It would take me almost twenty-five years, on a 2020 trip to climb Mount Kilimanjaro, to remember the gifts that my dad had given me and forgive him. In many ways, I still miss him, and part of the reason why I've dedicated this book to him is so that he's remembered.

On that November day, my body, my family, and my life changed. I describe the events surrounding the car accident now as multiple layers of grief: loss of a loved one, loss of the way my right arm used to be, and loss of childhood innocence.

I call this sort of scenario a disability origin story. It's the story of when our disability happened, whether it was congenital (from birth), an accident, cancer, or something that emerged over the course of our lives.

I'm reminded of a quotation from Brené Brown: "Our stories are not meant for everyone. Hearing them is a privilege, and we should always ask ourselves this before we share: 'Who has earned the right to hear my story?'"[1]

Thing is, we don't owe anyone our disability stories. Some of our disabilities may be a result of traumatic events that we don't want to revisit or relive. As the daughter of Asian immigrants, I internalized that I should not share anything that might seem shameful for fear that it might make my family look bad. Through the lens of this East Asian culture, death in the family, disability, and the car accident were all examples of such things. For twelve years after the accident, it became my shameful secret. I wore long sleeves year-round to "hide" my arm and told everyone my dad was away on a trip.

A lot of the people I grew up with didn't know what had happened to my dad. It sucked to not be able to talk about him. They also assumed that my arm injury was from birth. Two decades later, I was diagnosed with post-traumatic stress disorder (PTSD), a mental health–related disability. I suspect that not talking about the car accident exacerbated my mental health in a way that became PTSD.

So, then, why am I sharing my story when I don't owe it to anyone?

We all have varying levels of comfort around how much we share. Part of why I'm so open about my disability story is that I remember what it felt like not to honor my truth. For twelve years, I felt like I was operating as a shell of myself, keeping track of all of the lies. Now, I want to take control of and reclaim my narrative rather than let others make assumptions. As Emily Ladau says so eloquently, "If we want the world to be accessible to the disability community, then let's make the ideas and the experiences surrounding disability more accessible to the world."[2] But just because I'm open about my disability story doesn't mean that every disabled person is—or that they have to be.

When I was a senior in high school in 2005, I wrote a letter to my guidance counselor titled "It's Time." We were beginning the college application process, and I had begun reflecting on what life after high school might look like. I shared my hopes, dreams, and aspirations for the future. I also wrote about how maybe one day I'd write a book.

That dream stayed in the letter for many years afterward.

There was not only a massive amount of imposter syndrome—me, a writer?— but also the logistics of it all. At the age of nine, I had to learn how to write with my non-dominant hand—not because I wanted to but because I had to. Becoming disabled impacted the way I wrote and the way I typed. And while I initially thought it would diminish my voice on the page, I would later find out that that wasn't the case.

Now, I'm reflecting on my unconventional journey: from the way my literary agent reached out rather than me pitching him to using speech-to-text technology in drafting my proposal. It was all similar to how I've navigated daily life with a paralyzed arm in a two-armed world—different but creative and, most importantly, presented in a way that works for me.

So how did I get here, from twelve years of silence to telling my story on global stages at TED and the World Economic Forum in Davos, across social media, and within the pages of this book?

Accidentally.

I didn't set out to be a disability advocate.

More than a decade after the car accident, I was invited to speak on a student panel about disability as part of a half-day event at Georgetown University called Accessing Difference: New Politics and Pedagogies of Disability. It was October 22, 2009.

I took a seat at the front of a conference room along with two of my fellow classmates. I had never spoken about this topic before, and I felt like my heart was beating out of my chest. I was so nervous. When it came time to introduce myself, through tears, I shared the story of the car accident publicly for the first time.

A few things also happened before October 22, 2009, that led to what felt like a watershed moment for me and my advocacy journey.

When I was a freshman at Georgetown, in 2007, I cocreated a Taiwanese American club with a few classmates. When we first decided to start the club, we were told by another organization, the Chinese Student Alliance, that there wasn't a need for a Taiwanese club. We persevered, and until my junior year, I was part of the leadership team. Cofounding the Taiwanese American club introduced me to pride, culture, and community in a part of my identity that I had thought I had to erase in order to assimilate. As I write, the club is still active. From this experience, I learned what it was like to start a community group. Starting a Taiwanese American club gave me the confidence that it was possible to start a disability club.

I had a summer internship in investment banking at Goldman Sachs after my junior year. Each week, we received performance feedback from a recruiter. A few weeks in, I remember leaving my session feeling a little low because I was having a tough summer and making a lot of small mistakes in tasks. Sending calendar invitations was the bane of my existence, and I couldn't seem to get them right. Those small mistakes were reflected in my feedback. As a perfectionist at the time (though I feel that I am currently in recovery), I was being extra hard on myself. The Goldman recruiter, Jenny, had known me for a few years, since one of the schools she covered was Georgetown. She said, "Tiffany, you deserved your place here. You don't need to have a chip on your shoulder."

I call this a gentle callout. Jenny's comment pushed me to start thinking critically about the ways in which I thought I wasn't operating at my full potential. Because I had internalized society's views and the media portrayal of disabled people that said we could not measure up, I had set the bar too high for myself, wanting to prove them wrong.

In August 2009, at the start of my senior year, now with a full-time offer to return to Goldman, I decided to apply for a Fulbright research fellowship in China, where I had studied abroad. In my research on China, I came across a statement that students there needed to be physically, mentally, and emotionally healthy in order to pursue their education.[3] I was curious about how this requirement would impact the educational outcomes of the students who had become physically disabled during the Sichuan earthquake in 2008. Putting together the proposal for the fellowship was strenuous and required several letters of recommendation. Prior to asking for these letters, to help guide my professors, I shared my personal statement, which included my personal story and connection to disability. One told me that while he knew my topic might be controversial, he thought I was the best person to pursue it, given my personal experience with disability.

Spoiler: I didn't get the fellowship, but the process made me realize that there was value in my experience as a disabled person.

Also in August 2009, I was a resident assistant, and we went through a diversity training exercise called The Big 8, where we were asked to cut slices of a pie based on how important different aspects of our identity were to us. The slices represented race, ethnicity, sexual orientation, gender identity, ability, religion/spirituality, nationality, and socioeconomic status.

Being a woman was a big part of my pie. My Taiwanese identity had become prominent since creating the Taiwanese American club. Being disabled made up almost half of my pie.

I looked over at my neighbor and saw that being non-disabled was the thinnest sliver of his pie. I realized that if you're not disabled or not affected by disability, you don't really think about it. However, I thought about not being able to use my disabled arm on an almost daily basis.

An idea of creating a disability club sparked in me. Today, some of you might recognize me from Diversability, the disability-centered community business with more than eighty thousand members that we've built over the years to elevate disability pride, build disability power, and advance disability leadership. Back in 2009, Diversability started as the first student-run disability club at Georgetown University. Diversability continued as an active club until 2014, and in 2019, a new student club called the Georgetown Disability Alliance would continue this work.

After I graduated, I went on to work at Goldman Sachs, where I was actively involved in the firm's disability employee resource group (ERG). In my final year at the firm, I joined the investment banking campus recruiting team, which helped me understand what companies were thinking about when they recruited talent from underrepresented backgrounds.

After I left Goldman, I joined Bloomberg Television. During my off hours, I cofounded its disability ERG, pitching its creation to Bloomberg's chief diversity officer. At the time, Bloomberg was in the nascent stages of forming its ERGs, and having met the leaders of the Asian American, Native Hawaiian, and Pacific Islander (AANHPI) ERG, I knew there was an opportunity to bring my knowledge of disability communities to the company.

I left after a year to join the media network REVOLT and put my finance hat back on, working directly with REVOLT's chief financial officer as its director of business development. At a Black-owned company, I witnessed that it was possible to build a company that was racially and gender diverse. In 2018, the company was 67 percent Black, Indigenous, People of Color (BIPOC) with over 60 percent women in senior leadership.

While I was at REVOLT, itching to find a way to connect to the disability community, I relaunched and incorporated Diversability. Our earliest supporters were my colleagues at REVOLT. We started by hosting panel events and fireside chats in New York City. Our first event happened in a packed room of over seventy attendees, making me realize that there was a desire to create spaces for disabled people to gather and to build a stage for our voices. We then started hosting events in seven other cities, including Los Angeles, San Francisco, and Chicago. At the start of the pandemic in 2020, with support from Meta's Community Accelerator Program, we made all of our programming virtual and increased our digital footprint and community fourfold. Today, we see ourselves as the mostly virtual disability ERG for the world—one that exists outside a company.

At the same time, I started noticing that friends and people I'd meet in real life or on social media kept asking the same questions.

"How can I be a better ally to disabled people?"

"How can we get disabled employees to self-identify?"

"How can we get disabled employees to join our disability ERG?"

I have never been the biggest fan of disability etiquette trainings. I say this a lot throughout the book: the disability community is not a monolith. But I started having more conversations with friends, doing podcasts, and engaging with corporate partners about where we could begin to talk about disability inclusion and allyship. And I started thinking more about what it would look like to move from a disability-negative culture to a disability-positive one, phrases I have adapted from the sex-positive movement.

In 2020, in the wake of George Floyd's murder, many of us who were non-Black were trying to figure out how to support our Black peers. I was confronted with the ways in which I had upheld white supremacy in my own life. I read *How to Be an Antiracist* by Ibram X. Kendi. My friend Nicole Cardoza started *The Anti-Racism Daily* newsletter, which grew to over 300,000 subscribers in three years. In the years that followed, anti-Asian racism rose due to misinformation about the origins of the COVID-19 pandemic. All of this elevated my consciousness that I needed to do more than *not* be racist. I needed to be *anti*-racist.

As companies made statements about racial equity, I tried to better understand intersectionality in the context of anti-racism. *Intersectionality* is a term coined by Kimberlé Crenshaw to highlight the ways in which different aspects of our identity create a compounded experience of oppression.[4] As a disabled Asian woman, I sit at the intersection of ableism, racism, and misogyny.

In December 2020, I started *The Anti-Ableism Series* on TikTok, a video series highlighting the different ways we can be better allies to disabled people. There are so many ways that ableism shows up in our society, from not including captions in videos and building entrances that don't have step-free access to asking disabled people intrusive questions about our bodies and medical history. I wanted to create a digestible tool that people could use to start their own journey to becoming anti-ableist. The series currently has over two hundred videos with more than five million views.

The Anti-Ableist Manifesto was born out of that series and from talks I've given over the years to answer the aforementioned questions.

I came across an Instagram post from the United Nations entity for gender equality and the empowerment of women (UN Women) in 2020 that said, "Ending discrimination starts with self-reflection."[5] This has been the guiding phrase for my work and this book, because in order to know where we're going, we need to know where we're coming from. The work is as much about what you do as about what you value and how you think. To that end, you'll find prompts and reflection questions at the end of every chapter as you embark on this journey from self-reflection toward action. Consider these a version of the "gentle callout" that Jenny did for me, to guide you to a deeper understanding.

The book is divided into three sections organized through a framework called "Me, We, Us." It starts with your individual journey and ends with how we can come together as a collective to create systemic change. I was introduced years ago to this framework, which was influenced by a storytelling framework called public narrative,[6] developed by Harvard professor Marshall Ganz as a way of looking at how we can make impact and change as individuals, in our communities, and in the world.

For the purpose of clarity, I have adapted the framework in the following sections:

1. Anti-Ableism and You: What is disability, ableism, and anti-ableism? What does anti-ableism look like to you as an individual, and what can you do to be anti-ableist? These first couple of chapters will be more historical to create some shared context.
2. Anti-Ableism and Your Community: How can we be anti-ableist in our personal relationships, on our teams, and in our communities?
3. Anti-Ableism and Societal Change: What does anti-ableism look like in public spaces, such as the workplace and online? How can we collectively build anti-ableist systems and structures so that we live in a society that is equitable, inclusive, and accessible for all?

Whether you are a diversity, equity, and inclusion (DEI) professional or part of the disability community, a friend or family member of a disabled person, or just someone who wants to learn more, I hope this book provides you with the guidance to show up with more care and compassion for yourself and each other. The fact is, we live in an ableist society that influences the way we think, behave, live, and treat others. We're all impacted by ableism, whether we realize it or not. If we're fortunate to live the full extent of our lives, we'll all end up disabled. We'll also learn that many of the innovations that benefit disabled people, such as curb cuts, audiobooks, electric toothbrushes, and remote work, also benefit all of us. This book is for all of us.

This book isn't all-encompassing; it can't be. I'm coming at this from the perspective of someone who was born in the United States to immigrant parents, who acquired my disability at a young age, who was raised in a single-parent household, and who had the privilege to attend a private university and work in the corporate world. One thing I've had to learn is that I will not be able to single-handedly dismantle the system of oppression that is ableism. But we can take steps toward doing that together.

Throughout this book, I've made a decision to include a variety of stories from disabled people with unique backgrounds, experiences, and opinions. As many of us say, "Once you've met one disabled person, you've met one disabled person." My goal is to add color and share some of the challenges and triumphs that come with living with a disability in an ableist society. Though these stories may look different for everyone, when taken together, they provide a powerful and compelling picture of the disability community. And no matter how diverse or different these stories are, remember that we're all connected through our common humanity. I hope these stories will help to make our experiences more accessible to you and serve as a call for you to embrace the authenticity of your own. I hope this can be one resource in a choir of other disabled voices and resources that will help shape your perspectives.

Learning is never about shame, so I'm grateful that you showed up so we can all learn together. Thank you for being here and joining me on the journey to becoming anti-ableist.

PART 1

ANTI-ABLEISM AND YOU

CHAPTER 1

What Is Disability?

According to Merriam-Webster, *disability* is "a physical, mental, cognitive, or developmental condition that impairs, interferes with, or limits a person's ability to engage in certain tasks or actions or participate in typical daily activities and interactions."[1]

However, I don't like using the word *impair* to describe a person's body and/or mind. The term *impair* means to diminish, weaken, or worsen.[2] And when we say that disability *impairs* our life experiences, it suggests two things: First, it imbues disability with a negative connotation. Second, it suggests that our disability is the reason for or cause of any negative life experiences.

This is inaccurate. Disability itself is not the cause of our negative experiences, as we will come to learn in the next few chapters. Instead, it is the way that our society is built to favor non-disabled people and discriminate against disabled people that causes us to be harmed.

If something as basic as a dictionary definition can get it wrong, I knew we had to try to change it.

A few years ago, in partnership with the Link20 initiative of the Ruderman Family Foundation, a few disability advocates and I drafted a note to try to change Merriam-Webster's definition of *disability*. We were inspired in part by Drake University graduate Kennedy Mitchum successfully petitioning Merriam-Webster to change the definition of *racism* to incorporate systemic oppression in 2020.[3]

Unfortunately, we did not receive a response to our letter. But who knows—someone at Merriam-Webster read that letter. Perhaps they learned something new. Much of advocacy work looks like this: planting the seeds for work that others will take on in the future. Even if we do not achieve the original goal, it can bring about wins that we may not know about for years to come. This letter was the first of many I've drafted to my elected officials pushing for change and to corporate leaders urging them to champion disability inclusion, some of which have been very effective. At the very least, discussing definitions with our friends, family, and colleagues helps to widen the circle of awareness.

I define disability as a health condition of the body and/or mind that impacts the way a person participates in daily activities. There is no negative value judgment in this definition.

In my presentations and speaking engagements, I choose to share the definition of disability from the World Health Organization (WHO), which states that "disability results from the interaction between individuals with a health condition, such as cerebral palsy, Down syndrome, and depression, with personal and environmental factors including negative attitudes, inaccessible transportation and public buildings, and limited social support."[4]

And yet, even though we have this shared definition of disability, our experiences of disability are diverse.

To highlight this, I want to share a story from my own experience. In June 2022, I attended a camp hosted by the United Brachial Plexus Network (UBPN), which brought together people who live with brachial plexus injuries. I met with doctors who served our community, parents and family members who loved us, and other people with the same diagnosis. One of my most significant moments during the camp was confronting the fact that my injury is most severe in my hand. My hand looks different. There's a significant amount of muscle atrophy, and over time, my knuckles have hyperextended.

I remember telling one of my fellow camp attendees with a brachial plexus injury at breakfast, "I'm surprised that no one else's hands look like mine."

He responded, "Before I saw your hand, I didn't know that our injury could look like that."

While all of us had brachial plexus injuries, they all manifested in different ways. I realized that even if someone has a brachial plexus injury like mine, they might navigate and experience the world in a totally different way. To live with my paralyzed dominant arm, I adapted many daily activities, such as typing, tying my shoes, putting my hair up, and wearing a necklace. I have a steering knob requirement on my driver's license, but I learned that many other drivers with brachial plexus injuries don't. Similarly, life and access might look totally different for someone who can use both hands but has a disability that affects their ability to walk, see, or hear.

Although I've been in disability rights advocacy for years, I left the camp with a renewed understanding and appreciation of the sheer diversity of disability.

Disability doesn't have "a look," or at least not one look. Some of us are full-time wheelchair users. Some of us are ambulatory wheelchair users, which describes people with chronic illnesses or mobility issues who have some capacity to walk but who still use a wheelchair in certain situations. Some of us have speech- or vision-related disabilities. Some of us have disabilities that may not be obvious at all. Some of us have disabilities that are not always apparent but that may become apparent, such as the seizures in epilepsy, known as dynamic disabilities. As diversity, equity, inclusion, and accessibility (DEIA) consultant Catarina Rivera shared in a LinkedIn post on dynamic disabilities, "A person might need a mobility aid one day for their condition, while the next day they don't. People with dynamic disabilities might be able to perform a task one day, and then another day be unable to perform the same task. This doesn't mean they're faking their symptoms....People with dynamic disabilities want others to know that their conditions are real and that variation is typical."[5]

There are one billion of us globally,[6] and one in four American adults have a disability.[7] As Dr. Amy Kenny, inaugural director of the Georgetown University Disability Cultural Center, sees it, "Disability is a culture and a community, a way of being that invites us to reimagine a new world where all access needs are met without condemnation or critique; where rest is not earned, but relished; where we recognize that we move, think, and communicate in beautifully diverse ways; and where we know that time is a construct. Disability drives innovation and teaches non-disabled people the inherent wisdom of our bodyminds. We, the disability community, are the future."[8]

We are here, we are diverse, and we are more than Merriam-Webster's dictionary definition.

Reflection Questions

1. How have traditional definitions of disability influenced your perception of a disabled person?

2. Prior to reading this chapter, how did you define disability? Does your definition frame disability in a negative, neutral, or positive light?

3. Ask a couple of friends to share their definitions and see where there are similarities and differences.

CHAPTER 2

Not All Disabilities Are Apparent

Imagine this: you're sitting on the subway when the train arrives at a crowded stop. As people get on, a person who seems to be in their twenties eyes your seat meaningfully. You look closer: they aren't in a wheelchair, and they don't have a cane to signify that they might be blind or have low vision. There is no clear marker that would lead you to think they are disabled. *Surely they don't need my seat, because they don't have a disability*, you tell yourself.

Have you ever found yourself in such a scenario? But what if this person has a disability that isn't obvious or can't be perceived externally—a **non-apparent disability**?

Non-apparent disabilities are physical, mental, or neurological conditions that are not immediately apparent but can impact someone's movements, senses, or activities. Note: I use the term *non-apparent disability* instead of *hidden disability* or *invisible disability*. According to Disability:IN, a nonprofit resource for disability inclusion in businesses, *hidden disability* implies that the disabled person is "purposefully withholding this information," but "there is a difference between choosing to not self-disclose a disability versus actively hiding it." Meanwhile, *invisible disability* suggests that "the person is not visible or that you cannot discern that a person has a disability," which is not always true since "non-apparent disabilities may become apparent depending on the type of disability." In addition, "invisible disability" might make those with non-apparent disabilities feel invisible, overlooked, and invalidated in their disability experiences. *Non-apparent disability* simply says it as it is.[1]

It is estimated that 70 to 80 percent of all disabilities are not apparent.[2] Additionally, according to a 2017 Coqual report, 62 percent of disabilities in the workplace are not apparent.[3] The takeaway: the majority of disabilities are not apparent. Examples of non-apparent disabilities are mental health disabilities such as depression, anxiety, and schizophrenia; learning, attention, cognitive, and neurodivergent disabilities such as attention-deficit/hyperactivity disorder (ADHD), dyslexia, and autism; chronic illnesses and autoimmune conditions such as diabetes, asthma, lupus, and multiple sclerosis; substance use disorders such as alcohol addiction; hearing-related disabilities; and long-haul COVID. This list can help us gain a beginner's understanding of the sheer diversity of disability, but it isn't comprehensive. Furthermore, though I tried to categorize a few non-apparent disabilities previously listed, many people experience multiple disabilities—called comorbidities—that don't necessarily fit into a single category.

I have both apparent and non-apparent disabilities. My apparent disability—the brachial plexus injury in my right arm—helps people understand my condition because they can see that my arm looks different. However, my non-apparent disability—living with PTSD—isn't always perceived by others, so people sometimes focus more on my apparent disability without giving due attention to my non-apparent disability, even though PTSD impacts me more than the fact that I can't use one of my arms. While I'm grateful for ongoing mental health support, I'm still learning to better manage my response when I'm triggered and the unpredictability of when it happens.

People with non-apparent disabilities face unique challenges precisely because of this tension. Often, we are stigmatized, doubted, or disbelieved simply because our disabilities are not noticeable or obvious. For example, because mental health disabilities are not always apparent to others, they seem "less real" and are not always at the forefront of people's minds. We are perceived as being lazy or lying about our condition. Plus, the constant judgment, misunderstandings, and rude questions from others implying that we have to justify ourselves leave us exhausted and even ashamed.

Statements like "But you don't *look* sick!" or "You don't look disabled" reveal how others judge us based on what they perceive with their limited capacities, even if we *are* sick or have pre-existing conditions. Angie Collins-Burke, a nurse and coauthor of *Just Pick Up the Peg: A Nurse's Journey Back from Stroke*, explains the complex emotions that come with her non-apparent disabilities, which include brain injury, depression, chronic pain, and epilepsy: "I continually beat myself up because I'm unable to work. I frequently ask for help and am unable to function at the level that others expect. Feeling like a burden or that we're not achieving enough can lead to feelings of guilt."[4] Dealing with frequent questions and suspicions is draining and causes self-doubt. Collins-Burke continues, "Sometimes I let doubt get the better of me, and I wonder, 'Am I an imposter?' When others assume it's all in your head, it can make you question your reality."

The statement "You don't look sick," which you'll later learn is a type of ableist microaggression, invalidates our experiences because it suggests that we should look radically different from non-disabled people. It also perpetuates the belief that we need to put our disabilities on display and "prove" them in order to be accommodated. With such ableist beliefs, it is no surprise that non-apparent disabilities are often underreported, especially within the Asian American and Pacific Islander (AAPI) community. Members of the AAPI community are 50 percent less likely to seek out mental health support than members of other racial groups because the assumption is that if you can't perceive it, then it doesn't exist.[5] However, if a condition like anxiety makes it hard for us to get out of bed in the morning or affects our social interactions, that just shows how real mental health disability is, and it should be treated as such. Pushing through and masking our symptoms should not be the norm.

The stigma and misconceptions of non-apparent disabilities also affect society at large. We are often misdiagnosed or medically gaslit (meaning a medical professional dismisses or downplays a patient's symptoms). For example, when people casually use psychiatric or clinical terms to describe personality quirks, such as "I'm so ADHD" after forgetting to do one thing or "I'm a little OCD" (referring to obsessive-compulsive disorder) when describing their design preferences, they are furthering the stigma, says psychiatrist Sasha Hamdani. This makes it harder for people who actually need help to get it because society invalidates what real ADHD and OCD may look like.[6]

We also face a lack of resources to handle or treat our non-apparent disabilities. According to Nancy Becher, a chronic and autoimmune disease specialist, health care systems do not prioritize long-term management of and research on chronic and autoimmune diseases because people with those diseases are viewed as having a lower quality of life, and health care systems are mostly designed to focus on acute care and emergency services.[7] As former Centers for Disease Control (CDC) director Rochelle Walensky once said, we are "unwell to begin with"[8] and therefore not prioritized in terms of care.

People with non-apparent disabilities face another unique challenge: we sometimes have the privilege to choose whether to disclose our disabilities, which impacts how we are treated, something that people with apparent disabilities can't do. While choice is a good thing, it adds to the potential burden of "outing" ourselves in order to obtain the support we need. For example, whenever I take carry-on luggage onto a plane and ask for assistance to store it in the overhead compartment, a bystander can see my paralyzed arm and understand the situation. While some people with chronic conditions are also unable to lift their luggage, they might experience pushback if they ask for assistance unless they explain their disabilities. If I'm not wearing my wrist splint on my injured arm and someone doesn't notice it, I experience similar pushback. It's like that twenty-something person you encountered on the subway who might be experiencing debilitating pain and who requires a seat. When someone asks, if you are able, give up your seat.

Becca Lory Hector, an autism and neurodiversity advocate, explains the problem she has with this false choice: "Not disclosing...means I am not somewhere or with someone that I feel safe with. It also often means committing to ignoring or suppressing my needs and accommodations, or masking, through the interaction. Yet still, more often than not, that is the easier route."[9] Hector is not alone. According to a 2023 Involve study, 37 percent of people with non-apparent disabilities choose not to disclose at work due to a fear of discrimination and a lack of support.[10]

Eric Garcia, a thirty-three-year-old autistic author and journalist based in Washington, DC, shared an experience he had early in his career when he attended his first Senate hearing—and how his disability made it more challenging to read the social cues his colleagues might tacitly comprehend:

> They had to adjourn for votes. And I remember shouting across the dais to ask a senator a question. An officer said, "If you do that again—you'll

be thrown out," or, "—you'll be arrested." And I remember just being horribly mortified. And it was because…being autistic, I didn't understand a lot of the social cues. I didn't understand the rules.…It reminded me of how autistic people often have to…do a lot of guesswork with social rules, with social situations. Something that might have just been natural to a lot of my colleagues as reporters wasn't natural to me.[11]

Often, people with non-apparent disabilities choose not to disclose because we feel as if we shouldn't take up advocacy space, but this is a double-edged sword: as a result, people have a poorer understanding of non-apparent disabilities. Fortunately, more and more of us are speaking out, including celebrities who willingly spotlight their conditions. Pop superstar Selena Gomez, who was already living with lupus, canceled her Revival world tour in 2016 to deal with depression and anxiety and was diagnosed with bipolar disorder two years later.[12] In 2022, in addition to sharing her journey with mental illness in a documentary, she cofounded Wondermind, a platform that "destigmatizes and democratizes mental health,"[13] and joined the inaugural White House Conversation on Youth Mental Health led by the US Department of Health and Human Services and MTV Entertainment/Paramount.[14]

When more public figures disclose their disabilities, it makes it easier for the rest of us to do so, too. When I worked at Goldman Sachs, it was public knowledge that the president at the time, Gary Cohn, was dyslexic.[15] When someone so senior at a Fortune 500 company disclosed his disability, it made me feel that I could be more open about mine.

To become comfortable talking about non-apparent disabilities, our larger society has to collectively cultivate an anti-ableist environment that acknowledges and supports the reality of disability. According to the same 2023 Involve study, 50 percent of workers who did disclose their non-apparent disabilities shared that the difficulties they faced in getting support made the process not worth it. Hector adds, "The real conversation isn't about disclosure in the workplace; it's about discrimination in the workplace."[16] I discuss accommodations later in the book, but when the process to even request accommodations is demeaning, stressful, and overly complicated, it makes it more difficult for disabled people to participate.

Disability is diverse, and we must respect and make space for all types of disabilities, whether apparent or non-apparent. Just as the umbrella term *Asian American* came into being in 1968 to consolidate the voice and power of everyone in the diaspora despite the different cultures, languages, and experiences, I believe that the disability community has more power when we come together as a collective and in solidarity. I discuss more strategies on how to support people with non-apparent disabilities in the Anti-Ableism and Your Community section.

Reflection Questions

1. Prior to reading this chapter, what did you think disability looked like? How has this chapter challenged or reinforced your pre-existing perceptions?

2. Do you, or does anyone else you know, live with a non-apparent disability? What are the unique experiences that you/they face? How do you acknowledge or label your own non-apparent disabilities when you talk about them?

3. Can you think of other non-apparent disabilities that this chapter doesn't mention? Check out resources such as the Invisible Disabilities Association (IDA), Understood.org, National Alliance on Mental Illness (NAMI), and the Autistic Self Advocacy Network (ASAN).

CHAPTER 3

Disability Is Not a Bad Word

I often encounter people who are uncomfortable with the word *disability*.

They sometimes say that the root of their discomfort comes from the prefix *dis-* in front of *ability*. The etymology of *disability* dates back to the 1570s "as a combination of the prefix 'dis-' which connotes 'apart,' 'asunder,' 'away,' 'utterly,' or having a privative, negative, or reversing force; and 'ability' which connotes power or capacity to do or act physically, mentally, legally, morally, financially, etc."[1] Through this lens, disability is linked to the *inability* to do or act physically or mentally.

While we can't change the origins of the word, we can challenge the lens through which it was created and reclaim what it means to our community.

Not all words that start with *dis-* have negative connotations, says recording artist and disability advocate Lachi. *Distinguished, discovery, distinct*, and *discussion* are a few that come to mind.[2] While this exercise is not entirely accurate through a linguistic lens, it still encourages us to start unlearning the automatic association of *dis-* with "without" or "less than."

Therapist Meriah Nichols takes this conversation a step further by highlighting how *dis-* is also related to the Latin prefixes *bis-* and *duo-*, which connote "twice" or "two ways." *Dis-* is then reframed as "another way of doing and being," so that *dis-* plus *ability* becomes "the ability to do or be in another way."[3]

The fact is, *disability* is not a bad word but rather a neutral term. Disability just *is*.

I used to joke that people who are uneasy with the word *disability* should repeat it ten times in a row to become more comfortable saying it. I've now realized that this is actually a psychological phenomenon backed by science. *Semantic satiation,* coined by psychologist Leon James (Jakobovits) in 1962, refers to how the uninterrupted repetition of a word reduces it to meaningless sounds and enables the speaker to separate their thoughts and associations from the word.[4] Repeating the word *disability* again and again in everyday use causes it to lose the negative value judgment we may have assigned to it. The more we use the word, the better we can remove the stigma society associated with it and attribute new meaning as well as neutral or even positive value judgments to it.

For example, to me, the word *disability* now connotes a sense of pride, a source of strength, and empowerment.

There are two main themes I'd like to address when it comes to using language to describe disability. First, there are **identity-first** and **person-first language**, the terms most commonly adopted by the disability community to describe ourselves. Then there are **euphemisms**, words people use in place of *disability* because they think it is a bad word.

When people from the disability community describe themselves or self-identify, we usually pick one of two ways: identity-first language—"I am a disabled person" or "I am disabled"—or person-first language—"I'm a person with a disability." Person-first language was initially introduced in the 1970s among disability advocacy groups[5] by people with disabilities who said, "We are not our disabilities. We are people first. I'm a person first."[6] Non-disabled people needed reminders of disabled people's humanity. However, some people in the movement now believe that person-first language has ableist undertones because it separates the person from the disability, assuming our disability to be bad, negative, or undesirable. In comparison, identity-first language—"I'm a disabled person"—views disability as a core part of our identity, in the same way that I'm an Asian woman. I can't separate my personhood from my disability. And I wouldn't.

Next, we have euphemisms, which include phrases like "differently abled," having "unique abilities," or having "special needs" to describe disabled people. Though popular for a while, they were used during a period when disability was still highly stigmatized, which explains the desire to hide the word *disability* under alternative phrases.

Here is a list of euphemisms for disability in addition to those previously mentioned that are often used:

- Different abilities
- Handicapable
- Challenged
- People of determination (used in the United Arab Emirates)

Overall, terms like *differently abled, special needs, unique abilities,* and *people with determination* diminish the very real hardships that come with living with a disability in an ableist society or the pride people feel in our experiences. Describing someone as having "special needs" instead of simply "disabled" suggests that our basic human rights are "special" or out of the ordinary as opposed to simply necessary. You'll also hear people say, "We all have different abilities" or "We all have special needs" as a way to encourage people to see the humanity of the disability experience, but that also suggests that disabled people exist on a level playing field with the rest of society, which undermines the issue. It's called the Americans with *Disabilities* Act (ADA) for a reason. The ADA prohibits discrimination based on our legal categorization of "disabled," not any euphemism. "Disability" is what is enshrined in our civil rights. You can check out the #SayTheWord campaign and movement started by disability community activist Lawrence Carter-Long that encourages people to use direct and specific language when referring to disabilities.[7]

It is important to note that when referring to a disabled person as an individual, always check in with us first to see what type of language we prefer. Preferred language varies from person to person and is up to the individual. For example, I often find myself switching between identity-first and person-first language, though I prefer the former ("I'm disabled") for the many reasons I've shared in this chapter. Some time ago, I received a direct message from a stranger on social media who requested that I change my language to person-first language ("I'm a person with disabilities") because they had been taught this in a university class. An important part of allyship is being nuanced and appreciating the diversity that exists within disability—say it with me: we are not a monolith. So it's important to respect and defer to individual preferences.[8] In fact, some disabled people still prefer to identify themselves as "differently abled" and having "unique abilities," and you should honor that. However, when talking about the community broadly, the main takeaway is to use the word *disability* when referring to disabilities. Call it like it is.

Now, you might ask, *But Tiffany, why is your organization called Diversability? Isn't that a euphemism?* The short answer is yes. The longer answer is when I started Diversability in 2009, I often got blank stares when I mentioned that I wanted to start a movement around "disability pride." People were confused by how anyone could be proud to be disabled. I chose "Diversability" because disability for me is a natural variation of human diversity. I wanted to highlight that and the fact that disability itself is diverse. I suggest using *Diversability* only as a proper noun when referring to our organization and using *disability* otherwise.[9]

It is also important to know which terms have become outdated and should not be used, like *handicapped* and *crippled*. *Handicapped* in particular has negative connotations, probably due to the common belief that it is derived from the term "hand-in-cap" to describe beggars, though this etymology has proven to be false—*handicap* actually refers to actions that make a game more equitable. You might still see mention of "handicapped parking" in public spaces, but I suggest using "disability parking" or "accessible parking" instead.

As you progress on your anti-ableist journey and rethink the language you use, it's possible that you'll encounter some disabled people who say, "I personally don't have an issue when you use such language. It doesn't bother me." And there are exceptions of people with certain disabilities preferring to use outdated terms like *crip* to refer to themselves or people with mental illness using *mad* as a way to reclaim those terms. As Andrew Pulrang says, "When we 'reclaim' such terms for ourselves, we do so with a great deal of care and discretion. And this is not a privilege open to people outside of our disability communities."[10] Each individual disabled person is entitled to their own opinion on what type of language is used to describe them. However, it would be wrong to imply that it is therefore acceptable to do so for all other disabled people.

Such comments are an example of a type of ableism known as lateral ableism, which you'll learn about later. According to Aubrey Blanche-Sarellano, a designer of equitable processes, products, and operations, disabled people who are personally unbothered by ableist language cannot prevent the harm done to the wider community. "The fact that you are not personally harmed does not mean that others are not. Your focusing on yourself rather than the broader system of white supremacy-enabled ableism is...exactly what these systems of oppression want."[11]

If we are to truly become anti-ableist allies, we must start with language. If something as simple as the words we say and the phrases we use causes discomfort, how much more difficult will it be to change actual thoughts and behaviors? Our current situation exists partly because we have stayed silent, not knowing what to say or how to say it in a way that seems polite or perfectly informed. And when we stay silent, we don't learn, grow, or make progress. Instead, let's learn to sit with our discomfort and then move through it so that we can break down old, harmful associations and attribute new meaning and power to our words.

Reflection Questions

1. What do you think about when you hear the word *disabled*? Write down some of the feelings you've had.

2. If you have used or heard of a disability euphemism, why do you think it was used in that context?

3. What are some other words that you can think of that start with *dis-* that don't have a negative connotation?

4. If you notice yourself feeling uncomfortable with the word *disability*, say the word ten times in a row. *Disability, disability, disability, disability, disability, disability, disability, disability, disability, disability.* How does that make you feel?

CHAPTER 4

Disability Is Not a Bad Thing

In the previous chapter, we learned that *disability* is not a bad word. We talked about the importance of naming disability for what it is and confronting our discomfort. But why? What's the larger motivation behind this?

Disability is not a bad word because we need to realize that *disability is not a bad thing.*

We've been brought up in a disability-negative culture, where most of us view disability as a trait that is less than, broken, and in need of fixing. This produces a damaging social view of disability that continues to contribute to the marginalization of and discrimination against disabled people.

Take, for example, the conversations around whether autistic people and people with ADHD, depression, anxiety, or OCD belong to the disability community. We learned in Chapter 2: Not All Disabilities Are Apparent that autism and ADHD are examples of non-apparent disabilities that fall under developmental and learning disabilities, and depression, anxiety, and OCD are examples of mental health disabilities. However, some people continue to resist this categorization with responses like "Saying that ADHD and autism are disabilities sends the message to children and late-diagnosed people that they are less able and less than." As DEI consultant Julie Harris observes, "These common beliefs and statements show more about one's beliefs about disability than the actual diagnoses."[1] Her point is that people are riled up because of their preconceived notions of the word *disability* rather than because ADHD and autism are considered disabilities. Instead, if they can come to terms with this categorization, it might empower them to better understand the barriers people with neurodivergent disabilities face in a neurotypical world.

A big part of my work is dedicated to moving us toward a disability-positive culture, where society can view disability as simply part of the human experience with a neutral, or even positive, value judgment. If we want to change the culture, we have to first change our attitudes. A simple first step is to change the everyday language we use, not just around our disabled family, friends, and acquaintances but also within non-disabled spaces.

Let's begin with **inclusive language**: using language that avoids excluding particular groups of people or perpetuating harmful stereotypes based on gender, race, sexual orientation, age, or disability status. An example of gender-inclusive language is saying "everyone" instead of "you guys." Inclusive language "acknowledges diversity, conveys respect to all people, is sensitive to differences, and promotes equal opportunities."[2] The goal is to make everyone feel valued so that we can create a more welcoming environment for all with the words we use. For example, we should use the inclusive term *non-disabled people* as opposed to *able-bodied people*. *Able-bodied* assumes a binary and stagnant state that does not take into account people with non-apparent or dynamic disabilities. It also wrongly suggests that people with disabilities are not capable of using our bodies well.

We can't talk about inclusive language without bringing up the different types of non-inclusive language, whether they are subtle **microaggressions**, harmful **figurative terms** we use daily, or outright **insults**.

What is implied when someone says, "The only disability in life is a bad attitude"? While the sentiment might be well-intended, this **microaggression** equates disability with someone's bad attitude and conveys that actual disability does not exist or matter. Microaggressions are dangerous because although their subtle language may not be "obviously" or intentionally hurtful or damaging, they still inform the way we think—that disability is a bad thing. We will learn more about microaggressions in a later chapter.

I was on a podcast some time ago, and the press release mentioned that the featured disabled podcasters had "overcome their disabilities." Even if it sounds well-meaning, the phrase *overcoming disability* is another example of a microaggression because it suggests that disability is something negative that needs to be conquered or defeated. Plus, I am still disabled, and I am okay with it! An alternative phrase could be *overcoming adversity in the face of ableism*, which names ableism as the main problem rather than disability. Here are other examples of microaggressions in language and better alternatives:

Ableist Words and Phrases to Avoid	Alternative Words and Phrases
suffering from disability	living with disability
they accomplished this despite their disability	they accomplished this with their disability
handicapped parking	accessible parking / disability parking
wheelchair bound	wheelchair user
lost their battle with cancer/depression	died

Let's talk about some of the common **figurative terms** that we use daily, perhaps unthinkingly, that end up weaponizing disability as a negative experience. These phrases may be figurative, but for some disabled people, they are literal. As TV presenter and disability advocate Sophie Morgan says in her memoir *Driving Forwards*, "People often describe themselves as 'paralyzed by fear,' and as a paraplegic, I would agree, there is nothing more paralyzing than fear—other than paralysis itself, that is. But while one is real, fear, on the other hand, is imagined."[3]

Metaphors like "falling on deaf ears" to describe a statement that is ignored or "the blind leading the blind" to describe a directionless effort are harmful because they carry negative connotations. In an Instagram video, speaker and DEI consultant Catarina Rivera demonstrates how she leads her friend, accomplished author and activist Haben Girma, on the dance floor. As both women sway in rhythm, Rivera explains in a voice-over, "Being blind doesn't mean being ignorant. Haben and I think we should all get rid of this ableist phrase because the blind leading the blind can be quite fabulous."[4]

"It's just a metaphor! I don't mean it seriously," someone might say. But what does it mean when someone chooses to make light of terms that describe and make assumptions about the lived realities of disabled people? It demonstrates that they don't take our concerns seriously.

It might seem difficult, even tedious, to make a conscious decision to change the way we've been speaking for years, but this interruption to our personal thought patterns is part of our anti-ableist work. Luckily, language is fluid and ever changing, and there are so many alternatives we can make use of to express ourselves in creative ways.

Ableist Words and Phrases to Avoid	Alternative Words and Phrases
paralyzed by fear	terrified / frozen with fear / riveted with fear
blind leading the blind	directionless / clueless / going in circles
falling on deaf ears	not getting through / not resonating
tone-deaf	oblivious / ignorant / out of touch
blind spot	missing piece / gap in knowledge / bias / area of limited awareness
analysis paralysis	state of inaction
that's a real handicap	that's a real challenge

Finally, sometimes people use disability terms (whether current or outdated) as outright and overt **insults** or **jabs**. This contributes to the ongoing stigma and negative attitude surrounding disability.

Examples of Disability Terms Used as Insults

That's so lame.

Are you deaf?

He's a vegetable.

She's crazy/insane/psycho.

You're retarded/stupid.

Instead of using these figurative insults, just say what you actually mean, whether you mean "boring," "nasty," or "uncool" instead of *lame*; "absurd," "wild," or "ridiculous" instead of *crazy*; or "foolish," "immature," or "silly" instead of *retarded*. By making this linguistic switch, you're removing harmful stereotypes about the disability experience.

It's okay to make mistakes along the way. Ableist language and value systems have been ingrained in most of us since we were young, and it'll take years for all of us—whether we're just starting out or have been allies for some time—to unlearn it all. What's important is how we claim our mistakes and own up to them.

The good thing about correcting our mistakes when it comes to inclusive language is that all we need to do is change the words we use. It may feel hard at first, but to paraphrase Glennon Doyle, I know you can do hard things.[5] It is natural to react defensively when you're challenged—just breathe through it, and recognize that someone trusted and respected you enough to tell you the impact of your words on them. These shared understandings of disability provide common language so that we can learn more about the historical roots of disability rights and collective action next.

Reflection Questions

1. Have you used ableist language in the past? How can you be more mindful of your language going forward?

2. What are some other common ableist phrases not mentioned in this chapter? What better alternatives can you replace them with? How might these phrases contribute to ableism?

3. Are there examples you can point to of public figures updating their language? How can you learn from such instances and be open to evolving your language?

4. Find a news article about a disability-related topic and look at the language it uses. Is it written through a neutral lens or with negative value judgment of disability? How would you correct this language, if necessary? If you are unsure about alternatives, you can search disability journalism guidelines for suggestions.

CHAPTER 5

A Brief History of the Disability Rights Movement

The cosmologist Carl Sagan said, "You have to know the past to understand the present."[1] Even though this might be your first time learning about disability history, there is a long legacy of disability activism. None of this work exists in a vacuum, and I'm grateful for the disability activists who paved the way for me and those who will come after.

As a brief history, I encourage you to use the information laid out in this chapter as a catalyst to dive into areas that are of interest to you. Professor Kim E. Nielsen's book *A Disability History of the United States* could be a great place to start.

I first started learning more about disability history in 2015 around the twenty-fifth anniversary of the ADA. I was living in New York City when the mayor proclaimed July Disability Pride Month, and the city was celebrating its first Disability Pride Parade. Even in the process of researching for this chapter, I learned a few things!

So how did it all start?

In the ancient world, disability was viewed through the lens of superstition and religious beliefs. In some religious cultures like Christianity, it was seen as a manifestation of the divine, but it was viewed mostly as a curse or punishment from a god. During the periods of the Greek and Roman empires, which valued human perfection, disability was seen as inferior, undesirable, and disposable. Roman fathers were responsible for deciding whether a disabled child would live or die, and the child was often abandoned in the woods. In Sparta, the child was the property of the state, and abandonment of a disabled child was required by law.[2]

From the Middle Ages through the Renaissance, around 1000 to 1700, disability continued to be shunned as the devil's work or punishment for a parent's, and eventually the grown child's, sins. During this period of social and economic hardship, families couldn't afford to care for disabled family members—or they simply didn't know how to—and disabled people were evicted and often became beggars or were hidden out of public spaces. In 1247, Europe's first mental health hospital, Bethlem Royal, was founded in Britain, later gaining notoriety for its brutal "treatments" of disabled patients, such as bleeding and cold-water therapy,[3] that were a mix of punishment and religious devotion, and for its use of "chains, manacles, locks, and stocks."[4] Owing to the rise of witch hunts during the 1600s, many disabled people were also accused of witchcraft and sorcery.[5]

By the 1700s, the start of the Industrial Revolution, disability was commonplace. Long hours in horrible working conditions and a lack of workplace safety regulations, combined with a rise in population and poor medical facilities—as well as wars—left many disabled.[6] Technological advancement also exacerbated social inequities and increased poverty. Into the 1800s, disabled people continued to be scorned and cast off. As the number of people experiencing homelessness grew in cities, new policies were enacted to address the "problem." Cities began the practice of "warning out" disabled people, which meant telling them that they were no longer welcome. Disabled people were also loaded onto carts and dropped off at the next town.[7] In addition to forced displacement, disabled people were locked away in poorhouses or jails.

The 1800s also saw the first emergence of disability rights in the United States. Formal education for the Deaf community began when oral and manual schools were created in the early 1800s.[8] Oralism and manualism are two methods of teaching Deaf people to communicate, with oralism using speech and lipreading, and manualism using American Sign Language (ASL). Around the mid-1800s, nurse and advocate Dorothea Dix visited jails, poorhouses, and asylums across the United States and observed appalling conditions where disabled people lived.[9] Dix appealed to Congress to set aside land to accommodate disabled people, paving the way for the first publicly funded state institutions in the United States for people with disabilities. This was a turning point in promoting the belief that the US government had a responsibility to care for its disabled citizens.

Unfortunately, history would show that institutionalization was not an ideal solution. Like Bethlem Royal Hospital six hundred years before, these institutions had poor and overcrowded living conditions. Instead of providing care and rehabilitation, they abused and neglected the disabled residents, adopting cruel treatment methods that resembled torture, imposing isolation, and even using the residents as free labor. Additionally, institutionalization took away the choice and agency of disabled people, leaving them in the hands of their family members and doctors. Nevertheless, institutionalization became a widespread practice, keeping hundreds of thousands of disabled people segregated from the rest of the population in a practice known as "warehousing."[10] Meanwhile, outside institutions, "ugly laws" in certain cities banned disabled people who were "diseased, maimed, mutilated, or in any way deformed, so as to be an unsightly or disgusting object" from showing themselves in public.[11] Ironically, disabled people with "disfigured, disabled, or exaggerated bodies" were displayed as "oddities" in county fairs for the enjoyment of spectators.[12]

The early 1900s saw the rise of eugenics, "the science of the improvement of the human race by better breeding,"[13] according to Charles Davenport, a central figure of the movement in America. The belief was that certain "undesirable" human conditions like "feeblemindedness," epilepsy, and insanity were hereditary and should therefore be "bred out." Disabled people were on the front line of this attack, with seventy thousand disabled people in the United States undergoing forced sterilization without their consent after a 1927 Supreme Court ruling, *Buck v. Bell*, which states that governments have the right to forcibly sterilize people with disabilities.[14] Despite certain limitations, the ruling is still in place today. Most famously, the eugenics movement made its way to Nazi Germany, where disabled people made up one of the many groups targeted by Hitler in his campaign for racial purity. In 1933, people with what were believed to be "hereditary" conditions had to undergo compulsory sterilization. Hitler decided that the next step was to kill babies with congenital disabilities and later disabled adults. In total, the Nazi program Aktion T4 carried out the murder of 300,000 disabled people.[15]

After World Wars I and II, disabled veterans pressured the government to provide them with rehabilitation and vocational training as a way to thank and honor those who had sacrificed their lives and health for the country since they could no longer serve in the military. In the 1930s, economic growth, increased government assistance, and advancements in technology and medical care helped to bring disabled people closer to self-reliance. However, there was still a lack of accessibility in public spaces.[16] Significantly, in 1938, the Fair Labor Standards Act (FLSA) passed, with Section 14(c) legally allowing employers to pay disabled employees lower wages due to what was seen as limited productivity.[17] This was originally meant to incentivize employers to hire disabled people, but it resulted in unfair wages. As of February 2024, twelve states have phased out Section 14(c), and five states are in the process of doing so.[18]

By the Civil Rights Movement in the 1960s, disability rights advocates had joined forces with other minoritized groups to demand equal rights, treatment, access, and opportunities. Parent advocates were a big part of the disability rights movement, calling for their disabled children to be removed from segregated institutions and enrolled in schools where they could learn alongside other, non-disabled children.[19] When the Civil Rights Act passed in 1964, it protected against discrimination based on race, color, religion, sex, and national origin, leaving disability out of the picture despite the efforts of advocates. This exclusion pushed activists to call for laws specific to disability rights, which eventually led to the Rehabilitation Act of 1973 (Section 504), where, for the first time in US history, the civil rights of disabled people were protected by law. The law prevented disabled people from being discriminated against in federally funded programs, such as hospitals, public schools and universities, and public transit systems, and it also mandated equal access to public services. Crucially, this law focused on fixing the environment as opposed to fixing the individual.[20] Previously, for example, schools and libraries had been "available" to the public but not accessible to disabled people.[21] The law was signed in 1973 but was delayed due to the enormous financial costs it required of the government, such as updating public buildings to meet the new standards. Disability activists, including Judy Heumann, Kitty Cone, Brad Lomax, Mary Jane Owen, Corbett O'Toole, and Hale Zukas, wrote letters and lobbied lawmakers, and in 1977, they organized sit-ins, including a twenty-six-day action at the San Francisco federal building known as the "504 Sit-In," the longest non-violent civilian occupation of a federal building in US history.[22] That finally got the program moving.

Riding the momentum of this win, disability rights activists continued to organize and protest, fighting to represent and speak for themselves. In 1983, the World Institute on Disability was founded by Judy Heumann, Ed Roberts, and Joan Leon. It was one of the first international disability rights organizations led by people with disabilities. Judy Heumann, known as the "mother of the disability rights movement," was the first wheelchair user to become a New York teacher. She sued the New York Board of Education in 1970 at the age of twenty-two after she was failed on her mandatory medical exam because she could not walk.[23] And Ed Roberts, known as the "father of the independent living movement," successfully sued the state of California after the University of California, Berkeley, tried to reverse his acceptance after realizing that he was quadriplegic because it was unprepared to accommodate his needs. He became its first student to use a wheelchair.[24] Roberts went on to organize the first disability-led student organization in the United States, advocating for accessibility on campus, which later inspired him to found the country's first independent living community. In his words, "No longer would we tolerate being spoken for."[25] In 1988, a weeklong student protest at Gallaudet University, a university for Deaf and hard-of-hearing students, led to the election of the first Deaf university president.[26] On a national level, activists fought for specific laws like the Voting Accessibility for the Elderly and Handicapped Act of 1984, requiring accommodations for disabled people during elections, and the Air Carrier Access Act of 1986, prohibiting discrimination against disabled people by airlines, among others.[27] However, what was still missing was a wide-reaching and broad civil rights law that would protect the rights of disabled people in the United States.

In the 1980s, disability rights activist Justin Dart Jr. traveled extensively to collect stories about the injustices that disabled people faced. His ultimate goal was to create legislation that would address discrimination against disabled people in the United States.[28] Iowa senator Tom Harkin took this information and worked with other prominent leaders to author the ADA in 1990, thirteen years after Section 504 had paved the way. Dart is widely recognized as the "father" of the ADA. Businesses that disliked the new accessibility requirements lobbied against the bill. At one point, over a thousand disabled people gathered in Washington, DC, to protest, including an action known as the Capitol Crawl when protesters left behind their wheelchairs and crutches and crawled up the steps of the Capitol.[29] This protest was intended to be a physical demonstration of how inaccessible architecture impacted people with disabilities, forcing Congress to see disabled people. The late Michael Winter, who participated, said, "Some people may have thought it was undignified for people in wheelchairs to crawl in that manner, but I felt that it was necessary to show the country what kinds of things people with disabilities have to face on a day-to-day basis. We had to be willing to fight for what we believed in."[30]

The ADA passed four months later on July 26, 1990.

Today, the ADA extends protections to all private institutions and workplaces, ensuring "the equal treatment and equal access of people with disabilities to employment opportunities and to public accommodations," and intends to "prohibit discrimination on the basis of disability in: employment, services rendered by state and local governments, places of public accommodation, transportation, and telecommunications services."[31] This means providing accessibility in public services and infrastructure, such as ramps, elevators, automatic doors, handrails, and captions on TV and streaming services, which are accommodations that both disabled and non-disabled people benefit from. It also means mandating that private businesses and public services accommodate disabled employees, clients, and customers. Essentially, the ADA is landmark legislation because it mandates the "full participation, inclusion, and integration of people with disabilities in all levels of society."[32]

However, as you'll hear many advocates say, the ADA should be the floor, not the ceiling, of the disability rights movement. It is often poorly and inconsistently enforced across states, with multiple violations across the country.[33] While there are fines for non-compliance of up to $75,000 for a single ADA violation and $150,000 for additional violations, there are exceptions and exemptions, and many disabled people lack the time and energy to fight for our rights. Prejudice and bias against disabled people still exist within families, in media representation, and elsewhere. Enforcing laws is one thing; changing attitudes is another and is necessary to create lasting change.

In 2006, the United Nations (UN) adopted the Convention on the Rights of Persons with Disabilities (CRPD), the first legally binding instrument to address the rights of disabled people at the global level.[34] This was born out of a desire to shift from "viewing persons with disabilities as 'objects' of charity, medical treatment, and social protection toward viewing persons with disabilities as 'subjects' with rights, who are capable of claiming those rights and making decisions for their lives based on their free and informed consent as well as being active members of society."[35]

The passage of the Affordable Care Act (ACA) in the United States on March 23, 2010, was also significant because it improved access to health care for people with disabilities and chronic conditions and addressed disability discrimination. Because of the ACA, young adults can stay on their parents' insurance until age twenty-six, and insurance companies can't deny coverage or charge higher premiums to those with pre-existing conditions or comorbidities.[36]

I've been honored to meet some of the notable figures mentioned in this chapter, including the late Judy Heumann and Senator Tom Harkin, as well as many other pioneering advocates whom I hope you will read about in history books to come. I've also been learning about the ways that disability has been downplayed in history and erased from historical figures, such as Mexican artist Frida Kahlo, who developed polio as a child and acquired physical disabilities from a bus accident when she was eighteen;[37] President Franklin D. Roosevelt, who also had polio; and Harriet Tubman, who developed epilepsy. This erasure of their disabilities makes their stories incomplete. It now falls upon our generation to remember and honor those who have come before us and to continue on the path they've laid out.

Where do we go from here? In the modern era of the disability rights movement, we are still trying to combat negative biases against disability. Newer terms like *ableism* are at the forefront of our conversations, and notions like disability intersectionality and disability pride—as well as movements like disability justice, which emerged in 2005 from a group of disabled activists of color called Sins Invalid that included Patty Berne, Mia Mingus, and Stacey Park Milbern and which we will learn more about in later chapters—give us valuable context and expand on our centuries-long fight for inclusivity and equity. The American Association of People with Disabilities (AAPD) highlights a few advocacy areas we can focus on: community integration, health care, employment, and political participation.[38] I share more strategies later, in the Anti-Ableism and Societal Change section.

We must also remember to let disabled people lead the way. Haben Girma, a disability rights lawyer, author, and speaker—and the first Deafblind person to graduate from Harvard Law School—reminds us, "The disability community is diverse, full of rich stories of talented people improving their communities....It touches all of our lives."[39]

We are long overdue to be living in a time when our doctors, family members, and government authorities no longer make decisions for us. It is time to reclaim our stories. We have the agency and dignity.

Reflection Questions

1. Are there areas of disability history that you'd be interested in delving into more deeply? Read books and articles, and watch videos that deepen your understanding. The Oscar-nominated film *Crip Camp* is a documentary that follows the journey of campers who became disability rights activists and played a crucial role in the Section 504 Sit-In.

2. Did you learn about disability history in school?

3. Were there parts of this history that surprised you?

4. Learn more about Ed Roberts, Judy Heumann, and other notable activists who have made or are still making disability history.

5. How have legislative milestones like Section 504 and the ADA shaped the landscape of disability rights? Where might there be opportunities for improvement?

CHAPTER 6

Models of Disability

We all see and talk about disability in different ways. You probably have your own "mental model"—or way that you view disability—even if you don't realize it.[1] And these ways in which we see and talk about disability reveal our beliefs and social attitudes.

Over the years, activists and academics have studied the history and culture of disability.[2] Disability studies scholars call the different ways people talk about disability *models of disability.*

As theoretical frameworks, I note that these models are meant to be viewed as tools—they are not exhaustive, they may overlap, and they will shift and develop along with society's changing attitudes.[3] In this chapter, I share eight different models of disability—though there are more—so that we can better understand the social attitudes toward disability and why it all matters. The medical model, charity/tragedy model, and social model are the three most frequently referenced by advocates.

First, the **medical model of disability** views disability as resulting from physical or mental "impairments" that are located in an individual, unconnected to external environmental or social factors, similar to the Merriam-Webster definition. The medical model sees disability as a defect, deficiency, or abnormality that negatively impacts an individual's quality of life and prevents us from being "normal." In the medical setting, disability is viewed as a health condition that needs to be treated or cured. In other words, disability is a problem that needs to be fixed. Let's take the example of a person who is unable to use stairs. The medical model of disability attempts to cure the person's condition rather than address the inaccessibility of the stairs.

The medical model of disability has been criticized by advocates because it stigmatizes disability. Historically, it is the reason many disabled people were institutionalized, because the medical model saw us "as useless and hopelessly dependent on others."[4] The medical model also focuses on costly treatment, such as surgery or drugs, that may not always be in the disabled person's best interest. A CEO of a large tech company once told me that deafness would cease to exist because of cochlear implants, without addressing Deaf culture or the high cost of some cochlear implants. Advocates and critics argue that instead of unnecessary medical interventions driven by the medical model, more resources and effort should be put into "simpler inclusionary practices like universal design and social inclusion."[5]

Second, the **charity or tragedy model of disability** views disability as a tragic experience and disabled people as needing other people's help and goodwill. It treats us as "victims of negative circumstance"[6] and "objects of pity and charity."[7] The charity/tragedy model is often used by non-disabled people and organizations, usually charities that paint disabled people as suffering passively and in need of donations and services to survive. In the case of a person not being able to use stairs, the charity/tragedy model would encourage charitable actions like raising money to address the condition that prevents the person from using stairs or physically carrying them up the stairs rather than providing step-free access or a chairlift.

The charity/tragedy model has been criticized for causing more discrimination against disabled people by taking away our agency to make our own choices, especially when the charitable donor or do-gooder calls the shots. It lowers disabled people's self-esteem when it makes us feel indebted to or reliant on others. Like the medical model, in which a medical professional makes the decisions and focuses on curing the individual, the charity/tragedy model is a reactive and top-down approach that tries to "save" the individual from our problems. In this case, the "problem" is the person's disability rather than inaccessibility and ableism.

Third, the **economic model of disability** defines disability as an individual's inability to work. In this model, the inherent worth of a person is tied to our ability to produce, and disability is tied to a lack of productivity in the capitalist system. The disabled person is seen as unable to contribute to society, which results in a loss of earnings for the individual, lower profit margins for the employer, and welfare payments from the government.[8] This framework is used by the state to determine who can be considered "disabled" in order to receive benefits. In order to qualify for Supplemental Security Income (SSI), a needs-based federal program that provides monthly payments to disabled people, a disabled person can't have more than $2,000 in savings or other assets, keeping many of them living below the poverty line.[9]

This model creates often arbitrary definitions of who is considered "disabled," resulting in benefits being provided only to some. In our example, a person who cannot use stairs is defined as "disabled" by the state. However, this definition is flawed because a person with another type of disability who can use stairs may not be defined as "disabled," denying us access to state benefits that we require. The economic model is also related to the charity/tragedy model because both portray the individual as "needy" and reliant on the help of others.

Fourth, the **moral model of disability** views a person as morally responsible for our disability. This model is often tied to religious or superstitious beliefs—for example, a person or our ancestors did something "immoral" in the past that caused our disability. As a result, the individual is seen as being at fault for our disability and deserving of it. In the example of the person who cannot use stairs, they may be seen as "not trying hard enough" or undeserving of entering the building.[10]

Puneet Singh Singhal, a disability inclusion advocate who lives with dyslexia, dyspraxia, and stammering, was born and raised in a slum in India and experienced extreme poverty and domestic violence. Along with becoming a caregiver to his chronically ill mother, he shared that he experienced horrific bullying in school for his speech difference. Enacting the moral model of disability, he told me, "even parents got in on the act, fearing I'd 'infect' their kids with my stammer."[11]

Dr. Amy Kenny, a disabled scholar-practitioner who serves as the inaugural director of the Disability Cultural Center at Georgetown University, shared how the moral model of disability affected her experience, "Too often, people in my religious community have tried to pray me away. They interpret my disabled body as sinful and rope God into their ableism. We are not the 'before' picture of a prayer makeover or the symbol of sin used to guilt others into repenting. Disabled people are divine."[12]

These first four models of disability share a common underlying theme: they assume that an individual's disability is the problem. So these models can be categorized under the "individual approach," also known as the "deficit perspective," where the *person* is seen as having the problem. However, there is also a "social approach," which sees *society*, and not the person, as the problem. And the problem is that society has failed to accommodate all people.[13]

This brings us to the **social model of disability**, developed in response to the individualistic approach of the medical and charity/tragedy models. In 1983, disability rights advocate Mike Oliver, known as Britain's first professor of disability studies, popularized the model in his book *Social Work with Disabled People*. In the social model, the individual is seen as "disabled by society and their environment rather than by their own impairment."[14] What makes someone disabled is "not their medical condition but the attitudes and structures of society."[15]

This way of thinking shifts the focus from trying to "fix" a disabled individual to creating "best practices for equity, like universal design and social inclusivity"[16] within the larger environment. The priority is on removing barriers to participation, creating policies and practices like the ADA, increasing resources and accommodations, changing attitudes, and reforming society. You can see how this ties back to the WHO's definition of disability that we learned in Chapter 1: What Is Disability? Under the social model, in the example of a person who can't use stairs, a ramp or elevator would be installed to address the inaccessibility.

Then we have the **human rights model of disability**, developed by disabled people and officially recognized by the UN in 2006 under the CRPD.[17] This model takes the social model one step further: while the social model proposes that society's attitudes and inequitable structures are what make an individual disabled, the human rights model simply states that "disability is a natural part of human diversity that must be respected and supported in all its forms," that "people with disability have the same rights as everyone else in society," and that disability "must not be used as an excuse to deny or restrict people's rights."[18]

Simply put, disability rights are basic human rights, not special rights,[19] and disabled people are deserving of the basic human rights that everyone else enjoys.

We are citizens, we can make decisions in our own lives, we have dignity and value, and we deserve to live a life free from discrimination.

In some ways, the human rights model shares a similar spirit with the **affirmative model of disability** and the **identity model of disability**. The **affirmative model** emerged in 2000 as a response to the medical and social models of disability.[20] In contrast to those models, the affirmative model sees disability as just a "different way of living in and experiencing the world, one not characterized by its disadvantages any more than its advantages,"[21] and considers disability simply a part of our being.

The **identity model of disability** highlights disabled people as a unique community with a positive culture worth celebrating. Under this model, the disability community is a source of pride, and we share a common disability culture that allows us to explore our collective identity and unite around our lived experiences and a shared cause as we fight prejudice and advocate for change together.[22] The identity model encourages disabled people to "see themselves more as a social or ethnic minority than as victims of biology." Disability scholar and activist Steve Brown explains, "People with disabilities have forged a group identity. We share a common history of oppression and a common bond of resilience. We generate art, music, literature, and other expressions of our lives, our culture, infused from our experience of disability. Most importantly,...we claim our disabilities with pride as part of our identity." Promoting disability culture is a specific and powerful way to address barriers to inclusivity because "as the disability rights movement has shown, when disabled people have a sense of their collective identity and culture, they feel more empowered to fight for social change and resist discrimination."[23]

Instead of adhering to a single model or writing off a model completely, we can find a balance. For example, although the medical and charity/tragedy models are outdated, and although we should reject the individual approach of these models that teach us to view the disabled person as a problem, this does not mean we should stop going to the doctor and searching for life-enhancing treatments for certain debilitating health conditions or that we should not fundraise to support the improvement of a disabled person's quality of life. Instead, for example, we can apply key concepts from the social and human rights models in the medical setting to ensure that medical treatment is provided accessibly and inclusively through anti-ableist practices. For example, a pediatric hand surgeon who works with children with brachial plexus injuries once told me that he'd added a mental health professional to rehabilitation teams for children after their surgeries, acknowledging the interplay between physical and emotional responses to procedures and treatment. And even as we use the social model to address inaccessibility and build a more inclusive environment, we can keep in mind the frameworks of the affirmative and identity models that celebrate disability pride.

Although the models of disability grew out of disability studies, they don't belong just in the academic world. We can use them, too. If we have an understanding of the history and usefulness of these frameworks, we can better understand how to build an anti-ableist society as individuals and as a community.

Reflection Questions

1. Reflect on your own beliefs and attitudes toward disability. How do they align with or differ from the models discussed in this chapter? Which model (or models) of disability resonated with you? Why?

2. How have you seen these different models of disability play out in your perspective on disability? What experiences, education, or exposure have influenced the shifts in your own perspectives?

3. Which models of disability dominate in your community or social circles? How might these models influence the treatment and inclusion of disabled individuals?

4. How might different models of disability impact decision-making processes and help inform more equitable decision-making?

5. Identify a movie with one or more disabled characters.

    •   Which model does the disabled character follow?
    •   What perspectives do you think the people working behind the scenes on the film (screenwriter, director, etc.) have on disability?
    •   How would the movie be different if it were portrayed through another model of disability?

CHAPTER 7

Disability Intersectionality

When we talk about understanding disability, one important concept is intersectionality, which describes how different forms of inequity pertaining to race, class, gender, sexuality, disability, and other individual characteristics intersect with one another and overlap to create a compounded and unique experience of oppression.[1]

Building on this, *disability intersectionality* refers to disabled people's lived experiences that are "impacted by their other intersecting identities."[2] Additionally, it describes how different systems like ableism, racism, classism, sexism, xenophobia, homophobia, and transphobia operate together and reinforce one another.

An important takeaway is that our disability experiences are diverse because of this intersectionality—everybody's story is unique. As I've mentioned before, the disability community is not a monolith.

I am a disabled Asian woman. As an Asian woman, I feel fetishized, but as a disabled person, I feel infantilized and desexualized. During the height of the pandemic, I feared for my safety and being harassed during the rise of anti-Asian hate and misinformation about the origins of COVID; at the same time, as a disabled person, I feared getting COVID, and if my symptoms were severe enough that I needed to be hospitalized, I feared doctors making judgments about my quality of life (since many assume that simply because we are disabled, we must have a poor quality of life) and not giving me access to proper care.

Disability intersectionality doesn't just affect my current reality. It also influences my story, which is both a disability story and a story of what it means to be the daughter of a Taiwanese immigrant and a refugee from the Vietnam War.

When I was young, I was taught that our family had a collective identity and reputation. Disability is taboo in many Asian cultures, based on an antiquated cultural belief that it is some form of punishment, and disabled people are seen as outcasts.[3]

After my dad died, my mom told people he was away on a trip. So I started telling people that he was away on a trip, too, like a form of collective gaslighting. We believed it was a way to avoid bringing shame to our family. For my mom, being widowed meant that bad luck somewhere in her lineage had caused my dad to die. Additionally, I now had a physical disability, which added another level of shame to my Asian narrative. Because of my self-consciousness around my arm that now looked different, I wore long sleeves all the time, even in the humidity and heat of Washington, DC, summers, so I could hide my disability and not talk about it. I had internalized the shame of the physical and mental trauma of the car accident because of the ableist cultural beliefs I grew up with.

My mental health was never discussed. My parents, like many other Asian immigrants of their generation, had overcome many hardships to get to the United States, so I thought I should not complain and should be grateful for the sacrifices they had made. It was only in 2019, two years after I had begun therapy for the first time, that I was diagnosed with PTSD related to the car accident—a non-apparent disability. That was a twenty-two-year treatment gap. For over a decade after the accident, I felt that I couldn't talk to anyone about my dad or my disability, and I wonder if that exacerbated what ultimately became my PTSD diagnosis.

Research shows that Asian Americans are three times less likely to seek mental health support than white people, and only 8.6 percent of Asian Americans seek out mental health services compared to 18 percent of the national population.[4] Many Asian cultures simply do not view mental illness as a disability that requires treatment. Psychiatrist Geoffrey Liu explains,

> For some Asian Americans, there's a real sense that your value as a person depends on your ability to take care of your family and community....

Mental illness is seen...incorrectly...as taking away a person's ability to care for others. For that reason, it's seen as taking away someone's identity or purpose. It's the ultimate form of shame.[5]

The result is that many people do not get the support we need.

Another compounding factor is that Asian Americans deal with the model minority myth: the harmful belief that Asian immigrants or children of immigrants must assimilate to whiteness and perform better than other marginalized groups in order to belong and succeed in America. For disabled Asian Americans, the pressure to prove that we are hardworking makes it even more difficult to navigate society with our disability. As disability activist Mia Ives-Rublee remarks in a *Huffington Post* article, "We need to make sure our community survives and thrives wherever we're at, and part of that means putting our heads down and not complaining and working hard and being that American success story."[6] Because of this, Ives-Rublee finds herself in a paradox at the intersection of her Asian American and disabled identities: "Disabled Asian Americans will never fit the model minority myth. And I'm proud to say I subvert it."[7] While we know that the model minority is a myth, I thought this statement was fascinating because it put into perspective how much I had tried to achieve it in my own life. It always felt as if what I did was not enough because I wondered if, in my mom's eyes, being disabled made me not fit that "model."

Here's a look at communities at other intersections. A 2020 study found that one-third of LGBTQIA+ adults, 36 percent, self-reported having a disability. They were also more likely than non-LGBTQIA+ people (at 24 percent) to be disabled.[8] Disabled LGBTQIA+ people face compounded stigmatization as well. Unique challenges include both finding LGBTQIA+-inclusive and accessible community and health care services and facing bullying and harassment at school more than their non-LGBTQIA+ peers with disabilities and their LGBTQIA+ peers without disabilities.[9]

Yema Yang is a queer, mentally ill, autistic, and disabled Chinese-Burmese Buddhist woman and the child of immigrants. She is a critical mental health and disability justice scholar-activist-poet dedicated to collective refuge, love, and liberation. She shared with me her experience of seeking disability accommodations while at university and the struggle she faced both with older white therapists and a system that was already unfamiliar and alienating. Having already been denied a psychiatric verification—essentially, a letter stating that she had a diagnosable mental illness and that required disability accommodations in her academic setting—Yang began to question the veracity of her own experience:

> Here my therapist was, suggesting I was an imposter in disability. As a Chinese-Burmese woman who rarely saw herself reflected in mental health or disability spaces, I already was fighting to feel like I was legitimately mentally ill and disabled. I had to constantly remind and convince myself that my experiences and feelings were real and valid—that it wasn't all in my head.[10]

She was able to get her accommodations, but only a semester after she had requested them. Yang reflected on her frustrations:

> One of the most bitter parts of this whole experience came from realizing just how difficult this whole [expletive] process was. I am a queer, racialized, disabled woman and child of immigrants—in many respects, this whole American process of acquiring academic accommodations was already new and difficult to me. Yet, I am also privileged in other ways—upper middle class, English as my main language, in higher education. Additionally, because of my organizing work, I was familiar with advocating for myself and others, especially in mental health contexts. But even with those privileges and backgrounds that allowed me to get into a therapist's office, be understood when I articulated my experiences, and identify my need for support, I was *still* rejected and doubted for disability accommodations.
>
> I have a theory that this old white man therapist saw some Asian girl doing "well"—this face of the "model minority"—and didn't require accommodations as a result. Would he have given psychiatric verification if the student was white? I may never know for sure, but I do know how his decision impacted me.[11]

Yang's experience is an example of the clash between her intersectional identity and institutional ableism: a clinician and an academic institution created barriers to her access, perhaps specifically because of the way she presented.

Within the Hispanic/Latinx community, adults with mental illness receive treatment at a lower rate than the US average, with an estimated more than half of Hispanic young adults ages eighteen to twenty-five living with severe mental illnesses because they do not receive treatment.[12]

This is what Dior Vargas, a Latina mental health activist and the creator of the People of Color and Mental Illness Photo Project, experienced:

> As a child, I never saw any non-white, positive representations of mental health. It made mental illness seem like a curse or punishment or a lack of strength. I felt extremely alone because no one in my Latine family talked about mental health, nor did we think that mental health was important given what immigrant family members had gone through in the past. A lot of the thinking behind well-being was prayer and believing in God.[13]

Meanwhile, one in four Black people has a disability, according to the CDC.[14] Keri Gray, founder of National Alliance of Melanin Disabled (NAMED) Advocates, told me about her experience as a child cancer survivor:

> Now I was not only this…Black girl growing up in the South, but now I'm this Black disabled girl. And I honestly didn't know how to navigate that identity. On one hand, I had a lot of representation of what it meant to be Black; of what it meant to be a woman. But I did not have much, if any, representation of what it meant to be openly disabled. And to be okay with that.[15]

The struggle to navigate an additional minoritized identity heaped on top of others can absolutely send anyone into a crisis. But as she navigated the experience, Gray landed in college and found herself surrounded by disabled peers, many of whom were achieving incredible things. It was because of the understanding that she came to, recognizing that "there's a whole community here, where I can learn and grow," that Gray became an advocate herself and got involved in education around disability and racial justice.[16]

While Gray was able to transform herself into an advocate, not every Black and disabled person will have or want the same experience. More than half of disabled Black people in the United States will be arrested by the time they reach their late twenties, a "horrifyingly high" number that is double the 28 percent rate of white people with disabilities, according to Erin McCauley, the author of the study.[17] In 2019, Elijah McClain, an autistic twenty-three-year-old Black man who was deemed "suspicious" by three police officers while he was walking home from a convenience store listening to music, was restrained and placed in a chokehold and later died.[18] Disability is often falsely viewed as a threat of resistance to and non-compliance with law enforcement, especially when police officers do not know how to deal with disabilities like epilepsy, deafness, or autism, leading to unnecessary escalation or use of excessive force.[19] When we consider this on top of America's long history of overpolicing Black people, it is no wonder that disabled Black people are especially at risk. The combination of disability and Blackness leads to "a double bind," according to Talila Lewis, where the US government uses "constructed ideas about disability, delinquency, and dependency, intertwined with constructed ideas about race, to classify and criminalize people."[20]

And just because a Black and disabled person isn't being arrested doesn't mean they're not being othered. Eric Harris, a thirty-six-year-old Black disabled advocate and the director of public policy at Disability Rights California, was born with his disability and is a wheelchair user. He told me a story that still pains him:

> After wheelchair basketball practice, I had to stop for gas. I stopped at a local gas station and asked the gentleman behind the counter if I could use the restroom. I figured that there might be a key to access the restroom like at most gas stations. This person told me that the restroom was not working and that nobody could use it right now. I went on to fill up my gas tank, but while I was waiting, I saw someone go into the restroom to use it. I then went inside to confront and question the person behind the counter, and they acted like they did not understand me and still

would not let me use the restroom. I did not know if this was because of my disability, my race, or a combination of both.[21]

In 2005, Sins Invalid, a collective of disabled queer women of color, developed the concept of disability justice. Evolving from the disability rights movement that began in the 1960s, disability justice is a more comprehensive and sustainable approach to the fight for the rights of disabled people that is rooted in intersectionality.

Sins Invalid recognized that earlier disability rights movements had leadership that was "historically centered [around] white experiences" and were "single-issue identity based," centering people who could already "achieve rights and access through a legal or rights-based framework." These movements therefore "invisibilized the lives of peoples who lived at intersecting junctures of oppression," such as disabled people of color, immigrants, LGBTQIA+ people, people experiencing homelessness, incarcerated people, and people whose ancestral lands were stolen by colonizers.[22]

In response, disability justice lays out a ten-principle framework, focusing on tenets such as intersectionality, anti-capitalism, and cross-movement organizing while recognizing how systems of oppression interact with and reinforce each other.

Here is an example of this in action: disability justice is climate justice because the climate crisis impacts vulnerable communities like the disabled community the most. I learned more about this after attending former US vice president and Nobel laureate Al Gore's thirty-sixth Climate Reality Leadership Corps training in 2017. Rising temperatures and extreme heat are dangerous to those with multiple sclerosis who experience greater pain on hot days and to people with certain spinal cord injuries who cannot sweat to cool down. Air pollution exacerbates health conditions like asthma, and power outages threaten disabled people who rely on electricity-powered medical equipment like ventilators. Evacuation from natural disasters impacts those who have mobility issues, and accessibility devices are often lost in fires and floods. Droughts that cause food shortages and water insecurity also impact disabled people due to the disproportionate number who are already caught in an endless poverty cycle.[23] Additionally, the climate crisis is caused by capitalism, an "extraction-based economy" of "endless consumption" that is not only destroying the earth we live in but also operates on the basis of the lie that "disability is individually tragic and collectively burdensome." In a dying world fueled by capitalism, disabled people are often the last people to be saved, if we are saved at all.[24]

Disability intersects with many other social issues. Disability justice is not just climate justice but also reproductive justice, racial justice, economic justice, and police reform, to name but a few.

Intersectionality must inform how we understand disability. If we want to live in a world where we recognize that no bodies are superior to other bodies and that all lives are valuable and equally deserving, we must fight for justice and the liberation of disabled people, all other oppressed people, and the earth we live on.

Reflection Questions

1. Reflect on your own intersectionality. How do various aspects of your identity, such as race, gender, religion, sexuality, and disability, intersect and shape your experiences?

2. If you are an advocate for women's rights, gay rights, or racial justice, reflect on how intersectionality plays a role in your advocacy efforts. Are there areas where you can broaden your focus to address the interconnected nature of various forms of oppression, such as ensuring that the Women's March or LGBTQIA+ Pride Parade is accessible?

3. What are some causes or social justice movements that you care about, such as reproductive justice, voting rights, or climate change? Do some research on how these movements impact disabled people and how they might also be disability justice issues.

CHAPTER 8

What Is Ableism?

"Identifying [ableism] by name is only the beginning of the process of counteracting it," says Lisa Diedrich, professor of women's, gender, and sexuality studies at Stony Brook University.[1]

When many of us, including me, were younger, we knew we were being treated a certain way because of our disabilities. For me, it was the countless times I was picked last for sports teams during gym class. Jamie Shields, a self-described "Registered Blind AuDHD Rhino" (after being told his whole life how he could or couldn't identify),[2] shared a similar early experience from his childhood, which, much like my own, involved feeling othered without having the language to express it:

> Being Disabled embarrassed me. It made me feel like I was less than. I was treated differently, and not in a good way. I learned that being Disabled was a bad thing. It indicated to others I was not "normal," and that I was an easy target for their aggression. Adults also seemed to want to wrap me in cotton wool or talk about my Disability like it was a bad thing to be discussing.[3]

These experiences led him to "binge drinking, skipping class, and feelings of being worthless" while at university, where he continued to struggle with internalized as well as institutional ableism. "But still, I didn't know how or what ableism was, nor that my internalized ableism had me self-sabotaging and self-destructing."[4]

So what *is* ableism?

Let's start with the dictionary again. According to Merriam-Webster, *ableism* is "discrimination or prejudice against individuals with disabilities."[5] I, too, used to see my negative experiences from navigating the world solely as a result of others discriminating against me because of my disability. However, the truth is that ableism is much more than just prejudice on the basis of disability.

Ableism is an entire system of oppression, with nuanced meanings and a complex history.

The earliest known use of the word *ableism* was in 1981, when it appeared in Yvonne Duffy's *All Things Are Possible*, a text on disability and sexuality. The term appears only once in the book, during an interview with a disabled lesbian woman who remarked that she had experienced "ableism" in both lesbian and straight communities.[6] Since then, disability advocates and scholars have increasingly used *ableism*, especially in 2020 during a period of renewed consciousness, when people were starting to grapple with their understanding of racism. In 2022, the term gained more widespread media coverage through John Fetterman's US Senate campaign: a stroke left Fetterman with an auditory processing disorder right before a debate, prompting a national conversation on what ableism is, how it affects our interactions, and how it is represented in our culture.[7] Although the term is fairly modern, it is important to note that ableism has always existed, even in antiquity, as we have seen in Chapter 5: A Brief History of the Disability Rights Movement.

Today, I use the working definition of *ableism* from abolitionist and disability advocate Talila Lewis:

[Ableism is] a system of assigning value to people's bodies and minds based on societally constructed ideas of normalcy, productivity, desirability, intelligence, excellence, and fitness…[that] are deeply rooted in eugenics, anti-Blackness, misogyny, colonialism, imperialism, and capitalism. This systemic oppression leads to people and society determining people's value based on their culture, age, language, appearance, religion, birth or living place, "health/wellness," and/or their ability to satisfactorily re/produce, "excel," and "behave." You do not have to be disabled to experience ableism.[8]

Ableism can also affect people who are not disabled, such as in the way the media has dissected women's bodies for years (ableism and sexism) or our mistreatment of Black bodies throughout history (ableism and racism). This is where intersectionality comes in: ableism, racism, sexism, and other systems of oppression all operate together.

Other definitions of ableism point out that our society assumes that there is a "default" or "norm" that is superior to any experience that falls outside it. According to the Disability & Philanthropy Forum, ableism "is a set of stereotypes and practices that...[assume] that the bodies and minds of non-disabled people are the 'default,' placing value on them based on society's perceptions of what's considered 'normal.'"[9] In its definition, Salem State University adds the idea of power and privilege: "Ableism is prejudice plus power....In North America (and globally), societally enabled or non-disabled people have the institutional power."

Today, as I look back on my past understanding of ableism, my takeaway is that disability is not the problem that needs to be fixed; ableism is.

So what does ableism actually look like in practice? What are some examples of an ableist society in action?

Systemic or institutional ableism is a form of ableism that is often overt and structural. It manifests as "the physical barriers, policies, laws, regulations, and practices that exclude disabled people from full participation and equal opportunity."[10] This includes a lack of accessibility in public spaces, for example, no wheelchair-accessible entrances, a broken elevator, no braille on signs, or a lack of sign-language interpreters or closed-captioning technology. This lack of accessibility creates barriers to participation for people with certain types of disabilities. This type of ableism also includes limited health care coverage for people with "pre-existing" conditions or the fact that it's still legal for employers to pay disabled people below minimum wage through the FLSA.

Systemic or institutional ableism also harms disabled people, damaging our quality of life and even killing us. For example, in June 2020, Michael Hickson died when he was denied treatment for COVID because doctors determined that he had a "lower quality of life."[11] And in November 2021, disability activist Engracia Figueroa died from complications of injuries sustained when an airline destroyed her custom wheelchair.[12]

Then we have **ableist microaggressions**. This form of ableism is indirect and subtle but just as harmful. In later chapters, we will address some common ableist microaggressions and what we can do to interrupt them. Microaggressions, as defined by Kevin Nadal, a professor of psychology at John Jay College of Criminal Justice, are "the everyday, subtle, intentional—and oftentimes unintentional—interactions or behaviors that communicate some sort of bias toward historically marginalized groups. The difference between microaggressions and overt discrimination or macroaggressions is that people who commit microaggressions might not even be aware of them."[13]

Ableist microaggressions occur in our interpersonal relationships and how we interact with one another. The three types of interpersonal ableist microaggressions are microinsults, microinvalidations, and microassaults.[14] Microinsults are insensitive remarks or backhanded compliments that are often made unconsciously, such as "You're so inspiring because you're disabled," offering unsolicited prayers or advice to disabled people, or doing what you think is best rather than asking a disabled person what we need.

Microinvalidations deny or exclude real experiences, such as "I don't see you as disabled" or "But you don't *look* disabled." What this actually sounds like to disabled people is "You don't see me—my identity makes me invisible," "You don't hear me—my thoughts and opinions don't matter," or "You accept me only because my disability doesn't always make me visibly different."[15]

Finally, microassaults are explicit verbal attacks intended to hurt. They aren't ambiguous. Examples are mocking someone's disability, belittling someone's need to use assistive devices or mobility aids, complaining about accessible parking spots inconveniencing your ability to park, or deciding not to hire a qualified candidate because we are disabled.

A type of ableist microaggression is known as **everyday, minor, or casual ableism**. Casual ableism is "subtle ableism, usually hidden in seemingly innocent phrases, conversations, and actions."[16] Examples are when someone chooses an inaccessible venue to plan an event, posts a video without closed captions, uses an accessible parking space or bathroom stall when they are able to use non-accessible spaces without pain or risk of injury, or calls someone "psycho" or "crazy" in a casual or pejorative manner.

Black disabled advocate Eric Harris told me about the numerous occurrences of ableism that he experiences on a day-to-day basis, "including the regular occurrence of having taxi cabs pass me up for either my skin color or wheelchair, entering restaurants through the back or kitchen because the main entrance was not accessible or having to sit in the corner, and especially in school when teachers would crack jokes and make light of my disability." He reminds us that these examples "hurt deeply."[17]

Underlying casual ableism is someone's privilege to not think further about making accommodations for disabled people. As diversity, equity, inclusion, and belonging (DEIB) consultant Becca Lory Hector puts it, "It is one of the most painful parts of my job to have to silently process a microaggression, carefully educate surrounding it, and continue to remain professional all at the same time. And yet, when it happens, it reminds me of exactly how much work I have to do."[18]

Catarina Rivera, creator of @BlindishLatina, a disability advocacy platform, has Usher syndrome, which means she has both hearing and vision disabilities; she wears hearing aids and uses a white cane to navigate the world. Rivera told me about an experience she had while on a walking tour in Amsterdam. Carrying her white cane to make her way around, she struggled to understand the tour guide, who spoke without eye contact amid the ambient noise from the street. She approached him and asked, "Can you please face me when you're speaking so I can read your lips?" He didn't skip a beat when he looked at her—and her cane—and quickly replied, "How can *you* read lips?" Looking back on that experience, Rivera said, "I couldn't believe that I expressed what I needed and that he questioned it instead of listening to me. I don't have time to explain how my disability works to everyone I interact with, and I shouldn't have to. He put me in a position where he held the power to decide whether to accommodate me or not, and it was like he was asking me to prove my need."[19]

This, of course, is just the tip of the iceberg. Many other firsthand experiences of ableism have been submitted by different users on the Instagram page @CasualAbleism.

Ableist microaggressions are harmful because they assign "inferior worth to people with disabilities, limiting their potential"[20] and lead to a lack of psychological safety that has a lasting damaging effect on the mental state of disabled people. They are both the symptoms and causes of larger structural inequities—remarks or behaviors that are subtle or unconscious can easily develop into more overt forms of systemic ableism over time.

Living in an ableist world also creates **internalized ableism**, a form of internalized oppression. *Internalized oppression* is defined as the "internalization of negative messages and beliefs about oneself and one's group that are perpetuated by a society or system that oppresses them. It can manifest as self-hatred, low self-esteem, self-doubt, and a lack of self-worth, and can lead to individuals internalizing negative stereotypes and biases about their own group and accepting the dominant narrative about their own worth and value....It can be a significant barrier to self-empowerment and the ability to challenge and resist oppression."[21] For example, it means thinking that we should lower our standards for romantic relationships because "who would want to be with someone with a disability?" or not asking for accommodations, accessibility, or the support we're entitled to because we believe we are a burden.

Finally, **lateral ableism** is when certain disabled people do not consider or fight for the rights of all disabled people. More simply, it is when a disabled person is ableist toward another disabled person. Andrew Pulrang, a contributor at *Forbes*, uses the example of "people with physical disabilities bolstering their own social status and acceptance by emphasizing that they don't have mental impairments, with assertions like, 'My legs are disabled, not my brain!' or, 'At least there's nothing wrong with my mind!'"[22] Statements like this reinforce harm toward people who have mental disabilities. Another example is when we label someone "high functioning," such as "high-functioning autism" or "high-functioning anxiety," ultimately denying us the support that we might need. At the same time, those who are labeled "low functioning" are seen as not being capable of doing anything. Tackling lateral ableism is necessary to our collective liberation because, as Fannie Lou Hamer said, "Nobody's free until everybody's free."[23]

Once we know what ableism looks like, and once we recognize the ways that we might personally be contributing to an ableist society, then we can work on the ways to dismantle it through an anti-ableist practice.

Reflection Questions

1. Have you witnessed or participated in ableist behaviors, even unknowingly? How did these experiences impact you, and did you recognize them as ableist at the time?

2. Were you aware of these different types of ableism and ableist microaggressions? Can you think of other examples?

3. How might you actively interrupt and challenge ableist micro-aggressions? We will discuss strategies in the next section.

4. In what ways have societal messages influenced your perception of yourself (if you are disabled) or others with disabilities?

5. Have you observed examples of lateral ableism, and how can you promote solidarity in the disability community?

CHAPTER 9

What Is Anti-Ableism?

The only way to dismantle ableism and build a disability-inclusive world is to be anti-ableist.

To me, anti-ableism is rooted in action. It is not enough to simply be "not ableist." Although he speaks on racism, the author and antiracist scholar Ibram X. Kendi shares a very useful concept that we can apply to anti-ableism. In his book *How to Be an Antiracist*, Kendi says that the problem with being "not racist" is that it signifies neutrality: "I am not a racist, but neither am I aggressively against racism." As a result, people who proclaim that they are "not racist" do not feel the need to engage in the fight against racism. On the flip side, being antiracist means active participation in the work toward racial equity and justice.[1]

In the same way, anti-ableism means developing a whole philosophy and practice to combat ableism. This aligns with the definition from Salem State University: "Anti-ableism is strategies, theories, actions, and practices that challenge and counter ableism and inequalities, prejudices, and discrimination based on developmental, emotional, physical, or psychiatric disability."[2]

So why should we be anti-ableist?

First, ableism affects and harms us all, as Talila Lewis says—"You do not have to be disabled to experience ableism."[3] Dismantling ableism—alongside racism, sexism, classism, transphobia, and other systems of oppression—is in everyone's best interest and key to our collective liberation.

Second, ableism creates negative social impacts. When you exclude disabled people or make us invisible, you deny the diversity of the human experience, lose out on precious innovation and talent, and create barriers to equitable participation. Negative stereotypes and misconceptions result in social exclusion and limited opportunities in all areas of life, such as education, employment, health care, and public spaces, whereas anti-ableism allows diversity and creativity to flourish in a way that benefits everyone. As disability design advocate Liz Jackson wrote in a *New York Times* article, disabled people "are the original lifehackers."[4] We are simply some of the most adaptable and innovative people out there.

Third, there is a whole distinct and unique culture in the disability community that we should celebrate and be proud of—and that society should not exclude or deny. We are not invisible and should not be treated as such. Disability history matters, disability culture matters, and disability pride matters. We matter.

Fourth, it is illegal to treat disabled people as less than in the United States. When you treat people as less than, you are denying us our basic human rights, which, according to the ADA, breaks the law.

So, you ask, *what actions can I take to begin practicing anti-ableism?*

Throughout the rest of the book, you will learn the practical steps toward becoming anti-ableist. You've already started with this foundational section on owning your personal education and unlearning pre-existing ideas and myths about disability (Anti-Ableism and You). In the next sections, you will learn how to live out these lessons in your interpersonal relationships and interactions (Anti-Ableism and Your Community) and, finally, how to take actions that impact the collective and lead to lasting change (Anti-Ableism and Societal Change).

Reflection Questions

1. What does being anti-ableist mean to you?

2. Write out this phrase: "I am unlearning ableist behavior" or "I am becoming anti-ableist." How does that make you feel?

3. What has come up for you as you have worked through these reflection questions over the last couple of chapters? What steps can you continuously take to commit to anti-ableist practices?

4. What are you learning about yourself or the disability community so far that reveals some of your pre-existing assumptions or practices? How can you shift them into becoming anti-ableist?

CHAPTER 10

Why You Should Care About Disability

B ack when I was at Georgetown in 2009, I applied for the Reimagine George-town Grant to help fund the first student-run disability club at the university. As part of the application, I went through an interview with a selection committee of my peers.

I will never forget the moment when one of the members of the committee looked at me and said, "How are you going to get people to care about disabled people?"

I felt devalued, dehumanized, and discarded. Memories from my adolescence came rushing back—memories of feeling erased, insignificant, and invisible. The sad thing is that disabled people are no strangers to these emotions whenever we encounter resistance or are denied our basic human rights or equitable participation in daily activities. At that moment in the interview room, I told myself that I didn't want anyone else to feel like that. I told the committee that because I cared, I knew other people would care, too. Despite that offensive question, we did receive the grant.

I threw myself into the creation of Diversability. Our goal from the beginning was to create not a support group but rather a disability pride movement.[1] But people approached me, confused.

"What's disability pride?" they asked. "How can you be proud to be disabled?"

As Ardra Shephard writes on her blog, *Tripping on Air,*

> Being proud to be disabled isn't about liking my disability. It isn't about
> pretending that disability doesn't straight-up suck. Rather, claiming dis-
> ability pride is a rejection of the notion that I should feel ashamed of my
> body or my disability....Declaring my pride means that I don't accept
> society's definition of disability. Loving my disabled body is a radical act
> that can challenge the way people think about disability; one that pro-
> motes the idea that it's normal to be imperfect.[2]

I agree with Shephard. Disability pride doesn't mean loving every aspect of
our disability, body, mind, or experience. It is nuanced and varied and means
something different to each of us, but it means we get to be part of a vibrant community that we can be proud of.

Disability pride was still a new concept for some people in 2009, but it has been
around since 1990. Not to be confused with LGBTQIA+ pride, which is its own historic and essential movement, disability pride is for anyone who identifies as a member of the disability community, whether we exist at the intersections of disability
and LGBTQIA+ identities or not. After the ADA was signed on July 26, 1990, Boston held the first-ever Disability Pride Day on October 6 that year. Almost fifteen
years later, the first Disability Pride Parade kicked off in Chicago in 2004. In 2015,
to celebrate the twenty-fifth anniversary of the ADA, New York mayor Bill de Bla-
sio declared July Disability Pride Month, which has since consisted of events held
throughout the month and a parade and festival.

In 2019, ahead of the thirtieth anniversary of the ADA in 2020, I began drafting a letter to San Francisco mayor London Breed in my capacity as a member
of the Mayor's Disability Council, hoping to get similar recognition: "Disability
Pride enables people with disabilities to redefine their identity with self-worth,
serves as a tool to tackle ableism, bias, and discrimination, and reshapes false
negative perceptions of individuals with disabilities as people with value, talents,
and significance."[3] We were successful in obtaining a mayoral proclamation of
July as Disability Pride Month in San Francisco,[4] but we still have some way to go
before Disability Pride Month is formally recognized in other major cities as well
as in every state in the United States.

The way I see it, disability pride is an example of an anti-ableist mindset and behavior because it helps us to combat ableism by making disability visible and worthy. It is rooted in action rather than neutrality. And it helps us to move toward a disability-inclusive world. More than just a call for acceptance, it celebrates the intrinsic worth and meaningful contributions of disabled people.

This is why you should care about disability.

As we've learned, there are over a billion people globally who are disabled.[5] In the United States, 61 million Americans, or one in four adults, have a disability, according to the CDC.[6] We are not a small or insignificant group; in fact, we are the largest minority in the world.[7] Even if you are not disabled, it is certain that you know or are close to someone who is.

Here's the other thing: the disability community is the only minoritized group that anyone can join at any time.[8] Anyone can become disabled at any point in our lives. This was what happened to me: I was born able to use both of my arms, but a sudden car accident paralyzed one of them, leading me to relearn how to navigate life as someone who can use only one arm—and my non-dominant one at that. The COVID pandemic also reminded us of this with the phenomenon of long-haul COVID. Long COVID, defined as "the continuation or development of new symptoms three months after the initial infection, with these symptoms lasting for at least two months," has over two hundred known symptoms, including intense fatigue, shortness of breath, chronic pain, and brain fog. According to medical research, long COVID may also reactivate latent viruses in the body or cause chronic inflammation that triggers other health conditions.[9] As of late October 2023, 9.5 percent of the 134 million American adults who had COVID were still experiencing symptoms of long COVID.[10]

The truth is that many of us are what some call "pre-disabled," meaning that we have yet to become disabled, something most of us will likely face as we age or depending on various circumstances in life. In a *Daily Show* interview with the late author and disability rights advocate Judy Heumann, Trevor Noah used the term *able-bodied*, to which Heumann replied, "I call you 'non-disabled' because the likelihood of you acquiring a disability, temporarily or permanently, is statistically very high." Noah responded, joking but not joking, "Did you just threaten me?" Heumann responded, "Yes, definitely."

His answer revealed an uncomfortable truth that Heumann acknowledged in another interview with the *Washington Post*: that non-disabled people fear disability or feel threatened by what they don't know, causing them to avoid meaningful discussions about disability even when it affects and impacts them.[11]

The reason I bring this up is not to scare people but to emphasize that if disability can happen to anybody, then all the more reason to push for accessibility and inclusivity. As advocate and YouTube personality Molly Burke says, "The disabled community is something that everybody should be caring about because you shouldn't wait until it impacts your life to care about it."[12]

There's another fundamental reason why all this matters: caring about disabled people matters because we should just care about other people as human beings, period.

"We're not getting normal back, but we can do better...by one another," said disability rights activist Imani Barbarin in an interview with the Try Guys on how COVID has impacted the disability community and why we all should care. "We have the opportunity to do better because we can all see it now....So, take that as an opportunity to change where you live, change the policies that affect your community, and change this country for the better [because] we can." In response, host Zach Kornfeld added, "If you center those who are most vulnerable in your considerations, it will make life better for everyone....And if nothing else, I hope that people can take away some [expletive] empathy."[13]

What about the people who simply don't care? Writer and activist Michelle MiJung Kim provides a simple answer: "I no longer believe we should be spending disproportionate energy trying to 'convert' those who are simply unwilling to care, learn, or change. Instead, I choose to work with people who are genuinely interested in change—even if they are not 'perfect' (nobody is) and even if they fumble (we all do). There are so many people who do care, and there is so much work to be done among us."[14]

When you understand the different reasons why this matters, then you will understand why we need to do the work to dismantle ableism—whether it's because you are disabled, you have loved ones who are disabled, or you acknowledge that you may become disabled in the future. We *can* build an anti-ableist and disability-inclusive world together.

Reflection Questions

1. What does "disability pride" mean to you? How can embracing disability pride challenge societal norms?

2. Why do you personally care about disability? You can consider the different reasons highlighted in this chapter for inspiration or have your own.

3. What does an anti-ableist world look like to you? What specific actions can you take to bring this vision to life?

CHAPTER 11

Recognize and Use Your Privilege

Privilege is like air—you don't notice it until it's missing.[1] This is why it's often so hard to recognize the privileges you benefit from—they can be as natural to you as breathing. But it's crucial to be aware of your privileges, especially in an ableist world. You have to understand how you continue to benefit from ableism before you can combat it.

After seeing a BuzzFeed video in 2015, I was inspired to start facilitating the "privilege walk" activity in my communities.[2] In the video, a facilitator reads a list of thirty-five statements to a group of people who start out standing in a line together, holding hands. With every statement, each participant takes a step forward or back based on how they identify with it. The statements include phrases such as "If you took out loans for your education, take one step back" or "If you can show affection for your romantic partner without fear of being ridiculed, take one step forward." The privilege walk is an exercise that helps participants better visualize and understand what privilege looks like for each person, though this exercise has also been criticized for retraumatizing people for the benefit of privileged people's education. At the end of the exercise, the participants find themselves spread out in the room, standing in different positions relative to their privileges, a stark visual representation of inequity in our society. And it is no surprise that the people who stand at the very back of the room usually find themselves at the intersections of different compounding marginalized identities, including their race, gender, and disability status.

Now, let's apply this concept to non-disabled privilege. What does non-disabled privilege look like, and how much of it do you have? See the following for a few examples. Does anything on this list describe your experience? You can find more robust "non-disabled privilege" lists online, including one from activist and organizer Lydia X. Z. Brown.[3]

1. When speaking with medical professionals, your medical problems are believed and taken seriously, and you can expect doctors to respect your decisions.

2. If you are out in public, you are spoken to directly rather than the people you're with.

3. You can spontaneously attend an event, restaurant, or social outing without wondering whether the venue will be accessible to you, if you have the transportation to get there, or if you will be able to sit with everyone in your group.

4. If you have children, your ability to be a parent is not questioned.

5. People don't assume, based on your body and/or mind, that you are non-sexual.

6. You can buy children's books and toys featuring people like you.

7. No one thinks the way your body and/or mind works needs to be fixed or cured.

8. You are not considered a burden for simply existing.

9. In case of an emergency, you are able to evacuate a building on your own.

10. You do not have to think twice about how to get to an in-person appointment if the building has stairs or the elevator is out of order.

11. You do not have to worry about going to a space with food and whether people will be able to accommodate your dietary or chemical access needs.

12. Growing up, you had celebrities and role models whose bodies and/or minds were like yours.

13. You do not have to rely on strangers to help you bathe or use the toilet.

14. You do not have to think about whether flashing lights will cause sensory overload or seizures.
15. You won't experience sensory hypersensitivity, triggers, or flashbacks from loud noises or fireworks.
16. It is presumed that you deserve at least a minimum wage for your labor.
17. You know that public safety information will be provided in a format that is accessible for you.

The goal of this exercise is not to make you feel bad or guilty about your privilege—that sensation is real, though, and we'll cover it in the next chapter. It is not your fault that you experience the privileges you were born into. Many privileges are unearned. However, you do have a responsibility to educate yourself and be aware of the privileges you *do* benefit from.

As investor Arlan Hamilton says in her book *It's About Damn Time*, "I think when some people hear the word *privilege*, they get defensive, but I'm here to tell you that having privilege, or being privileged, is not the problem. Entitlement is the problem....Privilege is a hand-me-down heirloom, rooted in the circumstances you're born into; entitlement is something you procure and choose to wear."[4] Writer Gina Crosley-Corcoran adds, "Recognizing privilege simply means being aware that some people have to work much harder just to experience the things you take for granted (if they ever can experience them at all)."[5]

It is important to note that privilege is not clear-cut, and it does not simply split the room into haves and have-nots. Privilege can be defined as the "unearned access or advantages granted to specific groups of people because of their membership in a social group."[6] As we learned in Chapter 7: Disability Intersectionality, the notion of intersectionality describes how different forms of inequity pertaining to different identities can intersect and be compounded in a person's experience. As a result, people can be privileged in some ways and not in others, depending on their intersecting identities. For example, Crosley-Corcoran argues that poor white people still benefit from race privilege. Similarly, in the diverse disability community, many disabled people benefit from privileges that other disabled people do not. According to disability writer Andrew Pulrang, for example, "Physically disabled people tend to be better accommodated and socially accepted than people with cognitive impairments or mental health conditions." Then there are disabled people who "experience compounding layers of prejudice," such as a poor, Black, queer, quadriplegic woman compared to a white, wealthy, quadriplegic man.[7]

I benefit from many privileges, too. I was born in the United States. I attended college and graduated without student loan debt. I have work experience at recognizable companies like Goldman Sachs, Bloomberg, and REVOLT. I am not reliant on disability benefits that would create income caps and income limits for me (we'll talk more about the issues with disability benefits in a later chapter). There's even the notion of attractiveness privilege, where I've had people tell me, "At least you're pretty," for fitting conventional Western beauty standards, and that I'm "well-spoken" and "eloquent," which demonstrates the privilege I have over people with speech-related disabilities.

At Diversability, I've leaned into the social capital I've built from my collective work experiences to provide job references and write letters of recommendation for our team members when they are ready to pursue their next opportunity—and many of them have gone on to get their dream jobs, scholarships, and internships. We use Diversability's reach to create visibility and speaking opportunities for leaders and advocates in the disability community.

The same idea of using my privilege and my background in finance came into play as I began exploring economic empowerment. Disabled activist and founder of the Disability Visibility Project Alice Wong and I started the Awesome Foundation Disability Chapter, where disabled trustees contribute $100 each month to fund a $1,000 microgrant for disability projects. As of February 2024, we have awarded over $80,000 worth of grants to more than eighty projects across eleven countries. The inspiration for this goes back to when I founded Diversability in 2009 as a student club, made possible through that modest $500 Reimagine Georgetown grant. And over the last couple of years, thanks to Arlan Hamilton and the Backstage Catalyst apprenticeship program, I've become an investor in startups and a few venture capital funds to support underestimated and disabled entrepreneurs.

So how can you use your power and privilege to fight for disability equity? A big part of becoming anti-ableist is honestly reckoning with the power and privilege we hold, even if it feels uncomfortable. And working through this discomfort is what will light a fire under us and allow us to grow and take action, which we'll discuss in later chapters. As author Ijeoma Oluo says, once you "identify where [your] privilege intersects with somebody else's oppression, [you'll] find [your] opportunities to make real change."[8]

Reflection Questions

1. How does thinking or talking about privilege make you feel?

2. Think about all of the ways in which you might benefit from privilege. Write out as many as you can. Here are a few that you can start with: race privilege, gender privilege, sexual orientation privilege, class privilege, and education privilege.

3. If you are non-disabled, how do you benefit from non-disabled privilege?

4. What are some ways that you experience both privilege and marginalization simultaneously?

5. Have you encountered situations where your privilege may have inadvertently perpetuated ableism? What could you have done instead? For example, saying that you don't need a microphone at an event and can speak loudly instead without knowing whether there might be attendees who would benefit from you speaking into a microphone so that the audio can be amplified and heard in all parts of the room.

CHAPTER 12

Overcome Your Non-Disabled Guilt and Shame

"I'm just feeling really guilty. It feels uncomfortable, and I'm not sure what to do with that feeling now," one participant said to me after one of my privilege walk exercises.

I have often received this response. Feelings of guilt are very real and valid, and sometimes it is hard for someone to move beyond their guilt because of how uncomfortable it can feel. Guilt can become so overwhelming that it drives people to inaction and silences them, preventing them from moving forward in a constructive way.

We can categorize guilt as two different types: **unhealthy guilt** and **healthy guilt**.[1] Here, I use pre-existing frameworks and discourse on racial justice and white guilt and adapt them to anti-ableism and non-disabled guilt.

Unhealthy non-disabled guilt leads to inaction, as I previously described, because it is overwhelming to learn the truth of how our privilege reflects, facilitates, and entrenches ableism in every sector of society. When our guilt makes us feel bad—for example, when we use an ableist term and are called out for it—we sometimes start to laser-focus on how ableism makes us feel, as opposed to the injustices of ableism itself. We decide we don't want to engage in anti-ableist discussions because we simply don't want to feel bad, which is a self-absorbed act.

Then there is healthy non-disabled guilt, where the experience of guilt leads to the desire to change. Guilt can open our eyes to injustices we've never noticed before—for example, when someone calls us out for using an ableist term, we realize that ableism has infiltrated our language and shaped our thoughts. And when we allow ourselves to sit with the discomfort of our guilt and acknowledge what causes it—ableism—we can be mobilized and inspired to address the root cause. As theologian Letty Russell says, "The poor do not ask us to feel guilty, for they can't eat guilt. What they ask is that we act to address the causes of injustice so they can obtain food."[2]

This, of course, is easier said than done, especially because feelings of unhealthy guilt are often accompanied by shame. If guilt is feeling bad about a certain behavior, then shame is feeling bad about who you are as a person. In other words, guilt over non-disabled privilege can turn into shame when non-disabled people realize that they automatically benefit from ableist structures in a way that they can't separate from their self-perception. When someone feels shame, "the whole self is under attack, not just [their] behavior that is something [they] can change," says June Tangney, a shame and guilt researcher at George Mason University.[3] This type of thinking can cause one to spiral into a self-focused and selfish state, where people cope by becoming defensive to protect their identity or by doubling down and seeing themselves as an "irredeemable villain."[4] Unfortunately, both of these outcomes prevent people who experience shame from getting out of the hole of this vicious thought cycle.

The good news is that it is possible to harness shame and guilt to move forward and make positive change, even if it means having to be uncomfortable first. Feelings of discomfort are incredibly jarring, since non-disabled people's version of "normal" in an ableist world is defined by *their* comfort. In fact, we disabled people often spend time and effort making the non-disabled people around us feel comfortable, even if it means going out of our way to do so.

I can think of a few examples from my own experience. In the early years of my advocacy, I would describe my paralyzed arm as my "funny hand" as a way to acknowledge my disability and bring levity to the situation. I have since stopped using that phrase because I would not want anyone to label any part of my body "funny," nor would I use that language to describe others. However, I still do some things today for non-disabled people's comfort. When others notice me wearing my wrist splint and ask about it, I explain, "It's from a car accident a long time ago.

Don't worry, it doesn't hurt!" in an attempt not to elicit more concern about my lifelong injury. You would be surprised by the number of people who ask me if my hand hurts, and even after I've explained that it does not, they respond with "Well, it looks like it hurts," dismissing my response and doubling down on their own projections about my experience.

There's a phrase going around DEI and education circles: "Get comfortable with being uncomfortable." Lily Zheng, a DEI speaker and strategist, aims to clarify this statement: "It's not the *experience* of discomfort that creates positive change, but instead the *resolution* of it."[5] According to Zheng, it is not enough to feel uncomfortable without any follow-up, which can exacerbate pre-existing ableist attitudes and behaviors. Instead, we need to focus on resolving the dissonance of our discomfort through constructive action and attitude shifts.

Here are some strategies to do so:

1. First, acknowledge that we all, including you, have ableist tendencies. We live in an ableist society, and ableism largely dictates the way we think and live. Spoiler alert: I'm unlearning ableism, too.

2. Second, instead of allowing shame to beat you down or turn you inward, acknowledge that your non-disabled identity and non-disabled privileges do not define you. We are all capable of change, and you have the power to redefine your thoughts and actions.

3. Third, stop focusing on how the reality of ableism makes you feel bad and allow the discomfort to open your eyes to how ableism hurts disabled people, which should fire your resolve to combat ableism. Convert your guilt into action. Tangney adds that while the inward-looking nature of shame interferes with empathy, "guilt and empathy go hand in hand," and guilt can push people toward constructive actions like apologies, donations, education, advocacy, and organizing.[6] While guilt can't be the long-term motivator of your anti-ableist work, it can be the start of propelling you into action. Revisit your responses to the reflection questions on your own motivations in Chapter 10: Why You Should Care About Disability.

4. Fourth, remember that you can sometimes redistribute your non-disabled privileges to those who lack them, as we discussed in Chapter 11: Recognize and Use Your Privilege. Instead of locking your privilege away because you believe it is stained with guilt or shame, wield it strategically to empower others. As bell hooks says, "Privilege does not have to be negative, but we have to share our resources and take direction about how to use our privilege in ways that empower those who lack it."[7] I discuss concrete ways to do this in later chapters.

5. Fifth, if you still find yourself stuck with feelings of guilt and shame, try to engage in self-reflection through journaling or by talking with other non-disabled people who share similar experiences. Shame is an often debilitating emotion that can affect your mental health, and you might also consider seeking professional help to work through it.

Reflection Questions

1. Write out this phrase: "I have ableist tendencies." How does it make you feel to know that you have ableist tendencies? Note: I suggest this phrasing over "I am ableist" because how we talk about ourselves influences who we become.

2. What is the difference between healthy and unhealthy guilt to you? Do you have examples from your own life? How can you tell the difference?

3. Think back to a time when you felt guilt or shame over an interpersonal incident. How might you respond differently next time to transform guilt into learning and action and not get stuck in shame?

CHAPTER 13

Accurate Disability Representation Matters

When I saw the 2019 film *The Farewell*, it put into words what I couldn't convey for a long time. In the movie, a young Chinese American woman returns to China to visit her grandmother, who has just received a terminal cancer diagnosis. However, the rest of the family has decided not to tell the grandmother that she is dying, partly because of their cultural beliefs. As the credits rolled, I realized how the film helped to illuminate the behaviors of my own Asian family: the stigma and taboo surrounding my dad's death and the reason we had kept it a secret for so long. When people who didn't share my cultural background asked me about the circumstances of his death after I saw *The Farewell*, I referenced the film as a way to help them understand my story.

Representation matters. In this case, representation of my AAPI heritage in a film written and directed by a fellow Asian American made me feel seen, heard, and validated. It not only helped name what I was going through and showed me that I wasn't alone but also helped better explain my experiences to others who didn't share my cultural background.

Asian American representation in TV, film, and other media has grown, and I hope disability representation will follow suit. We've already learned that people with disabilities are the largest minority group in the world—27 percent of adult Americans[1] and 15 percent of people worldwide are disabled[2]—yet we still find ourselves underrepresented in the media. And if we do appear, we are often inaccurately or insensitively portrayed.

Nielsen found that in September 2022, just 4.1 percent of all titles on TV included disability themes, and when shows did feature disabled characters, their total screen time was significantly lower than that of non-disabled characters: 8.8 percent of screen time for characters with non-apparent disabilities and 0.4 percent for characters with apparent disabilities. In the movies, only 2.3 percent of all speaking roles across the one hundred top-grossing films in 2019 featured a character with a disability, with no meaningful changes to the statistics over the prior five years.[3] With these abysmal numbers, it's no wonder that disabled people are 34 percent more likely than the rest of the population to report that we feel underrepresented on-screen.[4]

Underrepresentation in media is an example of an exclusionary microaggression that can make us believe that our stories don't matter. Unfortunately, underrepresentation isn't the only issue we deal with. Disappointingly, the representation that *does* make it to the screen is often rooted in inaccurate or insensitive stereotypes of disabled people as "abnormal," "pitiful," or "charity cases."[5]

"Disabled people either play villains or happy snowflake angel babies. We're either charitable, inspirational, never do naughty things in our life, or we're murdering babies because we lost an eye in a dart accident," says actor and comedian Maysoon Zayid.[6] In the 2016 film *Me Before You*, based on the book by Jojo Moyes, a man becomes quadriplegic in an accident and chooses assisted suicide, reinforcing harmful stereotypes that just because we are disabled, we would not want to live. Another example is the 1988 film *Rain Man*. Dustin Hoffman's character is autistic and portrayed as a savant, perpetuating the stereotype that all autistic people are solely defined by exceptional skills. Because of such extreme media depictions, it is no surprise that disabled people are still seen as one-dimensional tropes rather than real, multifaceted human beings, both in fiction and in real life.

The media we consume has a profound power to shape the way we think. The constant stereotypical portrayals of disabled people perpetuate ableism in our society, and we easily inherit these harmful beliefs because they are all we see and know.

To make things worse, the reason these inaccurate media portrayals exist is that, more often than not, non-disabled people are the ones who write, produce, direct, or act out our stories. Disabled people are underrepresented not only on-screen but also behind the scenes, which means we are not in full control of our narratives. A 2018 study from the Ruderman Family Foundation found that almost 80 percent of all disabled characters on TV were portrayed by non-disabled actors[7]—what the disability community calls "cripping up." According to actor and filmmaker John Lawson, nearly half of all actors who were nominated for the Academy Awards for playing a disabled character went on to win; however, of the almost thirty Oscar-winning acting roles featuring a character with a disability, only three were portrayed by someone with that disability—Harold Russell in 1947, Marlee Matlin in 1986,[8] and most recently Troy Kotsur in 2021.[9] Behind the scenes, disabled screenwriters represent only 0.15 percent of first-look and overall deals, 3 percent of upper-level TV writers, and less than 1 percent of the Writers Guild of America (WGA). Without disabled writers in the room, our stories are told without us.[10]

Accurate and *authentic* representation matters. Representation alone will be empty and performative if your characters are disabled but the people who create them are not or if these disabled stories promote negative and untrue stereotypes of us. As Vilissa Thompson, disability rights activist and founder of Ramp Your Voice!, says, "In order for disabled characters...to be authentically portrayed, we need actually disabled people consulted, writing, producing, directing, and casted to tell our experience the way it should be....Nothing about us without us."[11]

It is not difficult to cast disabled people as disabled characters or to make films written and directed by disabled people. Although the industry has a long way to go, recent success stories include Zack Gottsagen in *The Peanut Butter Falcon*, playing a young man with Down syndrome who runs away from his care facility to become a wrestler; the Academy Award–winning *CODA* about a hearing child with Deaf parents that cast Deaf actors; and *Crip Camp*, an Oscar-nominated documentary about a summer camp for teens with disabilities who went on to become activists. The British comedy-drama series *Sex Education* has been praised for its inclusive approach to topics like sexuality and disability, with George Robinson, an actor who uses a wheelchair, cast as Isaac and Alexandra James, a Deaf actress, cast as Aisha.

Matthew Von Der Ahe and Kennedy Garcia, a couple, are actors and public speakers who have Down syndrome. They were cast in a 2023 McDonald's commercial for the Super Bowl. Von Der Ahe shared,

It's so important for people to see couples like us, represented in film and television, in a light that makes us more alike than different. The portrayal of intellectually or physically disabled persons in relationships is crucial for challenging stereotypes and fostering a more inclusive society. It helps break down misconceptions, showcasing that individuals with disabilities are fully capable of experiencing and contributing to the beauty of love and companionship, just like anyone else. This representation not only promotes understanding but also empowers those with disabilities to pursue and embrace fulfilling relationships, reinforcing the idea that love knows no boundaries.[12]

Studies have found that increased visibility and positive representation in media help to reduce harmful stereotypes and play a significant role in changing social attitudes. For example, a 2017 study found that higher media exposure to homosexuality fostered more accepting attitudes toward the LGBTQIA+ community.[13] As of 2024, the Academy of Motion Picture Arts and Sciences has established new rules that films must meet at least two out of four standards for representation—on-screen, creative leadership, industry access and opportunities, and audience development (meaning, community and fan engagement)—in order to qualify for a Best Picture award.[14]

It is also important to remember that disabled people don't belong just on a screen or behind it—we also belong in every field and industry, whether it is entertainment, education, tech, business, science, or politics. We belong in all spaces, like restaurants, gyms, and concert venues. Just because you don't see us doesn't mean we don't exist—we've always been here, and we demand to be seen and heard in an ableist world that erases us.

For example, in 2021, the deodorant brand Degree published an open letter in the *New York Times* calling for more disability representation in the fitness industry. According to the Lakeshore Foundation, 81 percent of people with disabilities said we did not feel welcome in fitness spaces, a two-pronged problem because disabled athletes already "face heightened discrimination and bias," which is "compounded by the lack of representation of disabled trainers and coaches in the fitness industry and the limited access to inclusive fitness spaces."[15] In response, Degree launched the #TrainersForHire initiative, encouraging fitness companies to hire disabled trainers in various athletic fields, from CrossFit and powerlifting to paracycling.

I was part of that 81 percent for a long time. That has changed as I've become more involved in the disability community, met adaptive athletes, and been introduced to different adaptive sports programs that have made fitness spaces less intimidating. I am officially a triathlete, having completed my first triathlon in March 2024!

In medicine and research, disabled people are systemically excluded from and underrepresented in clinical trials,[16] which ironically further drives the health disparities of people with disabilities even though some disabled people expressly wish to participate in such trials to further medical research. In 2017, actor, athlete, and ambassador for the Global Down Syndrome Foundation Frank Stephens testified before the US Congress about the importance of including people with Down syndrome in medical research on diseases like Alzheimer's, autoimmune disorders, and cancer because of the extra copy of chromosome 21 that they have. "I cannot tell you how much it means to me that my extra chromosome might lead to the answer to Alzheimer's," Stephens said, to a standing ovation.[17] Four years later, a medical team at Linda Crnic Institute for Down Syndrome received a $4.6 million grant to recruit young adults with Down syndrome to study Leukine, a promising drug for Alzheimer's.

In education, representation is especially crucial because students are learning valuable lessons from their society, environment, teachers, and peers at an impressionable young age. Disability representation in the classroom can look like diverse course material and educational topics, diverse educators, and diverse teaching and engagement styles with students. Such representation helps students to feel a sense of belonging, which increases their confidence and academic achievement.[18] Representation also empowers students and shows them what is possible. For example, when students don't see disabled people represented in career or academic opportunities, they may receive the message that such professional roles are not available to them. But when they do see successful role models, it paves the way for them to realize that success is possible for them, too.

When Ali Stroker became the first wheelchair user to win a Tony award for her role in *Oklahoma!* in 2019, she said in her acceptance speech, "This award is for every kid who is watching tonight who has a disability, a limitation, a challenge, who has been waiting to see themselves represented in this arena. You are." In an interview, she added, "As an eleven-year-old girl pursuing this dream, I was looking to see who is there and who is working and has disabilities or is in a wheelchair, and there was nobody. It makes me feel amazing to be able to be that...because I did not have that."[19] In 2023, the musical *How to Dance in Ohio*, inspired by Alexandra Shiva's 2015 HBO documentary, made history as the first Broadway musical to cast autistic actors as autistic characters.[20] I even made a trip to New York City just to see the show and witness history in the making.

As a disabled person of color, even the fact that I get to write this book is a win for representation. We are seeing more children's books featuring disabled characters and more disabled authors publishing books, but there's still much to be done. The root of this is the lack of diversity in the publishing industry. According to the 2019 Diversity Baseline Survey from Lee & Low Books, 76 percent of the publishing industry is white and 89 percent identifies as non-disabled.[21] This matters because books shape culture, similar to film and TV, and those who work in publishing are the gatekeepers who determine which stories are amplified. When you don't have disabled editors or disabled literary agents, there might be a disconnect in understanding disabled characters or stories written by disabled authors that might make such books less likely to get published. "We can't get these books published until we have more decisionmakers and people involved throughout the entire production process who come from all these different backgrounds," says Alice Wong, author of *Disability Visibility*.[22]

If you have gotten this far, thank you for your support of this book. Reading and consuming content by disabled authors like me creates more possibilities for other disabled authors to have their books published.

And when we can't find ourselves represented in traditional media like TV, film, and books, we turn to social media. Social media representation, including digital formats like podcasts and blogs, validates our experiences, gives us a platform to own our stories, and helps us find our voice and community. When disabled people show up on these apps and platforms to talk about our lives, we are debunking misconceptions and filling in gaps in classroom and industry conversations elsewhere. Our content not only shapes broader societal attitudes about disability, especially among the majority Generation Z audience of TikTok, but also has a positive impact on the disability community itself.

"The act of posting a TikTok helps [disabled people] reclaim their narrative and find a community," says Meryl Alper, an associate professor of communication studies at Northeastern University. "This normalization can be really powerful for young disabled people and can really change the trajectory of their lives in terms of self-advocacy," adds Elizabeth Ellcessor, an associate professor of media studies at the University of Virginia.[23] I even noticed a shift in myself when I first started making content on TikTok. It was the place where I first got comfortable talking about my brachial plexus injury. Through constant video engagements as I shared with others how I lived with my paralyzed arm, I learned how to better embrace my body and myself.

Studies have also shown that some of the best ideas for inclusive assistive technologies and design concepts come from TikTok disability content creators who share videos of our creative "life hacks" or the adaptive games we come up with, such as a person with quadriplegia holding a fork with a hair tie or two wheelchair users pushing a yellow block into each other's territory in a strength competition.[24] Nicola Swann, owner of Made with Mud, designed the Digni-TEA (dignity) mug in 2021 at the request of a customer whose partner had Alzheimer's and needed a mug with two handles—the only other options at the time were plastic sippy cups. The mug went viral on social media, and since then, she has introduced new designs that benefit people with different disabilities.[25]

Here's the thing: disability-inclusive content is good for business. Research shows that social media posts from disability content creators scored 21.4 percent better in average media value and had 20.5 percent more interactions than posts from creators without disabilities.[26] Disabled content creators have shown that we can provide big brands with an authentic way to connect with disability-centered audiences.[27] However, representation in traditional media, such as advertising, is still lagging, with only 1 percent of prime-time TV ads featuring disability-related themes or visuals, while only 3 percent of ad spending went to disability-inclusive ads.[28] A lot of this hesitation comes from brands' fear of getting it wrong and reinforcing problematic depictions, which they deem risky business, or thinking that disability is "beyond their scope" or not their responsibility or that the disability audience doesn't have dollars worth capturing.[29] Stephanie Thomas, disability fashion stylist and founder and CEO of Cur8able, tells me, "According to *Vogue Business*, DEI budgets are practically non-existent.[30] Many managers are tired of being 'lectured' about the need for diversity while not being trained to ethically, profitably, and authentically develop long-term DEI goals."[31]

But some brands have paid attention. One success story is Tommy Hilfiger's adaptive collection, which focuses on inclusive design for the needs of all people, such as one-handed zippers, magnetic buttons, and open seams to accommodate prosthetics. The #TommyAdaptive campaign "benefitted from the support of 26 different influencers, including three with disabilities":[32] Jillian Mercado, Lauren "Lolo" Spencer, and me. On social media, the campaign received a 40 percent higher engagement rate and average media value per post than the fashion industry average,[33] demonstrating the power of disability representation. As Stacie de Armas, senior vice president of Nielsen, says, "Inclusion is not a trend but a necessity that must be understood and valued....The success of disability-inclusive content on social media should be a signal for traditional media."[34]

We live in a culture where people are quick to cancel a person or a brand for getting it wrong, but brands need a little grace and space to get things wrong before they can get things right—as long as they are open to feedback. James Embry, an advertising creative director who has a seven-year-old son with Down syndrome, says, "Things might need to get a little uncomfortable before we get to a point where it's typical to have people with disabilities in adverts.... Because that conversation is an important conversation to have. [Clients and agencies] should stand up to that conversation and say, 'We're including people....If you don't like it, tell us how you would like to see it, and we'll remember that for next time.'"[35]

Of course, it's better to avoid getting things wrong altogether if you can manage it, and a great way to do that is to partner with disability organizations from the get-go and work directly with disabled consultants and talent.

There is no excuse not to work toward authentic disability representation, no matter what space or field you find yourself in. Disabled people exist everywhere, and we should be represented accordingly, with the power to control our narratives.

Here are a few things you can do to increase disability representation:

1. Hire disabled talent in front of and behind the camera and for your social media campaigns. You can check out several initiatives and organizations focused on increasing disability representation in media and entertainment, including the Easterseals Disability Film Challenge, the Media Access Awards, and Making Space Media.

2. Actively seek feedback from the disability community through the creative process in your advertising and marketing campaigns.

3. Support disability representation in education by elevating diverse course materials (such as books, podcasts, and films by disabled people) and hiring disabled educators. Disability in Kidlit is a website dedicated to discussing portrayals of disability in middle-grade and young adult literature, where all book reviewers must share the same disability as the characters in the books they review. The hashtag #OwnVoices, coined by sci-fi writer Corinne Duyvis, is a way to easily identify books written by authors who belong to the same historically excluded communities as the main characters in their books.[36]

4. Different initiatives and organizations have emerged to increase representation in different industries. For example, Disability Victory works to develop the political power of disabled progressive candidates, the Disabled Academic Collective supports disabled academics in their work, the Disability & Philanthropy Forum creates a space to learn about disability inclusion in philanthropy, and the Docs with Disabilities initiative aims to increase representation of disabled clinicians and scientists in the biomedical workforce. See if something like this exists in your field and if there are ways you can amplify and support its work.

Reflection Questions

1. Have you witnessed inauthentic disability representation in the media? What are some examples? How has that affected your perception of disability?

2. In what areas of your life are disabled people most underrepresented? What can you do to contribute to better representation? For example, in your professional field, what can you do to ensure representation in the materials you share or create?

3. Reflect on your media consumption habits. How can you support and amplify content created by disabled individuals on social media and other platforms? We'll dive deeper into this in the next chapter.

CHAPTER 14

Diversify Your Feed

Take out your phone, open the social media app or apps you use most, and do a quick scroll through your feeds. What are the first fifteen to twenty posts or videos that pop up? Is there a particular type of content or account that appears the most? What themes or trends do you observe? Do you notice a pattern in the demographics of the voices that keep showing up?

Chances are the content you consume on social media reflects your current interests and belief systems as well as your pre-existing circle, which most likely consists of people who look like you, think like you, and live like you. Your algorithm is showing you content that it thinks you will enjoy and consume.

"If you've ever participated in unconscious bias training...you might have been asked about your closest contacts," says DEI manager Siobhán Kangataran, "and then asked to consider how diverse they are in comparison to your race, ethnicity, age, ability, background, gender, sexual orientation, and so on. Often these exercises are surprisingly unsurprising—we surround ourselves with people who look, sound, and live like us. Familiarity equals comfort, safety, and security."[1]

This is our echo chamber—a metaphorical term that describes an environment where beliefs are reinforced by constant communication and repetition—and it's no surprise that closing ourselves within it can feel very comfortable. For example, my own echo chamber consists of graduates from Georgetown University or people who have a similar university education level; women entrepreneurs; people who are passionate about social justice, racial justice, and diversity, equity, and inclusion; millennials; disability advocates; and those living in large metropolitan cities like New York, San Francisco, and Los Angeles. In other words, people who are very much like me.

Social media companies reinforce the comfort of our echo chamber by designing algorithms that define what type of content shows up on our feeds to compel us to keep scrolling. These companies make more profits by keeping us on their apps for longer. It's a competition for our eyeballs and attention—the attention economy.

Remaining stuck in our social media echo chambers means we see only what we are predisposed to see. It is an example of confirmation bias that reinforces old beliefs, narratives, and ideologies. Because of this "mere exposure effect"—"a psychological phenomenon in which people prefer things that they are familiar with"[2]—this bias creates a vicious cycle that becomes increasingly hard to break free from. These echo chambers then contribute to increasing social and political polarization and extremism in a society that is already governed by partisanship.[3]

Our social media feeds are showing us a version of reality that is different from everyone else's. This means there's a whole world of other truths, opinions, and realities out there that we will likely never be exposed to if we don't seek it out. By remaining within our echo chambers, we lose the opportunity to encounter diverse perspectives and expand our worldviews. This prevents us from thinking critically, making our own decisions based on facts, and considering the viewpoints of others.

Dr. Jess Rauchberg, an expert on digital media cultures, adds that social media algorithms are not neutral technologies: "If disability is represented as something negative offline, such beliefs, representations, and tropes will influence the development and design of digital platforms."[4] For example, TikTok's algorithm continues to promote content and hashtags that further ableism, such as the #NewTeacher challenge, where users showed their children photos of people with facial differences or other apparent disabilities while recording the children's frightened or disgusted expressions.

Rauchberg also argues that social media platforms take things a step further by actively erasing certain types of content, including disability content. One way that TikTok enforces what Rauchberg calls "digital eugenics" is through the practice of shadowbanning, a strategy that social media platforms use to suppress the visibility of a user's content without formal notice, resulting in lower over-all engagement even if the user has a large follower count. "Shadowbans are not random, isolated, or coincidental; rather, they are intentional and deliberate... [and] are intended to surveil and control marginalized communities. They are reflections of our own offline cultural beliefs about who 'naturally' belongs, and who does not." Rauchberg cites the example of TikTok's "Auto R" moderation guidelines, which "mark certain vulnerable or minoritized user populations into 'risk groups' as a means to prevent cyberbullying," such as disability content cre-ators being placed in the "Risk 4" category, which limits any videos they post to other accounts based in the same country. The result of these "risk protections," of course, is lower engagement—because these accounts are hidden, censored, and eliminated from the app's #ForYou home page.[5]

For all of these reasons, I encourage people to interrupt their social media algorithms. It may be hard to expand your circle beyond your comfort zone from the get-go, especially in terms of your daily interactions and the spaces you navigate. However, a good first step is simply going into your social media apps and diversifying your feed. You might have noticed the popularity of #Diversify-YourFeed in 2020, encouraging people to follow Black creators. I'm adapting it here, as the guidance also works for disabled content creators.

Essentially, teach your algorithm new ways of showing you information out-side your bubble. You can do this by choosing to follow people who do not live like you, people who challenge your preconceived beliefs, and even people who make you feel uncomfortable at first. Note that this is different from accounts that intentionally cause harm and spread misinformation—please don't follow those accounts. It is okay to not absorb content that is harmful to you, your iden-tities, and your community. Remember that there is a difference between feeling uncomfortable (this is where growth happens) and experiencing harm.

In the context of becoming anti-ableist, follow a choir of disabled voices, not just one, to hear what we collectively have to say as well as what we agree or dis-agree on. (Remember, we are not a monolith!) Then, reflect on the root of what might be making you uncomfortable, and with time (and the frequency of seeing this content on your feed), you may notice that what once felt uncomfortable will start to feel familiar. This is the exposure effect at play again, but this time in a helpful way.

Increasing exposure and awareness is one of the early steps we can take to learn more about diverse disability experiences. For example, chronic illness advocate and host of the podcast *Uninvisible Pod* Lauren Freedman made the conscious choice to follow disabled creators with experiences that differed from her own when she launched her show in 2019, which has helped her find new guests.[6]

Here are some other concrete steps to bring disabled voices into your feed:

1. Take a look at the hashtags #DisabilityPride, #DisabledAndProud, #DisabilityAdvocate, #DisabilityAwareness, and #WhenICallMyselfDisabled. Follow accounts that resonate with you.

2. If you enjoy a particular type of content, such as sports, follow a disabled athlete or an account that creates disability sports content. Amy Purdy @AmyPurdyGurl, Annika Hutsler @AnnikaTheAmputee, and Angel City Sports @AngelCitySports are a few that I follow. Similarly, if you like travel content, you can follow disabled travel accounts like Cory Lee @CurbFreeCoryLee, Marcela Marañon @TheJourneyOfA-BraveWoman, and Wheel the World @WheelTheWorld. There are disabled creators in all niches!

3. Ask yourself, "Who's missing?" Use an intersectional lens when you decide which accounts to follow so that you can make sure to include a diversity of disability voices in your feed. For example, take a look at some of the demographics. Are the disabled creators you're following mostly white, mostly Gen Z, etc.? Are there BIPOC disabled creators you can follow?

4. Use a search engine to find lists of accounts to follow. For example, search "top disability voices on LinkedIn," "Black disabled people on Instagram," or "queer disabled people on TikTok." It's a plus if the list has been written, curated, or vetted by a disabled writer.

5. To start building your knowledge of anti-ableism, follow these accounts by disability activists: Alice Wong on X/Twitter (@SFDireWolf), Imani Barbarin on TikTok (@Crutches_And_Spice), Catarina

---

Rivera on LinkedIn (linkedin.com/in/CatarinaRivera), Haben Girma on Facebook (@HabenGirma), and Mia Mingus on Instagram (@MiaMingus), to mention just a few. Other good accounts to follow are those that create educational content, like Instagram accounts @DisabilityTogether and @DisabilityReframed by Ashley Harris Whaley. And if you're not following me yet, you can find me at @ImTiffanyYu across social media.

6. If you are not active on social media, you can use similar strategies to diversify your "feed" in books, podcasts, films, TV shows, newsletters like Peter Torres Fremlin's *Disability Debrief* (disabilitydebrief .org) and Kevin Gotkin's *Crip News* on Substack (cripnews.substack .com), or any other media. I enjoy reading Andrew Pulrang's column on *Forbes*.

There is no denying the power of social media. And while social media algorithms have harmed, and continue to harm, disabled people, social media has also given us a platform to showcase our own narratives and make our disability experiences more accessible to the masses, even when traditional outlets haven't deemed our stories worthy of coverage. It has made the world a smaller place, allowing us to transcend physical boundaries and access communities and viewpoints we might never have been able to see in real life. By using social media intentionally and consciously, we can transform it into a tool to expand our perspectives and gain a better understanding of anti-ableism.

Reflection Questions

1. Think about the five people you spend the most time with/talk to the most. What are some commonalities among them? Who is in your echo chamber?

2. Take a look at the first fifteen to twenty posts that appear on your feed on the social media platform you frequent the most. What common themes do you notice? Do they all show you similar content? What are some of the demographics of those content creators?

3. Identify a cause that you are passionate about but that might engender diverging opinions, and do an internet search for it. Take the opposite stance and do a search on that. What did you notice about the two searches?

4. If a disabled content creator shows up on your feed, engage with their content by liking, commenting on, and/or sharing the post. It helps to support that disabled creator and train your algorithm to see that disabled voices matter on these platforms.

PART 2

ANTI-ABLEISM AND YOUR COMMUNITY

CHAPTER 15

Interrupt Ableist
Microaggressions and Harassment

In many ways, microaggressions are where ableism starts. They're both symptoms and causes of larger structural inequities in an ableist world. When we become complacent and let microaggressions slide, we perpetuate harm and microaggressions lead to normalizing more overt examples of ableism. Learning how to recognize and interrupt microaggressions whenever we encounter them will help get us started on our larger anti-ableist work.

As we learned previously, *microaggressions* are "indirect, subtle, possible unintentional discrimination" against individuals based on our disability that can take the form of "statements, actions, incidents, or exclusions."[1]

I appreciate the naming of "exclusions" in this definition because people often imagine that a microaggression is something negative that someone has said or done. But sometimes microaggressions are things someone has not said or done at all. In my TEDxBethesda talk, "The Power of Exclusion," I recount the story of no one wanting me to be on their team during gym class when I was growing up.[2] At the time, I called it "chronic exclusion," and I later realized that this personal experience of being excluded is a microaggression felt throughout the community—disabled people are one of the most socially excluded groups around. It's when the blind colleague is not invited to the baseball game because someone else assumed they would not want to attend or when no captions are provided for Deaf or hard-of-hearing employees during a video presentation.

In Chapter 8: What Is Ableism?, we learned about the different types of microaggressions—microinsults, microinvalidations, and microassaults. And in Chapter 4: Disability Is Not a Bad Thing, we learned why the microaggressions we use in language are harmful and how we can avoid them in our inner thoughts and external speech. There are many types and manifestations of microaggressions, but autism and neurodiversity advocate Becca Lory Hector summarizes some of the biggest ones in a LinkedIn post: patronization ("You're such an inspiration"), infantilization ("Let me just do it for you"), denial of personal identity ("I can't believe you're married and have kids"), and denial of the disability experience ("That's no big deal, we're all a little disabled").[3] Over the next few chapters, we will continue to explore other common ableist microaggressions in specific scenarios, such as making assumptions, not believing people with non-apparent disabilities, providing unsolicited advice, and telling a disabled person that we're inspiring. We will learn how to respond effectively and practically.

How can we do our part to interrupt these ableist microaggressions when we observe them in our interactions, whether it's in a conversation with someone else or we've committed the microaggression ourselves?

Before I share some practical advice, let's chat a little more about the practices of calling out and calling in. *Calling out* someone or something typically happens in public, and usually as the microaggression is happening. It lets someone know that their words or actions are unacceptable. It can feel uncomfortable to call someone out, but callouts are usually necessary to interrupt the microaggression that is unfolding in the moment so that we can hit "pause" to prevent further harm and break the momentum.[4] In contrast, *calling in* typically happens in private. In this case, the goal is to seek to understand each other across difference and learn together. We call people in when we want to help them imagine different perspectives, possibilities, and outcomes and allow for paradigm shifts. Call-ins are typically phrased as questions focused on reflection rather than reaction.[5]

I believe there is a time and place for both callouts and call-ins. Depending on each nuanced scenario, you will have to make a decision regarding whether you should call someone out or in. For example, if someone adopts a belligerent attitude and targets a disabled person with a microinsult in public, a callout might be necessary to interrupt the microaggression in the moment. However, if a friend engages in a microaggression in the workplace, and there is a prior relationship and mutual respect between the two of you, you might choose to call them in to prioritize their education.

I prefer to call people in—in the right situations—because I acknowledge that an interruptive callout may sometimes elicit a defensive response that takes away from the larger conversation (if a larger conversation is already happening). For example, someone who worked at an AAPI nonprofit once sent me an email asking if I could recommend a list of "differently abled" leaders whom their nonprofit wanted to honor on their annual list of impactful AAPI leaders. I replied with my suggestions, and at the end of the email, I explained that we don't really use the phrase "differently abled" anymore since it further stigmatizes *disability* as a bad word. I encouraged them to use the word *disability* when referring to disability, provided them with links to journalism guidelines, and offered my help if they had any questions. They were receptive to the feedback and responded, "That is super helpful and great to know—I'll use that moving forward!"

We can turn to callouts in the public arena in the cases of celebrities or government officials who have a greater responsibility and need for accountability due to their public image and influence. In the 2020 movie *The Witches*, Anne Hathaway played the evil Grand High Witch, who has three fingers on each hand, a condition similar to ectrodactyly, a limb difference. Although adapted from Roald Dahl's children's novel *The Witches*, the movie deviated from the book's description of witches as simply having "thin curvy claws, like a cat."[6] In response to public callouts led by disability advocates, including the Lucky Fin Project, a nonprofit organization that raises awareness and celebrates children and individuals with limb differences, Hathaway and Warner Bros. issued public apologies. Although the movie had already done damage by perpetuating the negative cinematic trope of villains having disabilities—inherited from outdated Western belief systems in which disability is viewed as a representation of evil—the callout led to Hathaway sharing a video from the Lucky Fin Project on her Instagram and committing to doing better in the future.[7] Most important, it elevated these discussions in the public consciousness and revealed the ways that we have used disabilities as costumes associated with something scary.

In 2022, CDC director Rochelle Walensky said in a *Good Morning America* video interview that it was "really encouraging news in the context of omicron" when a study found that 75 percent of deaths occurred in people who had at least four comorbidities, whom she described as "unwell to begin with." In response, disability advocates rallied in a public outcry. Danielle Connolly, a twenty-nine-year-old disability advocate who creates humorous and educational content under the name Daniellevates and who was born with a muscle disease of unknown origin, describes the visceral feeling of being on the receiving end of these kinds of micro-aggressions: "It's being told, 'If you're afraid, then stay home,' from the same people who would get health resources over me if rationed care ever came to be."[8] To help disabled people share our experiences of feeling forgotten and betrayed during COVID, writer, TikToker, and activist Imani Barbarin started the hashtag #MyDisabledLifeIsWorthy,[9] and almost 150 disability groups came together to sign a letter from the Disability Rights Education & Defense Fund (DREDF) to Walensky, outlining demands for a disability-inclusive pandemic response.[10]

We later learned that some context had been edited out of the video clip: Walensky had prefaced her reply by explaining that the figure came from a study of 1.2 million vaccinated people that had found that only 0.003 percent had died of COVID, and the "really encouraging news" she referred to was the fact that vaccinations were effective and not that the people who had died had already been in poor health.[11] Nevertheless, the power of social media and public call-outs prompted ABC to replace the clip with the longer, unedited version, and in response, Walensky met with disability advocates to discuss their concerns and apologize for the impact of her hurtful statement.

Many of us think we don't commit microaggressions because our original intent was not to insult or offend someone, and our natural inclination is to become defensive whenever we are called out. However, remember that impact over intention matters. What matters is how our statement or action was received, and in these cases, our words and behaviors can have negative impacts. So if someone brings a microaggression that you've committed to your attention, whether it's through a call-in or a callout, it's natural to feel confused at first, but make sure you follow up your first reaction by listening to how you have impacted the person. (Remember not to lose yourself in shame; instead, convert your guilt into action.) Then, validate that person's feelings, seek to understand why what you said or did was hurtful, apologize, and commit to changing your behavior in the future. We'll discuss accountability in a later chapter.

What should you do, then, when you observe microaggressions happening around you? How can you interrupt them with a call-in, if appropriate, to keep people accountable? Before we start, a quick caveat: some disabled people may choose not to do this interrupting since we've had to deal with microaggressions our whole lives, and we may not have the resources, energy, or desire to educate others—and that's okay. The following list targets non-disabled people (though disabled people can still use it if they choose, of course). While disabled people are at the forefront of disability advocacy, non-disabled allies should also take ownership of interrupting ableist microaggressions so that they can support us and lift some of the burden from our shoulders. An interruption from a non-disabled person can also help hold up a mirror to the behaviors and words of other non-disabled people, an effective way to call them in and create behavioral change.

I like to use this story from Brian Anderson, cofounder of Fathering Together, even though it talks about homophobia and his reflection on his role as an LGBTQIA+ ally, because I think it can be applied to ableism: "I'm a…cisgendered white man who is heterosexual, who has a Christian background," Anderson starts in a LinkedIn video. Many years ago, Anderson was part of a multicultural education class that was tasked with a role-playing activity to talk about LGBTQIA+ issues, and a heterosexual man in the group chose to wear a dress to represent being gay. Afterward, one of Anderson's gay friends approached him separately and said, "I know that you're friends with him, so I need you to talk with him about how that wasn't cool." At first, Anderson didn't understand why his gay friend couldn't just talk to the perpetrator himself. The friend explained, "This is where you become an ally. This is where I need you to talk to him because he'll hear you before he'll hear me."[12] Anderson's friend was implying that the perpetrator would respond better to a request to stop the harm if another heterosexual person instead of a gay person called him out. Often, harm is most effectively prevented when perpetrators are interrupted by people who look like them and who benefit from similar privileges.

When we allow seemingly "minor" behaviors or attitudes to go unchecked, these "low-level" forms of disrespect can accumulate and create a larger culture that enables and even rewards all-out abuse.[13] It is on us to stop such harm by intervening early to stamp out low- or midlevel forms of disrespect before it can escalate.

Here is a general guide for what you can do to interrupt microaggressions:

1. *Do* respond to the problematic statement or behavior in a calm but clear and direct way.
2. *Do* help the person to think through the reasons why their words or actions are an ableist microaggression by asking prompting questions.
3. *Do* be patient and give them space and time to reflect if the situation allows for it and if they are open to listening to your point of view.
4. *Do not* ignore, remain silent, or laugh off their microaggression without addressing it, even if you feel uncomfortable. (The only time it might be okay to do this is if you find yourself in a sensitive or potentially risky situation. In some scenarios, it might be better to plan to engage with them later in a safer space.)
5. *Do not* become belligerent or angry, especially if there is capacity for mutual understanding and respect between the two parties. Emotions can ignite defensiveness, which can get in the way of learning.
6. *Do not* speak from a position of superiority or self-righteousness or with the intention to shame, which can obstruct the other person's learning. This is a good reminder that we are all on our own learning journeys.

Additionally, here are some strategies and scripts we can use to call people in based on specific microaggressions that disabled people hear all the time.

You might hear someone say something like "They accomplished this despite their disability" or "They overcame their disability," ableist phrases that diminish the (sometimes significant) role that disability plays in our lives. To call the person in, encourage them to reflect on their words with some prompting questions:

- "What do you mean when you say that?"
- "What are the assumptions you're making when you use those words?"
- "What preconceived notions do you have about disability?"

- "Have you listened to a disabled person to learn more about what their reality/situation is like?"

As you engage in conversation to uncover pre-existing biases and educate the microaggressor, you can offer these alternative statements that say the same thing in a better way: "They accomplished this *with* their disability" or "They overcame *ableist attitudes*."

Then there's what sounds like praise but absolutely isn't: "You look great despite your disability" or "I don't think of you as disabled." Like the aforementioned statements, these continue to associate disability with a negative value judgment and connotation and suggest that disability has a definitive look. To interrupt these microaggressions, call the person in with these questions that will hopefully lead to more conversation:

- "What does disability look like to you, and why?"
- "What is it about the disabled person you're speaking to that doesn't fit your view of disability?"
- "How do you think disabled people feel in response to that phrase?"
- "How can you avoid painting disability in a negative light with the words you use?"

Here's an example of how this might look in practice, adapted from an Instagram post from the UBPN:

Jane: "*I didn't know you had a disability. I never would've guessed. You don't look disabled at all!*"

Tiffany: "*I know you probably didn't mean any harm, but complimenting someone for not looking disabled sends the message that looking disabled (whatever that means) is a bad thing or an insult. There is no one way to look disabled. Disability exists on a wide spectrum, and every disabled person's experience is valid regardless of how visible their disability is. I am disabled, and it's not my goal to look non-disabled.*"

Jane: "You're right. I'm sorry! I never thought about how that might come across. Thank you for helping to educate me."[14]

Another type of microaggression is when people use outdated or inappropriate language, such as "parking in the handicapped spot" or "the blind leading the blind." When you witness such outdated language, interrupt the speaker with questions that invite reflection:

- "Do you know the harmful history or connotations of that word/ phrase?"
- "Can you think of an alternative word or phrasing?"

You can also provide them with alternatives such as "accessible parking" or "disability parking" instead of "handicapped parking" or "lacked direction" instead of "the blind leading the blind." As we learned in Chapter 4: Disability Is Not a Bad Thing, there are a myriad of creative ways that we can express ourselves with language, and the least we can do is ensure that the way we speak does not contribute to ableism.

I've found that when I share my disability story with others, someone often replies with "I can't imagine." For example, many people tell me that they can't imagine having to relearn how to write with their non-dominant hand. To that, I reply that when you have no other choice, your body adapts, and odds are you will figure it out. The statement "I can't imagine" assumes that disability is an impossibility or an unimaginable situation, or that our situation is horrifying, when in fact disability is an everyday reality if you look hard enough. For me, it's a core part of my lived experience. Others in the disability community may receive statements like "I can't imagine losing my eyesight. That would be the worst" or even "I would rather be dead." When you hear these ableist statements, interrupt them by asking,

- "Is having a disability a stretch of the imagination?"
- "If you had to imagine this happening to you, don't you think you would have figured it out, too?"
- "Are there specific aspects of living with a disability that you find hard to imagine?"

- "How do you think a disabled person would feel if you told them you'd rather be dead than disabled?"

I believe these statements happen because most people are not quite sure how to respond when a disabled person shares our disability experience. They try to find something well-meaning and empathetic to say. Unfortunately, if they don't reply with "Well, I can't imagine," then they probably reply with "You're amazing" or "You're an inspiration," which is another type of microaggression—using disabled people as "inspiration porn"—which we'll discuss in more detail later. Instead of falling back on these responses, practice being an active listener and witness to the disabled person's story, and you can always simply respond with "Thank you for your willingness to share."

Jennifer Chassman Browne is an educator, DEIA consultant, and founder of New Ground Educational Consulting and More Than a T-Shirt Company. She related a story about one of her non-disabled friends offering to use their privilege to respond productively to ableist microaggressions:

With one friend in particular, she wanted to know if she could step in when she is present to witness...ableist actions and comments. Of course, I said yes. We have agreed that if she wants to step in, she briefly checks with me first, asking something like, "Is it okay if I respond?" If I say yes, she addresses the person who made the comment or took the action, explaining to them how their behavior was ableist. It is so encouraging to have allies like her who are willing to address ableism. She is able to step in with less emotion than I would have, and I think that, along with the fact that she is able-bodied, makes her an effective ally.[15]

If all of this feels like too much to memorize, especially if you witness a micro-aggression happening in real time and you want to interrupt it immediately but don't remember these specific scripts, all you have to do is remember five simple words: "What makes you say that?" This effective interruption, which I got from the *Better Allies* newsletter run by Karen Catlin, is especially helpful when you're a bystander in a conversation and you witness someone making ableist comments while talking to a disabled person.[16] "What makes you say that?" hits the pause button to stop the microaggression, invites reflection and a continuation of the conversation, and is open-ended but also probing enough to call the person in instead of making them defensive. Catlin provides a few other stock phrases that you can use: "We don't do that here"; "I don't get it. Can you explain the joke to me?"; and "Wow, that was awkward."[17]

Finally, it's important to prepare for situations that are more harmful and may require a more serious callout. If we want to be allies to the disability community, we have to learn how to be active bystanders. The bystander effect is the social psychological phenomenon of "the presence of others discourag[ing] an individual from intervening in an emergency situation, against a bully, or during an assault or other crime."[18] Notably, the more people are present during the event, the less likely it is that any of them will provide help because of what psychologists call the diffusion of responsibility: if there are many bystanders or onlookers present, individuals feel less personal responsibility to take action.[19]

When you witness harm as a bystander, there is no neutral position. As a bystander, you can be either part of the problem or part of the solution.[20] A passive bystander witnesses harm but chooses not to do anything to counter the violence, and their silence enables and provides tacit approval for the perpetrator's hurtful actions. On the flip side, an active bystander acknowledges a harmful situation and chooses to respond in a way that interrupts the harm, signaling to the perpetrator that their behavior is unacceptable and problematic.

How can you be an active bystander? A helpful strategy is to follow the six Ds for intervening—direct action, distract, delegate, document, delay,[21] and dialogue.[22] Each strategy is suited for different circumstances depending on the level of risk or danger. Your personal safety is important, and you should always assess the situation before stepping in to ensure that you can intervene safely. However, it is also important to note that your safety does not equate with your comfort. Oftentimes, intervening requires you to step outside your comfort zone to disrupt the status quo.

Here are the six Ds of bystander intervention:

1. **Direct Action:** Intervene directly by calling out the harmful behavior and telling the perpetrator to stop. You can also describe why

the behavior was offensive. Keep calm, call things what they are, and don't become emotional or aggravate the situation. You can also keep things brief, for example, by stating, "I don't find that funny," "That's inappropriate/not okay," "That's ableist," "Please stop that," or "Leave them alone." Use this strategy only if you feel you can do so safely and if you feel the person being harassed will also be safe from escalation or further retaliation. This can work well in group situations.

2. **Distract:** Interrupt the harm by distracting the perpetrator in subtle or creative ways. For example, ignore the perpetrator and the harassment that is happening and focus on the person being harassed. You can engage the person directly by bringing up a new topic, or you can pull them away from the hostile space under the pretense of asking them a private question.

3. **Delegate:** If you're unable to step in yourself, delegate the task to someone else. You can approach other people who are present and work together as a group to interrupt the harm, or you can approach an authority figure in the space, such as a teacher, HR representative, or venue staff. However, note that calling the police might be a sensitive issue for some people, and it is important to check in with them, if possible, before engaging with law enforcement.

4. **Document:** Record the harm as it happens with a cell-phone camera or take notes. This is a helpful supplemental strategy that should be employed only if someone else is already helping the person. The first strategy should be to actively stop the harm. After the incident, ask the person being harassed what they want to do with the recording—do not post it online without their consent. Documenting harm can be a powerful way to spread awareness and galvanize support, but it can also retraumatize or disempower the person who experienced the harassment.

5. **Delay:** If the situation is too dangerous to be stopped immediately, or if it happens quickly and is over before you can intervene, delaying might be your last resort. Delaying isn't about engaging in the moment but rather checking in on those affected after the harm has been done.

> When the episode is over, return to the impacted person and care for them instead of moving on with your day. Ask if you can help to support them or follow up in any way.
> 6. **Dialogue:** Continue to speak up and continue the conversation about abuse and harassment with your friends, colleagues, and community.[23]

Finally, remember that you can use and apply these active bystander strategies to different examples and levels of harm. Not every instance of harm will look like a hostile encounter. Sometimes harm for disabled people looks like a lack of access. Take it from Dr. Sophia Graham, lecturer on employment law and HR management: "There is quite a bit of guidance out there for people to support others that are being harassed....Unfortunately, there is less available guidance on how to support someone that is asking for access."[24]

When a disabled person asks a venue or organization for access, Graham suggests that allies offer to be active bystanders or witnesses. This approach is intended for situations when access is being denied so that active bystanders can take cues from the person to support us in our moment of asking, document the harm that is happening (such as taking pictures of access barriers like steps or noting the perpetrator's tone of voice), intervene if the perpetrator attempts to put their hands on the person to forcibly remove us, and follow up with the person after the fact to ask how to support us further, whether by making a complaint or taking things to social media. As an active bystander, you can also take the initiative to raise the problem with staff if you notice independently that access information provided for a business or an event is inaccurate or unsubstantial, and you can ask your disabled friends whether we would like you to take the lead in dealing with the issue.[25]

When you proactively interrupt microaggressions and ableist harm when they occur, these constant interventions will one day add up to dismantling an ableist culture because you're modeling the behavior that others should start using. Technology executive and workplace equity expert Aubrey Blanche-Sarellano reminds us, "It is often not the big gestures that create the most belonging, it's the tiny acts of humanity."[26]

Reflection Questions

1. Have you witnessed or spoken any of the microaggressions mentioned in this chapter? What do you think your intention was? What stories have you been told about the disability experience that made you think this way? How do you think that message may have been received by a disabled person?

2. Have you called someone out or called someone in, in person? What were those experiences like?

3. Can you see yourself using any of the sample response phrases mentioned in this chapter? If not, what are some other phrases you might use to address microaggressions?

4. Reflect on a past situation where you were a bystander. Were you an active or passive bystander? What could you have done differently? What fears and assumptions stopped you from being an active bystander? How can you challenge them?

5. How can you apply the six Ds (direct action, distract, delegate, document, delay, dialogue) in different situations to be an active bystander?

CHAPTER 16

Stop Making Assumptions

"If you're disabled, then why are you dancing?" This was a real comment I received on TikTok after I uploaded a video of myself dancing.

People make many assumptions about disabled people and the lives we live. As I mentioned in a 2018 TEDx talk,[1] the truth is that many people are uncomfortable around disability because they don't understand it. But instead of engaging with us directly to learn more, most people find it easier to fall back on assumptions because they're so afraid of saying the "wrong" thing or something offensive to our faces. Because of this fear—and the subsequent lack of conversation and communication—people rely on stereotypes in the media to inform their understanding of disability. Unfortunately, these stereotypes often portray disability as a medical diagnosis, a tragedy, or a charity case that is very much rooted in pity.

The problem with these mindsets is that they're rooted in assumptions. They perpetuate the myth that our disabilities prevent us from dreaming or achieving our goals and we are not given the chance to succeed. As someone who acquired my disability as a child, I even started to internalize these myths. I made a lot of assumptions about what living in a disabled body would be like, such as never being able to participate in physical activities again or never being in a relationship because no one would be attracted to me romantically. Fortunately, since then I have challenged my own assumptions about my disability and overcome these ableist myths to live my life the way I want to.

Biking was something I loved as a kid. It's one of the few memories I have of my dad, who was an avid bike collector. So it felt especially meaningful when I decided to embark on relearning how to ride a bike in 2016. I had won a scholarship to learn how to code in Amsterdam, and I didn't know much about it except that it was a big biking city. At first I thought I would rely on public transit, walking, or rideshare when I arrived, but then I decided to buy a bike. With every bike ride, I gained a little more confidence, from riding only on carless streets to using my bike as my main method of transportation. I biked to class, to the grocery store, and even in the pouring rain. Since then, I've biked in Chicago, Ireland, and Cambodia, and even at Burning Man. I have an entire series on TikTok about my adventures biking in San Francisco through the adaptive biking program for people with physical disabilities, and I even completed a twenty mile bike ride in February 2024. I learned how to adapt to riding a bike one-handed.

When people hear that I'm going to bike, they often respond with "How are you even going to do that? That sounds dangerous." Buried in that statement is something even more dangerous: an assumption about what I can or can't do because of my disability. In this case, they assume that I cannot bike safely—or even bike in general—with just one hand. Have you ever seen a biker going down the street while holding their phone to look up directions? They're biking with one hand. I also like to remind people that I'm not the first person who can't use both arms who has ridden a bike. If you search "one-handed biker" or any similar term online, you'll find a variety of stories featuring different disabled people riding not just road bikes but also dirt bikes and motorcycles. And even if I didn't feel comfortable riding a two-wheeled bike, there are adaptive bikes, such as seated trikes, that work well if someone has difficulty balancing on a two-wheeled bike.

Today, not only have I relearned how to ride a bike, but I'm also relearning how to swim; I've gone rock climbing; and in 2020, I hiked to the summit of Mount Kilimanjaro.

Here are a few examples of common myths and assumptions about disabled people, adapted from the Easterseals website:[2]

1. "Disabled people are brave and courageous." Living with a disability requires adaptation, not bravery or courage. We are not brave or courageous for simply existing. (Though, of course, disabled people *can* be brave and courageous, just as non-disabled people can.)
2. "All people who use wheelchairs are chronically ill, and they are confined to their wheelchair." A disabled person may use a wheelchair for various reasons—for example, as a temporary personal assistive device that helps ambulatory wheelchair users to get around in certain situations. A wheelchair is not indicative of sickness or inability to walk. Also, wheelchair users are not "confined" to their wheelchairs, which provide mobility, access, and freedom.
3. "Disabled people cannot have sexual relationships." Like everyone else, disabled people exist everywhere on the sexuality spectrum. Anyone can have a sexual relationship by adapting the sexual activity to their needs and desires, as both disabled and non-disabled people do.
4. "The lives of disabled people are totally different from the lives of non-disabled people." We have more similarities than you might think. Disabled people go to school, work, fall in love, have children, do our laundry, pay taxes, and dream like everyone else.
5. "Disabled people always need help." Many disabled people are independent and self-sufficient. All people are interdependent.

The first thing you can do to combat these stereotypes is to stop making assumptions and start making connections, as I discuss in a 2023 TED talk.[3] Engage directly with disabled people. Take the time to get to know us. Invite us to your gatherings. Ask us the same kinds of questions you would any colleague or friend. Don't treat us like we don't exist—we want to be seen and heard and accepted like anyone else. Then, listen to our answers and respect our boundaries. Sometimes we may not feel comfortable discussing something, and if so, we'll let you know. And if you're ever unsure about what to say, you can start with "I'm still learning how to get better at talking about disability."

The second important thing you can do is to presume competence. When people first learn about our disabilities, they often jump immediately to judging our capabilities and what they assume we can or cannot do, oftentimes without even asking. For example, some people still assume I can't type because I can't use one of my arms, even though I was at the top of my class as an investment banking analyst and could work on financial models just fine with one hand. Additionally, playwright and blogger Allie Funk encourages us to take this a step further and "assume personhood" rather than merely competence, because presuming competence contributes to the tendency that all of us—non-disabled and disabled people alike—have to infantilize people with intellectual disabilities.[4]

Once you've assumed personhood, you can always get additional clarification, since everyone's situation and experience are different. Proudly deaf since birth, Meryl K. Evans is a disability inclusion and accessibility advocate. As a deaf person who isn't fluent in ASL, she's had people enthusiastically sign for her, and she has had to let them know that it's not her preferred method of communication. She reminds us, "The best thing to do is to ask the person their communication preference. Don't assume....A better way is to ask, 'Do you know sign language?'"[5]

It's possible that a disabled person may need, want, and appreciate your help, but it's also possible that a disabled person is independent or simply does not wish for help in a particular moment. The important issue here is that you should not assume that disabled people need your help all the time, especially without asking for our consent first.

Mike Luckett, who goes by @MikeTheQuad on Instagram, says, "If you want to be a better ally, especially with those who are wheelchair users, ask before pushing." Even if you see someone who appears to be struggling, Luckett clarifies that the person may still wish to do things independently—and if they *do* need help, then they will usually ask for it directly.[6] Evans acknowledges that most people wish to help others and that they mean well. However, "imagine a stranger coming up to you, putting their hands on your jacket, and invading your space. This is uncomfortable. And that's what it feels like when someone suddenly tries to push a person's wheelchair without asking."[7] Disabled people have boundaries, too, and we need to be able to consider the request and give our consent.

A few years ago, I boarded a train in Switzerland. The luggage storage area was nestled in between and under the seats. As I tilted my luggage over on its side and prepared to slide it under, a fellow passenger pushed me aside and shoved my luggage in. Then he turned to me and said, "You should really ask for help."

I was shocked, confused, and hurt. I had been doing just fine with my luggage, even if it might not have looked that way to an observer. What ticked me off about this encounter was that the man had not only not asked whether I needed assistance or listened to my answer but also assumed what type of help I needed, done it without my consent—even pushing me out of the way—and topped it off by lecturing me on what I should have done. There's a reason I call myself an "expert lifehacker"—I've learned how to adapt in ways that work for me. I felt disempowered in the moment after a long travel day and chose not to engage with this interaction.

While some disabled people are proactive about asking for assistance, as Luckett mentioned earlier, there will be instances where you might want to be proactive as an ally.

Here is a three-step process you can use the next time you would like to offer assistance to a disabled person:

1. If you see a disabled person who might need assistance, proactively ask us if we need help.
2. Listen to our answer. We might say no or yes. The man in the luggage situation missed this step.
3. If we say yes, ask specifically how you can help instead of assuming what type of help we need. We might need assistance in a way that differs from what you imagine or assume.

The truth is that people with apparent disabilities sometimes feel offended if someone approaches us to ask if we need help—simply because we've already learned how to do these things over the course of our lives. The implicit assumptions and unsolicited offers of help further serve to patronize and infantilize us. They take away our autonomy and end up becoming microaggressions for some.

As I've mentioned, disabled people are not a monolith. Even in these anecdotes I've shared, we have different perspectives and preferences on what is the right way to offer assistance, especially in various situations with their own nuances. I remember attending an all-day conference a few years ago, and lunch was served in a large ballroom for a sit-down meal. We were seated at round tables while servers brought out the food. When my chicken dish was served, I experienced a moment of anxiety because I could not cut the entrée myself. This is something I've had to navigate throughout my career, from networking to client dinners during my investment banking days. However, this time was different. When the server brought out my chicken dish, he noticed my wrist splint and offered to help me cut the chicken. When I nodded, he went to the back, grabbed some cutting tools, and cut my dish. What I appreciated about this particular encounter was his proactiveness so that I didn't feel shamed by asking someone for assistance in public in a business environment.

When I shared the story about the conference lunch on my Instagram, I received a range of comments.[8] Some people responded that I should have just asked directly for assistance, as Luckett advises, while other disabled people chimed in to share their own experiences of navigating public meals and how refreshing it was that someone offered support proactively.

The diversity of comments made me think about the nuance of asking for help as a disabled person. For far too long, we've been made to feel like asking for help makes us a burden. Negotiating my access on my own can sometimes feel exhausting, as if I have to ask for permission just to show up. But I'm starting to learn to embrace interdependence, which acknowledges that our survival is connected. And what we can all do, as disabled people and non-disabled allies, is provide support and offer access to all—with the consultation and consent of the people we're trying to assist. If you're ever unsure about the nuances of a situation, a simple way to signal that you're willing to help without making assumptions about the disabled person's needs or desires is to say, "Let me know if you need anything" or "I'm here if you need support."[9]

Reflection Questions

1. Think about the assumptions you might make about a disabled person, for example, a wheelchair user, a blind person, someone with a mental disability, someone with an intellectual disability, or a Deaf person. (Feel free to choose a different type of disability to reflect on.) How might these assumptions influence your behavior or interactions?

2. With each of these assumptions, do a quick online search to see if there is a story of someone who is combating that assumption or stereotype. For example, if your assumption is that wheelchair users can't be parents or that blind people can't be engineers or that Deaf people can't drive, search for exactly that.

3. If you've ever offered a disabled person assistance, what was the context, and how did they react? If they did not react well, could your offer have been perceived as patronizing (remember, impact over intention)?

4. Have there been instances where you assumed that a disabled person needed help and received a negative response? How would the situation have unfolded differently if you had asked for consent first?

CHAPTER 17

Don't Give Unsolicited Advice

"**H**ave you ever tried surgery to fix your hand?" is a question I frequently receive on my TikTok content from viewers who do not have my injury.

If you go to any of my TikTok videos where I talk about my paralyzed arm, you might notice that I get a lot of comments from people who don't have my injury but who eagerly share advice: "Isn't there a surgery you can get?" "Have you thought about prosthetics?" "Why don't you just move your fingers?" Commenters have even gone so far as to say things like "You should just cut off your hand since it's useless."

Disabled people deal with unsolicited advice all the time—whether it's from our family, friends, colleagues, or even strangers in the store or on the internet. But what is it, exactly? Unsolicited advice consists of guidance or suggestions (sometimes well-intentioned) given to disabled people *without* our explicit request or consent. It is a type of ableist microaggression. Here are a few examples:

- The man on the train who assumed that I needed help with my luggage: "You should ask for help."
- The people who commented on my desire to relearn how to bike: "You shouldn't bike. It's not safe."
- "Have you tried yoga [or other treatment/therapy] to help with your pain?"

- "I heard about this person who had your condition, and veganism [or another activity/treatment] worked for them. You should try it."
- "Are you sure you can handle that?"
- "I'll pray for you."

The advice, which can include recommendations for medical treatments or lifestyle changes, usually focuses on how disabled people can manage our disability or improve our lives and make them easier. Additionally, it often comes from non-disabled people who may not share or understand the experience of the person they're speaking to. As disabled scholar-practitioner Dr. Amy Kenny puts it,

> Strangers and soon-to-be strangers always offer me unsolicited prayers and potions to change my disability. I've been recommended everything from "sleep with a bar of soap" to "eat more turmeric" to "use essential oils," but my personal favorite is "hit your other leg with a hammer." Somehow, I am still disabled. The constant unsolicited advice is dehumanizing and frustrating, as though my body is public property simply because I am disabled.[1]

Deaf disability inclusion and accessibility advocate Meryl K. Evans describes a common piece of unsolicited advice she receives:

> Just received another link to the sign language gloves asking if I had seen it. Yes. It's an old video that makes the rounds once a year. The way the sign language gloves work is that the signer puts on the thick gloves. The gloves have wires connected to a computer or a mobile phone [that] speaks the signs.... The deaf signer has to wear the gloves, not the person who doesn't sign.[2]

The root causes of unsolicited advice are the assumptions and stereotypes people have about disability: that disability is inherently negative and needs to be fixed and that disabled people need help. Most of the time, people give well-intentioned advice because they wish to help, but what they don't realize is how problematic and harmful unsolicited advice can be. In some ways, unsolicited advice, even if hidden behind encouraging words, is a form of judgment because it is an attempt to impart wisdom and apply it to another person's life based on ableist assumptions.[3]

In a thread, E Krebs, PhD (@SaltySicky), compiles a few of their own reasons (and some crowdsourced ones) for why chronically ill people become upset when they receive unsolicited advice.[4] *Many of these reasons are shared by other disabled people. Here are some examples, combined with my own reasons and observations. Note that the following list is largely paraphrased content based on the post, but anything in quotation marks is a direct quotation.*

1. It is condescending and judgmental. Unsolicited advice suggests that disabled people "haven't done our own research" or aren't "smart enough" to have already considered these ideas ourselves or in consultation with our doctors, family, and friends. It also suggests that we simply haven't done enough or tried hard enough. (@SaltySicky)

2. It disregards the autonomy and agency of disabled people and assumes that we lack the ability to make decisions about our own lives and are unable to help ourselves.

3. It presumes that there's an easy fix or "simple solution" that will solve our disability, which ends up "[trivializing] our complex experiences and conditions," especially when there are comorbidities. (@LilMxTangent)

4. It might be a sales ploy if someone is trying to sell specific products like a supplement. It sees the disabled person as a business "target" and potential customer instead of a person. (@GoldenC688)

5. It is often given "without ever trying to understand or ask questions about the disease [or disability] and how it works." (@hedonish) Besides not having a good understanding of the person's disability, people also often give unsolicited advice without asking what the disabled person thinks or feels about that particular topic.

6. It can be actually harmful, and even dangerous, to someone based on our specific condition, since everyone's situation is different. "Sometimes people (including alternative health practitioners) recommend echinacea to me—but people with my disease have ended up in the hospital after taking [it]." (@krinipi)

Disabled people have to deal with unsolicited advice so regularly, on top of the other types of ableism that we navigate and confront daily, that it adds to our stress and anxiety. Russell Lehmann, a motivational speaker and public advocate who has autism, OCD, and other non-apparent disabilities, says, "When you try to help me, please be sure that you know how to help me. Even if it's very well-intentioned…you can actually cause a lot of hurt…[and] now I'm in an awkward position between doing that at my own detriment or rejecting your offer of help."[5] Unsolicited advice contributes to a sense of being misunderstood, dismissed, and invalidated, and over time, it can erode our self-esteem and lead to a sense of disempowerment and dependence on others. It can even potentially fuel our own internalized ableism, where we start to feel defined by our disabilities and the need to fix them, as opposed to being individuals with our own unique identities. Another negative effect of unsolicited advice is that it often creates a barrier to deeper connection.

Remember that not every disabled person feels comfortable sharing the details of our disability with you (especially if your advice has the flavor of telling disabled people that what we're already doing is wrong or not enough). As disability community organizer Sarah Blahovec says, "While we know that you're just trying to help, this advice forces us to disclose intimate details of our health with strangers who know nothing of our individual medical situation, and to talk about whether or not we've tried what they're recommending. It's uncomfortable and frustrating." Instead, Blahovec says, "trust that disabled and chronically ill people and their medical teams are the most knowledgeable about their own health and their medical and lifestyle needs. Trust that they will seek out you or the proper sources if they're interested in what you have to offer."[6] Yes, there will also be times when I am *soliciting* advice and actively looking for suggestions, such as when I wanted to see how people put on over-the-ear headphones with one hand or when I asked the brachial plexus community for tips on relearning to swim with one hand.

So what can you do instead of offering unsolicited advice like "Have you tried [X] or [Y]?" Have you ever had a friend share a story with you, and you immediately provided feedback or went into problem-solving mode before being met with the response that they just wanted someone to listen? Sometimes what disabled people are looking for most is not advice but rather support; we just want to be seen, heard, and understood. It's worth checking before you launch into what *you* think is best, whether your friends are disabled or not.

And just as we learned in Chapter 16: Stop Making Assumptions, a good rule is to ask first, "Are you looking for feedback or advice or a shoulder to lean on?" Lehmann suggests asking, "How can I help?," which shows that you are aware that you may not know how to help, which "is a great thing."[7] Something like "Could I offer you some advice?" or "Are you open to some advice?" would also work. Then, don't forget step two: listen to the answer. Make sure that the disabled person is on board before you share any suggestions. Use active listening, practice empathy, and engage in self-reflection. You can do this by making an effort to genuinely understand the experiences and needs of disabled people (if we are willing to share), learning to ask open-ended questions, respecting our autonomy, and paying attention to your own assumptions and biases about disability—and correcting them.

Finally, if you are a disabled person who finds yourself on the receiving end of unsolicited advice, here are some answers you can use to close a conversation that is not helping you: "Thanks, but I don't really need advice." "There are many different ways of doing things." "I'm glad that works for you." "I'm already researching a solution." "I'll ask for advice if I need it."[8] Don't hesitate to set boundaries and assert yourself.

Reflection Questions

1. Reflect on a time you gave unsolicited advice. What was the response, and what impact do you think it had?

2. What are some of your own assumptions and stereotypes that underlie any unsolicited advice you might give to a friend or a stranger?

CHAPTER 18

Support People with Non-Apparent Disabilities

Disability inclusion and accessibility advocate Meryl K. Evans recalls feeling panicked when she joined her friend to run errands and they parked in an accessible parking space. Her friend had an accessible parking pass, but she didn't have a visibly apparent disability. She tells me,

> I know what happens when young and healthy-looking humans park in an accessible parking spot. And it's not pretty. The unofficial accessible parking police can be downright awful when they don't see visible signs of a disability. With all the different kinds of harassment people experience, this often leads those who need accessible parking to avoid using it.[1]

Maybe you have observed someone parking in an accessible parking spot, but when they got out of the car, you noted that they did not "look" disabled in the way that you assumed they should be. Or a fellow student in one of your classes requested extended time to take a test, and you wondered whether their disability claim was valid because it didn't seem to you that they had any disability.

I'm sometimes met with annoyance when I ask someone to help me put my carry-on luggage in the overhead compartment when I'm traveling by plane. I don't wear a wrist splint all the time, and in these moments, my paralyzed arm is not readily apparent. In all of these examples, it is possible that the person in the car and the student have non-apparent disabilities or even physical disabilities that are covered by their clothing.

Elena Keates, a social change advocate who has multiple non-apparent disabilities, told me, "In one workplace, when I informed the head of HR about my disability, she asked me if I had a disability parking tag. That was her bar for authentic disability."[2]

Puneet Singh Singhal is an accessibility professional in India who lives with multiple non-apparent disabilities. In 2021, he decided to seek a formal diagnosis for dyslexia and dyspraxia:

> During the diagnostic process, the professional, renowned in New Delhi, recognized my achievements and contributions to our society. Yet, his words, "You are so successful, why do you even need a diagnosis?" left me stunned. It was a stark reminder of how success is often misinterpreted as a sign of the absence of struggle. This encounter underlines a profound issue—the persistent disbelief and lack of understanding surrounding non-apparent disabilities. Unlike physical disabilities, conditions like dyslexia and dyspraxia are invisible to the naked eye, often leading to misconceptions and underestimation of the challenges faced.[3]

As you learned in Chapter 2: Not All Disabilities Are Apparent, people with non-apparent disabilities—which include mental health disabilities, learning and neurodivergent disabilities, and chronic illnesses—face the unique challenges of stigmatization, doubt, and invalidation simply because our disabilities are not immediately apparent to others who are quick to judge us based on preconceived assumptions of what disability "looks" like. This leads to misunderstandings at best or rude questions, gaslighting, and discrimination at worst, which causes people with non-apparent disabilities to feel constant exhaustion, shame, and self-doubt. This creates a vicious cycle of people with non-apparent disabilities being less likely to disclose or talk about our disabilities because of an ingrained fear of contempt and judgment, which exacerbates the problem, since non-apparent disabilities are then further misunderstood.

A good way to understand what people with non-apparent disabilities go through daily is to use the spoon theory, a term and concept coined by lupus patient advocate Christine Miserandino when she tried to illustrate what it means to live with lupus to a friend while they were at a diner. According to the spoon theory, people who have a chronic illness or non-apparent disability start each day with a limited amount of energy to expend on various daily tasks, represented by a number of spoons. People with non-apparent disabilities have many fewer spoons to use throughout the day than non-disabled people, and we must make intentional choices of which spoon to use for which tasks—even tasks as seemingly simple as getting ready in the morning, commuting to work, socializing, and eating—to ensure that we have enough energy to last without burning out. Miserandino explains,

> You cannot simply just throw clothes on when you are sick. I have to see what clothes I can physically put on. If my hands hurt that day, buttons are out of the question. If I have bruises that day, I need to wear long sleeves, and if I have a fever, I need a sweater to stay warm, and so on. If my hair is falling out, I need to spend more time to look presentable, and then you need to factor in another five minutes for feeling badly that it took you two hours to do all this.[4]

Each of these activities might take up an entire spoon or half of a spoon, depending on the amount of energy involved. By this time, the, say, twelve spoons she started out with could have dwindled to just six, and she hasn't even gone to work yet. As a result, the rest of the day has to be chosen wisely and split up among the limited number of spoons remaining, even if it means making impossible decisions such as choosing to buy groceries so that she can cook dinner (two or more spoons) or risk going without dinner entirely (which also costs spoons). "Everything everyone else does comes so easy, but for me it is one hundred little jobs in one....When other people can simply do things, I have to attack it and make a plan like I am strategizing a war."[5]

The spoon theory is a good way for people to visualize the different lifestyle demands that disabled people experience and non-disabled people do not. Miserandino adds,

The difference in being sick and being healthy is having to make choices or to consciously think about things when the rest of the world doesn't have to. The healthy have the luxury of a life without choices, a gift most people take for granted....It is the beautiful ability to not think and just do. I miss that freedom. I miss never having to count "spoons."[6]

Thea Touchton is a SAG-AFTRA actor and producer of comedies and mental health documentaries at Sueñito Media. Touchton has a mobility disability, has low vision in her left eye, and lives with complex PTSD (cPTSD). She provides an example of navigating limited spoons when she was growing up: "I've been disabled pretty much since I can remember. I had to sit out at recess in grade school. I often had to choose my resting for health over being able to play with my peers."[7]

If you wish to start taking steps to support people with non-apparent disabilities, your first task is to combat the assumptions you might have about non-apparent disabilities that cause you to unfairly judge or discriminate against us in the first place. Eliminate microaggressions like "But you don't look sick!" from your thoughts and speech. Even if you can't perceive any evidence of a disability based on your assumptions, the disability still exists.[8] And instead of scrutinizing the actions of people who don't fit your assumptions of what disability looks like, remind yourself that disability doesn't have a single or fixed "look."

Another common microaggression that people with non-apparent disabilities face is the accusation "This task is so simple. Why can't you do it?" Once I attended a workout class, and we were supposed to carry the weights back to their original places. The instructor, who knew about my paralyzed arm, handed me a light weight. However, she handed a heavy weight to the person behind me, who did not have a paralyzed arm but was navigating back issues. The other woman had a hard time carrying the heavy weight, probably more than I would have. Touchton shares a similar experience:

Although I had filled out the paperwork for accommodations [in college], they were not respected, and the professors' excuse was that they often forgot I was disabled because I didn't fit the stereotype. I eventually ended up having to leave that college as the students continued to mock my disability, screaming at me when I couldn't perform as fast as they wanted me to....The professors were aware of the bullying and even encouraged it, giving me a gag award at the end of the year titled "Cyclops! Thea Touchton"—I only have one eye.[9]

This leads me to my second point: Jess Cowing, PhD, whom I featured on Part 234 of *The Anti-Ableism Series*, says, "If you want to be a better ally to disabled people, believe us when we tell you about our experiences."[10] This is one of the most common microaggressions that people with non-apparent disabilities face: not being believed. In an environment where non-disabled people suffer mental and emotional exhaustion and self-doubt from being constantly judged and criticized, your belief can be powerful in helping to validate us and alleviating the emotional toll. We are the experts, not you. If we say we're unable to perform certain tasks that seem simple to you, take us at our word. If we open up to you about our non-apparent disabilities, don't assume we're lying or making them up. If we say we're in pain, believe us. It is hard enough for disabled people to get medical professionals to believe us, and it can take years to be diagnosed with some conditions. For example, studies show that people can wait seven and a half years on average to be diagnosed with endometriosis,[11] and it can take an average of ten years for someone living with a psychiatric or mental disability to get help.[12] It took twenty-two years for me to be diagnosed with PTSD.

Additionally, create space to believe and acknowledge any experiences you don't understand. Do not benchmark everyone using neurotypical standards.[13] For example, if someone with epilepsy asks you not to use the flash on your camera, respect their wishes—not everyone is okay with bright lights. If a person seems to be ignoring you when you're talking to them, instead of becoming annoyed, consider that they may have a disability that prevents them from hearing you, and get their attention another way.[14]

Of course, it's not enough just to unlearn your assumptions and believe people with non-apparent disabilities; you also have to proactively support us.

Here is a selection of strategies to support people with non-apparent disabilities:

1. If someone reveals our disability to you or tells you more about it, affirm us by saying, "I didn't know that; thank you for telling me." If you are close friends and we are willing to continue the conversation, you can ask follow-up questions like "Do you want to talk more about it?" or "What's it like to live with [disability]?" As the person shares more or talks about specific experiences, you can check in with us to see if we need additional support from you. Sometimes we may not need anything at all, in which case you can simply offer a listening ear and other forms of passive support.

2. Proactively ask people, "What are your access needs?" or "Do you have what you need to fully participate?" Support us by doing your best to address those needs, and use the "Let me know if you need anything" phrase we learned in Chapter 16: Stop Making Assumptions or "What do you need?" or "How can I support you?" Always practice active listening and support the person with our consultation and consent.

3. When you offer support, do not expect or demand that the person disclose our disability or give you the full details. Nobody owes you an explanation, and some people choose to keep this private. Reminder: you don't need to know the details in order to address the barriers someone is communicating to you. In public spaces, some people may choose to wear a badge to show that we have a non-apparent disability, such as a sunflower lanyard, a cue that communicates that a person might need additional support.[15] The Hidden Disabilities Sunflower initiative was launched in 2016 at Britain's Gatwick Airport and has grown to include nearly two hundred airports and other businesses.[16]

4. Rethink and reimagine what acceptable styles of working and socializing look like to you, whether in school or in the workplace, and allow space for a diversity of behaviors. For example, if you're interviewing an autistic person for a job, don't mark them down or judge their work capabilities if they don't look at you (some people with autism find eye contact uncomfortable). Instead, ask yourself, "How can I ensure that I'm evaluating a candidate solely on their capabilities and not their interview behaviors? How can we change the neurotypical benchmarks we use for interview success?" Similarly, some disabled people might

find open-plan workspaces difficult if they are sensitive to noise or high stimulation.[17]

5. Check in when you make plans with others to see if your plans work for us. Nitika Chopra, founder of Chronicon and a chronic illness advocate, says, "One of the things I appreciate the most is when I'm making plans with someone, and they actually don't assume that I have the same ability to get to the destination that we're meeting at that they do." Instead of assuming that it is easy for your friend to meet you at a particular location or walk a certain distance to a place, realize that the person may have different and fluctuating needs because of our non-apparent disability.[18]

6. Constantly build your awareness and make an effort to understand what people with non-apparent disabilities go through. Educate yourself by doing your own research on the wide diversity of non-apparent disabilities or by talking to people with non-apparent disabilities (if we are willing to do so) to learn more. You can start with the resources mentioned in Chapter 2: Not All Disabilities Are Apparent.

Finally, here are some tips for disabled people to advocate for yourselves in the workplace, especially if there is already a built-in level of psychological safety, inclusivity, and support. For example, if you have a non-apparent disability, you can reference your needs in email signatures or out-of-office responses, such as "I have ADHD, which comes with short-term memory and organization barriers. For internal employees, please message me privately or tag me in the email body if there's a delay" or "I have ADHD and dyslexia. I prefer meetings to emails. Feel free to book my calendar, and don't hesitate to bump an email thread if I'm taking some time to respond." These are two real examples I've come across from Thomas Frantz and Hannah Frankl, respectively, who both have non-apparent disabilities.

If you're not comfortable disclosing your disability, focus on the barrier and what accommodations or access requirements you'd benefit from. Remember, you can always advocate for yourself without the pressure of disclosing. This could look like conversations or emails that read, "I would benefit from [insert accommodation here]." For example, if you're in a meeting and you can't see the presentation on the board because of a vision-related disability, you could say, "I would benefit from sitting closer to the board," "I would benefit from using a digital whiteboard tool like Miro," or "I would benefit from an email summary of the meeting notes."

It is important to not make assumptions about people's disabilities, the way we live our lives, or what support we might need. When you proactively build in access, you are also supporting people with non-apparent disabilities.

Reflection Questions

1. Next time you are organizing an event or gathering, ask attendees at the time they are registering, "Do you have what you need to fully participate?" Make sure to emphasize that they can reach out to you privately rather than in the moment.

2. Did you grow up thinking that disability had a "look"? What were some of those assumptions?

3. What are some unique barriers that someone with a non-apparent disability may face that someone with an apparent disability wouldn't face?

4. Have you ever been surprised to learn that someone had a disability? What do you think was behind that? Did they challenge a stereotype you may have had about what it was like to live with a disability?

5. What are some ways you can challenge neurotypical benchmarks, such as calling someone a "culture fit"?

6. Have you made plans with someone without thinking about whether they might face barriers getting to your meeting location? How can you adjust your approach when making plans with others?

CHAPTER 19

Don't Treat Disabled People as Your Inspiration

When the late writer, comedian, and advocate Stella Young was fifteen, a member of her local community wanted to nominate her for a community achievement award. There was only one problem, according to her parents: she hadn't actually achieved anything at the time. In fact, Young had a fairly simple life of going to school, working at her mother's hair salon, and watching TV shows. "I wasn't doing anything that could be considered an achievement if you took disability out of the equation," she said in a 2014 TED talk. Many years later, when she was teaching a high school legal studies class, a student raised his hand and asked when she was going to give a motivational speech because the only time he had ever seen people in wheelchairs was when they had come to give inspirational talks.[1]

As disabled people, we are no strangers to the phrase "Wow, you're disabled? That's so inspiring." Disabled people and our stories are used as "inspiration porn," a term coined by Young to describe how disabled people are objectified by non-disabled people solely as a source of inspiration.[2] (Some people have since replaced this phrase with "inspiration exploitation" or "inspiration sensationalism" so as not to portray sex workers in a negative way.) Such thinking is rooted in the harmful belief that disability is a bad thing and that by simply living with a disability or existing as a disabled person, we are exceptional.

"But isn't being viewed as exceptional a good thing?" you might ask. "Isn't being seen as an inspiration a compliment?" The fact is that when people see disabled people as inspirational simply because of our disability and for no other reason—like that community member who wanted to nominate Young for the award—it reduces the person's entire identity to our disability. This type of misplaced admiration ignores the diverse experiences of disabled people, who are much more than our disability. It also objectifies and dehumanizes disabled people as symbols. When you tell disabled people that we're "so inspiring" just for getting out of bed, checking the mail, going to the grocery store, or having a job, it suggests that you're setting the bar lower for us.

Treating disabled people as your inspiration also perpetuates the problematic narrative that we exist merely to motivate or provide lessons to non-disabled people, which takes away our agency. It can even make disabled people feel that we need to constantly perform feats of inspiration in order to meet this exhausting social expectation. Another phrase in the community is the "super-crip" narrative, a term coined by sociologist Rebecca Chopp, referring to the expectation that disabled people must be extraordinary superheroes in order to be valued.[3] In the super-crip narrative, disabled people are expected to excel all the time, and when we fail to meet such expectations, we're seen as less worthy. So we find ourselves caught between a rock and a hard place: on one hand, we're seen as tragedies just for existing, and performing any daily task makes us inspirational; on the other hand, we're constantly expected to fit impossible superhero stereotypes.

Here's the other thing: when people say that disabled people are "an inspiration" or "inspiring," what they really mean is "I'm glad I'm not you" or "Thank goodness I don't have your problems." Essentially, they're not truly appreciating disabled people for who we are or for our genuine accomplishments; instead, they're relieved that they don't share our experiences. Embedded in this thought is the assumption that disability is inherently bad and that non-disabled people "have it better." This explains the many "inspirational" memes circulating on the internet, such as a picture of a child running with prosthetic legs under the words "Your excuses are invalid."[4] Imagine how a disabled person might feel when we see such memes: our existence is being used as a point of comparison and a motivational trigger to make non-disabled people feel better about themselves. It is reductive, inaccurate, invalidating, and hurtful. It also shames people who are not able to run due to their disability.

The fact is that disability is not exceptional, according to Young:

> I have lived in this body a long time. I'm quite fond of it. It does the things that I need it to do, and I've learned to use it to the best of its capacity, just as you have [learned to do the same in your own body]. And that's the thing about those kids in those pictures as well. They're not doing anything out of the ordinary. They are just using their bodies to the best of their capacity.[5]

Another meme, "The only disability in life is a bad attitude," is based on a quotation from Olympic skater Scott Hamilton[6] and casually uses disability as a metaphor to inspire non-disabled people. It's harmful for several reasons, including reducing the experience of living with a disability to a matter of attitude, blaming disabled people for our condition, and suggesting that a positive attitude can overcome any challenges. To this, Young says, "No amount of smiling at a flight of stairs has ever made it turn into a ramp....Smiling at a television screen isn't going to make closed captions appear for people who are Deaf. No amount of standing in the middle of a bookshop and radiating a positive attitude is going to turn all those books into braille."[7]

Young's point touches on an important detail: for all the talk about non-disabled people being inspired by disabled people, non-disabled people do not return the favor to prioritize accommodations that will combat ableism and support disabled people. While non-disabled people are being inspired, disabled people continue to live with barriers in a society that constantly places us at a disadvantage.

It is no surprise that the media helps to reinforce inspiration exploitation by highlighting stories of triumph, superheroes, inspiration, and goodwill. These public narratives feature either the accomplishments of disabled people (even if our accomplishment is just existing) or non-disabled saviorism, with non-disabled people doing a good deed for a disabled person that is elevated into a feel-good news story. In September 2023, Jon Hetherington, a longtime Beyoncé fan, took to TikTok to share that after twenty-five years of waiting, he had been forced to miss a Beyoncé concert because the flight he had booked had been unable to accommodate the size of his wheelchair by four inches. When fans heard his story, they rallied on social media to tag Beyoncé in their posts. Soon a member of Beyoncé's team reached out to arrange a new flight. Hetherington attended the concert and even had an opportunity to meet Beyoncé and her mother.

This was a great moment of allyship from Beyoncé's team and the Beyhive. However, once media outlets got wind of the story, they doubled down on the inspiration exploitation narrative by framing Beyoncé and her fans as the heroes instead of taking the opportunity to address the systemic ableism that had allowed this to occur in the first place. When this type of media coverage happens, the real issue—that air travel does not meet the accessibility needs of wheelchair users and those who use other mobility devices—is hidden under a sweet, innocuous, and heartwarming story meant only for non-disabled audiences. Here were some of the headlines: "Beyoncé & the 'Beyhive' Help Fan with Cerebral Palsy Attend Concert" (*Today*);[8] "When He Missed a Beyoncé Concert, the Hive Went to Work" (*New York Times*);[9] and "Beyoncé Fan in Wheelchair Will 'Treasure' Kind Words, Hugs from Singer After Long Odyssey to Attend Houston Gig" (*Billboard*).[10] Hetherington's own calls and advocacy to highlight the inaccessibility of airlines were largely buried in those articles under the main lede or sometimes not mentioned at all.

Media coverage written by disabled people looked very different. Lolo Spencer, actress, disability advocate, and founder of Live Solo, provided a more nuanced and accurate take by highlighting the systemic issues that caused the incident in the first place: "We are so happy that [Beyoncé] was able to make this moment happen for Jon and make it more than he ever expected. But we can't help but think about the cause of the issue which is [the] CONSTANT inaccessibility of airlines. We hope that the outrage that supported Jon will reach ALL airlines and have them do better to make traveling with devices a possibility."[11]

Words matter, especially in the media. When we paint non-disabled people as heroes for doing the bare minimum and erase systemic ableism from the story, we fail to address the root of the issue, which prevents change from happening.

If you're a professional in the media and journalism fields, what can you do? Kelsey Lindell, disability marketing expert and founder of Misfit Media, provides some suggestions:[12]

1. "Proactively learn about the stereotypes, stigmas, and tropes facing the disability community." The more you learn about inspiration exploitation, the better you can recognize it when it happens and stop yourself from perpetuating it.
2. "QC [quality control] your content by a disabled team or writer." Better yet, employ disabled writers and journalists to write your content.
3. Whether you're a writer or a reader, "pause and ask yourself what underlying issues contributed to [these stories] taking place originally." This will help you think critically and read past sensational headlines to get to the real issue.

Now, I do want to note that sometimes you can't control what makes you feel inspired. What I encourage you to do if you feel inspired by something (such as one of those headlines) is to convert that feeling into self-reflection and action.[13]

Is your inspiration rooted in genuine admiration for the person or objectification of our disability? To distinguish between the two, reflect on whether you're focusing on the whole person or primarily on our disability. Then, shift from simply being inspired to actively valuing our diverse experiences and contributions. You can do so by learning more about the historical contributions of disabled people in various fields or following disabled content creators. The more you learn, the better you'll be able to acknowledge that a disabled individual's worth extends beyond our disability.

Allyship, to me, is really about intimacy. It's about getting to know all the different facets of a person. That's why I've appreciated creating content on platforms like TikTok, because I use it as a video diary of sorts to highlight and document various parts of my life. I feature content around living with PTSD and navigating life with a paralyzed arm, but I also document parts of my daily life like the different experiences I've had since moving to Los Angeles. My followers don't know me just because of my disability; they also see me for who I am (as much as I'm curating on social media, at least!). I've had followers tell me, "I started following you because of your disability advocacy content, but I stuck around because I liked your personality and you as a person."

Next, convert your feelings of inspiration into actions you can take to either dismantle ableism and overcome barriers or make things more accessible. For example, when I was a keynote speaker at the 2023 Grace Hopper Celebration, the world's largest gathering of women and non-binary people in technology organized by AnitaB.org, I received a message afterward from an audience member that said, "Your story was so empowering to me today! You have inspired me to build and design for accessibility."[14] Now, that is the kind of inspiration I can get behind. While inspiration exploitation creates disconnection and dehumanizes disabled people, this type of inspiration leads to empowerment because it motivates people to take action to work toward accessibility.

Disabled people are not here to be your inspiration. We're real people, too, and we're valuable and whole regardless of what we accomplish. If you do find our experiences and contributions inspiring, then get inspired to join us in our fight against ableism.

Reflection Questions

1. Have you ever felt inspired by a disabled person? Why? Did your inspiration stem from genuine admiration or objectification?

2. What are some assumptions you make about the disability experience that might make you feel inspired?

3. Learn more about the accomplishments and contributions of disabled individuals in your field of choice. For example, research Stephen Hawking and his contributions to physics and cosmology, not only his diagnosis of amyotrophic lateral sclerosis (ALS), also known as Lou Gehrig's disease.[15]

4. As in the case of the Grace Hopper Celebration attendee, what have disabled people inspired you to do? How can you convert your inspiration into action to address systemic ableism?

5. Look up a media headline that features disability, and examine how it is framed. Does the headline frame the story through inspiration exploitation, or does it highlight the systemic barriers underlying it? If the former, do some research on what systemic barriers might exist that the article didn't highlight. (For example, if the headline is about someone with cerebral palsy running a marathon, does the article only highlight the runner's success; does it identify them by name; and does it mention systemic barriers the runner faces, such as whether there are enough adaptive running training programs or other accommodations available to disabled people who run marathons?)

6. If you are sharing disability content, how are you framing it? If the content focuses on "feel-good" aspects, can you also include the broader context that highlights systemic issues that create challenges for disabled people?

CHAPTER 20

Be in Community with Disabled People

When I first started Diversability, people asked about the types of advocacy issues we were tackling, whether it was closing the disability employment gap, working on education programs with schools, or calling for affordable housing and health care. While members of our community have done some of that, I like to think that our work at Diversability starts at the root by tackling the cycle of social isolation that many disabled people face.

I think of us as the "disability town square," where you can go to learn about all the different types of work being done in the disability space, from adaptive sports to independent living services to creative projects. Diversability, to me, is about the power of community, where we can provide a safe space to unlearn our own internalized ableism, interact with other disabled people, and foster relationships with non-disabled allies. Social health and being in community are, essentially, the why behind this work.

If we've learned anything from the pandemic, it's that social health is a key component in our overall well-being, which includes physical wellness, mental wellness, and social wellness.[1] During the early period of quarantine, many of us, whether disabled or non-disabled, were forced to isolate and stay within our individual household units, which sometimes consisted of just one person. This type of extreme social disconnection and isolation adversely impacts our mental health, which in turn compromises our physical health—poor social connections have been found to lead to a 32 percent increased risk of stroke, a 50 percent increased risk of dementia, and more than a 60 percent increase in the risk of premature death. Even before the pandemic, the loneliness epidemic was already seen as a public health crisis, with half of US adults reporting "measurable levels of loneliness."[2] The danger of loneliness is that it can move into an elevated state where the lonely individual perceives the world as threatening and not accepting of them, which creates a negative spiral that turns them inward even more while they push others away, affecting their self-esteem.[3]

Because of ableism, disabled people are still one of the most socially isolated and excluded groups in society.[4] The truth is that it is difficult for disabled people to make friends because of the access challenges we face, such as inaccessible physical and digital spaces that limit our participation at gatherings, differences in the way we communicate, or stigmas and stereotypes that prevent connection even if we are present. There's also a general lack of awareness, with many people simply forgetting that disabled people need relationships and social connections to thrive like everyone else, which results in events or meetups that are organized without considering our access needs. Sometimes people may not even see us as potential friends.

Growing up, I wasn't friends with other disabled people. I didn't know where to find them, nor did I even think to look for them. I thought that no one shared my experience, which was very alienating and disheartening for me as a disabled kid. It was for this reason that I started Diversability many years later: I knew it was something that nine-year-old Tiffany had desperately needed.[5] Today, I see similar sentiments of "I don't have any disabled friends" or "Where can I make disabled friends?" from other disabled people who are feeling equally isolated in their experiences. What I realize now is that you probably do already know disabled people; our disabilities just might not be apparent, or we might not feel safe enough to disclose or talk about our access needs.

As I became part of other communities along the way, like the Taiwanese American Students Association during my freshman year at Georgetown, I learned the importance of social connections and realized that the simple feeling of belonging had the power to change the way I viewed myself and my life. Interestingly, I became a disability advocate only after I created Diversability. Being a part of the disability community inspired me to engage in other disability advocacy efforts. This is why I believe that disability communities have the power to create systemic change. None of this anti-ableist work exists in a vacuum: community, solidarity, and allyship create coalitions and movements. For example, during the Section 504 Sit-In that we learned about in Chapter 5: A Brief History of the Disability Rights Movement, when the hot water in the bathrooms was shut off and the office phone lines were blocked for outgoing calls, it was groups like the Black Panther Party, Glide Memorial Church, Gay Men's Butterfly Brigade, Delancey Street, United Farm Workers, Gray Panthers, and Salvation Army that brought food, water, and other supplies to sustain the protesters.[6]

In addition to empowering me to do advocacy work, the disability community has helped to support me on my own personal journey. Through the friends I've met, I've built support systems that I can rely on and be accountable to in my various ventures, whether it's writing this book or taking part in different adaptive sports, such as rock climbing through the Adaptive Climbing Group, biking, or swimming. I also get support for living with my paralyzed arm from a Facebook group for people with brachial plexus injuries, which I use to exchange resources and solicit advice. And I'm part of other communities that support me in different ways, such as a community for entrepreneurs, one for AAPI content creators, and one for people focused on making social impact. I'm even in a community for people who are building communities!

For Nitika Chopra, the founder of the chronic illness community Chronicon, who has been living with multiple chronic conditions since she was ten, creating a community helped her to embrace her disability identity:

> Even though I struggled to walk without severe pain and spent the majority of my time bedridden for the first half of my twenties...I never knew that I could identify as someone who had a disability. In some ways, this might seem like a [good thing] because some people might find that word limiting or stifling. However, in a lot of other ways, it further perpetuated the amount of isolation I felt from not being understood or truly seen for the experience I was having or what I was going through. I also wasn't offered any accommodations that could have been life-changing for me at the time. It wasn't until years later when I started Chronicon

and began having honest conversations with people who were leaders in conversations around disability and chronic illness that I realized I had a disability all along.[7]

It is crucial for disabled people, who must navigate an ableist world that already isolates and excludes us, to have a strong and supportive community. According to an eighty-five-year-long Harvard study, the number-one thing that makes people happy and even helps them to live longer is not money, achievements, exercise, or a healthy diet—it is positive relationships.[8] There's something so powerful about community: it reduces feelings of isolation, provides social connection, promotes a sense of belonging, and contributes to our overall emotional well-being. When all of this happens, the effect of belonging to a community where we feel safe and supported can empower us further to foster inclusivity, advocate for our rights, and break down the barriers that limit opportunities for disabled people. A definition of community I like to use is "when a group of people come together to nurture their own growth and each other's growth," a concept I learned from another organization I'm part of, Friendly Nooks, founded by Tatiana Figueiredo.[9] When we work together with mutual support, we will grow together—both personally and as a community. All this leads to a greater empathy for and understanding of our diverse experiences, helping us to become a more effective force for change.

So where do non-disabled allies come in? When Diversability was created, I was intentional about opening the community to both disabled people and non-disabled allies. There were a few reasons for this. First, I wanted to include non-disabled allies so that they could witness the conversations we were having. Theoretical neuroscientist Dr. Vivienne Ming says that one of the best ways to tackle bias is through continuous real-life experiences with the people who challenge your assumptions and stereotypes.[10] So what better way than to interact with and learn from the disabled people in our community?

Second, I didn't want to create a disability-only group because I realized that some people might still be in the early stages of their disability journey. I wanted Diversability to feel like a welcoming community for them even if they weren't ready to subscribe to a label or identify as having a disability. Or maybe they just wanted to bring a friend with them. Yema Yang initially joined Project

LETS (Let's Erase the Stigma) in college because she wanted to do more hands-on mental health work, only to realize that she wasn't an ally after all:

> Just a few months of attending meetings at LETS and hearing people talk frankly about their mental illnesses...I realized I was mentally ill, too. When this thought first dawned upon me, I cried because the sudden influx of internalized fear and prejudice suffocated me....When I attended another LETS meeting and tentatively brought up what happened, I was met with nods and murmurs of affirmation. Reassurance that it made sense, that it was natural, that they've been there, too. And suddenly, being mentally ill wasn't so scary anymore....Mental illness was still difficult to navigate, but it was not as difficult as it could've been with added ostracization or isolation.[11]

Yang reminds us that becoming is part of belonging: recognizing who we truly are through experiences in new contexts and unlearning our own internalized ableism in the presence of community.[12]

Frequency creates familiarity, which in turn creates community. The more events you go to, the more you start to see familiar faces, and eventually you build a relationship and trust that become the building blocks of your own community. With Diversability, I noticed that there were people in our community who didn't engage much at first. However, through a mere exposure effect, as they witnessed others sharing their stories and resources over a period of time, this sense of community encouraged and empowered them to reach their second disability origin story, which is that turning point or defining moment when someone decides to accept their disability identity and takes ownership of their disability journey. I call these people the "longtime lurkers," and their journey toward self-actualization as a disabled person and becoming proud of all facets of who they are is a powerful reminder of why I do what I do. This is why Diversability has curated hundreds of events over the years, providing a platform for our disability community to humanize disability through our lived experiences and celebrate our shared humanity with non-disabled allies. Not only does this tackle disability bias on a regular basis, but it also helps people find their truth, pride, and purpose.

Here are some strategies you can use to be in community with disabled people:

1. Befriend disabled people. Connect in meaningful one-on-one relationships to get to know us better. Seek to foster a mutually vulnerable and honest relationship where you can share your experiences and perspectives with one another.

2. Ask questions and engage in non-judgmental conversations with your disabled friends. Listen actively so that you can gain valuable insights and understand our perspectives. However, you should also see your disabled friends for who we are as individuals.

3. Keep the access needs of your disabled friends in mind, especially if you're planning a hangout or an event. Be empathetic, flexible, and supportive depending on our needs at each moment, and remember to check in with us.

4. Support one another in each person's own unique journey and life path. Keep one another accountable, grow together, and build mutual trust.

5. Engage in community initiatives or advocacy work that promote disability inclusion, similar to how many communities showed up for us during the 504 Sit-In. Work together with disabled people, not on behalf of or independent of us, to achieve our collective goal of combating ableism.

6. Show up and join a disability community. In addition to Diversability, you can look up other disability-specific communities that resonate with you, such as Nitika Chopra's Chronicon for people living with chronic illness or Margaux Joffe's Minds of All Kinds for the neurodivergent community. Some of our events at Diversability are open to the public so that you can get to know the broader discussions we're having inside our communities. If these communities are not a good fit for you, my hope is that you have access to healthy relationships and social connections in other areas of your life.

7. Constantly educate yourself. Learn about the specific challenges of different disabilities so you can better support the people who live with

them. In turn, help to increase awareness and understanding of disability by engaging in education programs and open conversations in your other communities.

Disabled people need genuine friendships and community. We need people to share our lives with, to commiserate and laugh with. We need people who believe in us and root for us, and we also desire genuine connections with people whom we can trust to challenge and push us, who see us for our potential.

Reflection Questions

1. Reflect on the diversity of your own social circles. Are there disabled individuals among your friends?

2. What have your past interactions with disabled friends been like? Have your own friendships evolved after learning more about the disability community? How do diverse and intersectional friendships enrich your own life and perspective?

3. What can you do to actively contribute to building more inclusive spaces for disabled people to be in community with others?

4. What are some ways that you can inclusively and respectfully show solidarity with the disability community or with other groups of which you are not a member? How can you collaborate with disabled individuals to collectively drive change and combat ableism? This could include shopping at disabled-owned businesses, signing a petition, amplifying disabled content on your social media platforms, or listening and educating yourself.

5. Join some online communities that are open to non-disabled allies to learn more about the disability experience. If you are in the disability community but haven't really identified with your

community, reflect on what might be behind that. Are there communities you can join to lurk? Come hang out with us!

6. If you don't know any disabled people where you are, revisit Chapter 14: Diversify Your Feed to follow some disabled content creators on social media whom you can support, amplify, and engage with online.

CHAPTER 21

Ask Better Questions

"What's wrong with your hand?"

Can you imagine how many times people like me with physical disabilities get asked questions like that? When someone says this to me, they're suggesting that there's something bad about my disability, or that it is not "right." When we attribute negative value judgments to disability, as we've learned earlier, we perpetuate harm and ableism. I often respond to this exhausting microaggression by answering with my own question: "What do you mean by that?" My goal is to give the person an opportunity to reflect on their assumptions.

There's nothing wrong with asking questions. However, the way in which you ask questions matters. Before you open your mouth, reflect on why you're asking a question in the first place. What motivates it? Is it selfish curiosity, or is it a desire to learn more and offer assistance with the person's informed consent? Is your question an attempt to confirm pre-existing biases, and does it lead toward a specific answer you're trying to get out of the person? Or is it open-ended, where you're truly curious about what we have to say, excited about connecting more meaningfully, and open to gaining new insights that might challenge or surprise you?

The problem is that many non-disabled people have misused and abused these lines of questioning for so long that they have become hurtful and harmful to us. People—whether friends, colleagues, acquaintances, or strangers—like to ask about our medical history, whether we can have sex, and other invasive questions that we would not typically expect non-disabled people to entertain or answer. We are often asked intrusive and unnecessary questions about how we became disabled or the symptoms of our disabilities in order to "prove" our disabilities to someone. Even our employers ask us general questions about our disabilities as a condition for providing reasonable accommodations.[1]

We don't owe strangers on the internet or strangers in real life answers to questions about our personal lives. (You'd be surprised at how much you can learn about disabilities through a quick online search!) Instead, build intimacy and friendship with us first, and then let us choose how much we want to share.

Personally, for someone like me who is an educator in this space, asking questions is a great way for someone to learn from the myriad valuable perspectives of disabled people, and I usually feel comfortable talking about my disabilities in public. But that doesn't mean I'm okay with ableist questions like "What's wrong with your hand?" A better way of asking these questions could be "If you don't mind sharing, I'm interested to learn what happened to your hand."[2] However, asking, "What happened to you?" can also be a microaggression because it might force people to relive trauma or remind us of the hard experiences we've been through. For many years after my injury, I would start crying if people asked me about my arm. There was a lot of emotional pain I hadn't processed, and talking about my arm made me revisit those memories.

Or you could ask, "What's your story?"[3] This reframing comes from Keely Cat-Wells, an entrepreneur and disability rights activist. While "What happened?" suggests fleeting curiosity on the part of the asker, who simply wishes to have their curiosity satisfied in the moment, "What's your story?" creates connection and gives agency and autonomy to the storyteller. It also allows us to choose which parts of our story we feel comfortable sharing. The first type of question is often selfish, temporary, and a one-way exchange, while the second type of question invites an authentic conversation and allows the disabled person to control our narrative. "[It] empowers me to tell you how I handled those tough times, [and] it may give you an insight into my passions, mission, values, and other key traits that could be helpful and interesting to you," Cat-Wells says.[4]

I like to note that "What's your story?" can still feel like a microaggression to some people since it suggests that we are storytellers who exist for non-disabled people's entertainment. Remember, we don't owe anyone our disability story,[5] and nobody should be asked to explain or prove why we're disabled. We all have varying levels of comfort around how much we want to share, and that should be respected.

As you can see, there is a whole range of attitudes and opinions regarding asking questions about disability. Sometimes when I hear people asking about someone's disability, I guide them toward asking a more specific and helpful question: "Do you have what you need to fully participate?" This question allows the person answering to lead with what we need in a particular scenario without having to talk about our disability if we don't want to.

Many disabled people do not want to talk about our disabilities. Some of us want to talk about disability *our* way, in *our* time. As Annesley Clark, DEI associate of Save the Children, says, "I'd rather talk about the creative ways I've learned to participate in the world and coexist with my disabilities...than my medical history, diagnoses, or struggles."[6] The key takeaway is not to stop asking questions altogether but rather to stop asking harmful and ableist questions and to start asking *better* questions that will allow disabled people to express ourselves the way we want, address inaccessibility, and overcome barriers.

A big consideration is that we don't want to contribute to creating a prohibitive atmosphere, scaring away genuinely curious people who are open to learning because they're afraid of asking offensive or insensitive questions. Not asking any questions at all prevents connection, too. This is the moment when a child asks their parent, "Why is that person in a wheelchair?" only to be shushed immediately. Children have a genuine, uninhibited curiosity, but what they're learning from their parents in these situations is that talking about disability is taboo and shameful. Instead of silencing them, the parent should embrace this as a teachable moment so the child can learn that it is okay to talk openly about disability in a respectful way.[7] An alternative could be affirming the child's curiosity, educating them that some people might use a wheelchair for different reasons, and providing them with age-appropriate resources to learn more about disability.

Kelley Coleman, mom of two boys, one of whom has multiple disabilities, and the author of *Everything No One Tells You About Parenting a Disabled Child*, says,

> We have often had children (and adults) stare or ask questions about our
> son's feeding tube.... We emphasize that accommodations aren't something

extra that my child (or any other disabled person) is getting; they're what he needs in order to fully participate in his world. [I] can answer questions in real ways, and not pretend that my child is a superhero because he has a disability. He's a kid living his life, with some similarities and some differences from your child. If kids ask "What's wrong with him?" we can explain that having a disability is perfectly normal, and is just part of our everyday lives. We choose not to share our son's private medical information with strangers, just as they [do] not [share] their private medical information with us. The point isn't to ask someone their diagnosis, but instead to normalize disability and the child's curiosity. In doing this, you set your child up for future encounters with disability, which will of course happen throughout their life. Many parents need to unlearn their own ableism and the negative messaging around disability that they grew up with. Raising anti-ableist kids starts with acknowledging our own bias[es] and normalizing disability for our children every opportunity we get.[8]

I believe that the art of asking good questions is a practice that needs to be cultivated over time. It's okay to get things wrong or make mistakes—just don't let your mistakes guilt or shame you into never asking questions again. Try your best to ask good, respectful questions, but don't expect perfection. After all, disabled people have our own preferences. If someone doesn't want to answer your question, respect our boundaries and move on. If someone tells you your question was insensitive, take our feedback and learn from it. One of the best ways to unlearn our assumptions, grow, and tackle ableism together is by continuing to ask those questions and being willing to get things wrong so that we can work together to get things right.[9]

I often reflect on the fact that even though we've put out the invitation to others to ask questions, we're still not having radically honest conversations around disability as a society. I appreciate this sentiment from disability awareness consultant Andrew Gurza: "Please tell a disabled person if our disability makes you uncomfortable. Honestly, just name it. Kindly. The more we talk about it together, the better equipped we'll be to burn ableism to the ground."[10] You might be thinking, *This is super awkward and uncomfortable!* You're probably right, but we have to start somewhere. When asked how to go about this, Gurza responds, "I often ask people, 'Does my disability make you uneasy?' or 'Is my disability an issue for you?' And they'll tell me, 'Oh, no, it's fine.' Only to discover when we really get into what I might need from them that it is uncomfortable....I would ask, 'Why are you uncomfortable?' and 'Where does that discomfort come from?'"[11]

Naming the discomfort is a starting point and valuable opportunity to have a more meaningful conversation around disability, where you can reflect on your ableism and learn to be better.[12] Yes, hearing that our existence makes someone uncomfortable can hurt our feelings, Gurza says, but knowing that someone feels that way but is staying silent won't help anyone. There are mixed opinions about this approach, as it puts a greater demand on a disabled person's emotional labor, but I would love to see more spaces to explore discomfort in a way that doesn't shame people.[13]

We can't address the problem of ableism if no one is talking about it. Here are a few strategies and tips on how to ask better questions:

1. Ask yourself whether your question is relevant to the current conversation. Is it a natural segue from the other topics, or will it rudely interrupt the conversation? If the person has already raised the topic of disability, that is a good sign that you can continue to talk and express your curiosity. You can also pay close attention to the person you're speaking to; we might give good contextual clues in our words or behaviors that will tell you whether we're open to continuing a conversation or changing the topic. Be sensitive, aware, and considerate. Sometimes you can even ask directly, "Would you like to talk about this, or would you prefer that we talk about something else?"

2. Consider the specific context you're asking the question in, such as the relationship you have with the person and the environment. For example, are you already friends with the person, are we a professional acquaintance, or are we a stranger? Are you in a private space, such as our home, or in a public place, such as at the grocery store? Is this an intimate date, a catch-up among a group of friends, or a business event?

These nuances will help you to decide what question you should ask, whether it's a good time to ask it, and how you can phrase it.

3. Ask more empowering questions that respect the person's experience and preferences, such as "What are your access needs?," "What is your experience with this?," "What do you prefer to do in this situation?," or "Would you like any assistance?" Don't ask questions that rely on assumptions, reinforce stereotypes, or perpetuate ableism, such as "What's wrong with you?" or "Can you fix it?"

4. Check in with the person and respect our boundaries. If we've chosen not to answer your question, don't take offense, and don't let that stop you from asking questions in a different context.

Reflection Questions

1. What are you curious about regarding the disability experience? Are these questions you would ask a non-disabled person? If not, is this something you can search for online?

2. Is there anything about the disability experience that might make you uncomfortable? What do you think underlies that discomfort?

3. What challenges or fears do you personally associate with asking questions about disabilities? How can you overcome them?

4. Reflect on a time when you asked someone a question about their disability. What were you hoping to gain from the response? What made the interaction positive or negative? How do you think it was received by the person you asked?

5. If you asked someone a question and they did not want to respond, how would that make you feel?

CHAPTER 22

Treat Disabled People with Respect and Dignity

What does it mean to you to be treated with respect and dignity? Is it when someone addresses you politely and listens when you speak? Is it when someone values your opinions?

As disabled people, we know too well what it feels like to not be treated with respect and dignity. Most of us have our own versions of this hypothetical story: a couple of your friends are grabbing a nice dinner at a fancy restaurant, and you are a wheelchair user. When the server comes over to take the orders, he chats everyone up but does not talk directly to you, not even looking you in the eye. Or how about this one: you're out shopping at the grocery store. Soon people are whispering and pointing at you, and someone comes up to ask if you should be there or, worse, to tell you to leave because you're making others uncomfortable.[1] These stories are just examples of the lack of respect and dignity that disabled people face on a daily basis, and it can feel excluding, alienating, degrading, and dehumanizing.

Disability advocate and content creator Danielle Connolly, who was born with a muscle disease, describes the experience of being disrespected by non-disabled peers:

If someone makes a well-meaning comment like "get well soon," you should be grateful even though you aren't going to get well soon. If someone is patronizing you, you should be grateful because at least they are talking to you. If an organization or person is using your disability for clout or is being performative, you should be grateful that disability is even on their radar. While I may not always interrupt the outrageousness of these situations in the moment for a variety of reasons, I know that my feelings are real and that they are valid."[2]

We all want to be treated with dignity and respect. In 2005, then secretary-general of the UN Kofi Annan wrote, "While freedom from want and fear are essential, they are not enough. All human beings have the right to be treated with dignity and respect."[3] This concept is codified in the Universal Declaration of Human Rights of 1948, which reads, "All human beings are born free and equal in dignity and rights," and "everyone is entitled to all the rights and freedoms set forth in this Declaration, without distinction of any kind, such as race, color, sex, language, religion, political or other opinion, national or social origin, property, birth or other status."[4] This includes disability, as was recognized in 2006 under the CRPD.[5]

Disabled people are human beings with the same needs as everyone else, including the right to respect and dignity. Yes, we are unique individuals who have a wealth of knowledge, skills, and experiences that can bring diversity, resourcefulness, and creativity to society, and these qualities are worthy of respect and dignity—however, I also like to say that we are valuable and worthy simply because we exist.

Despite our inalienable right to dignity and respect, disabled people have a long history of being denied respect, which inspired a 2018 study by the Council on Quality and Leadership (CQL) that aimed to examine the relationship between respect and disability and how respect impacts one's quality of life. Carli Friedman, the author of the study, defines respect as "how we show our regard for each other" and an "[indication] that we believe someone is a valued person."[6] First, the study showed several disparities within the disability community, such as women with disabilities being 1.7 times less likely to be respected than men with disabilities, and people with 24-7 support being 7.7 times less likely to be respected than those with support as needed.[7]

The CQL study showed that the simple act of being respected improved disabled people's quality of life in various areas, such as realizing personal goals (1.8 times more likely if we were respected than those who were not respected), choosing where to work (3.1 times more likely), being in intimate relationships (3.7 times), being in our best possible health (4.2 times), being safe (4.3 times), having friends (4.6 times), participating in community life (5.3 times), and being treated fairly (8.4 times). The study also showed that when organizational supports are in place—when organizations know what is important to the person in terms of respect, ensure that interactions with the person are respectful, and implement supports that enhance the person's self-image—disabled people were 166.7 times more likely to be respected.[8]

Being treated with respect matters. On a flight taken by public speaker, DEIA consultant, and content creator Catarina Rivera, a flight attendant anticipated her needs by asking if she'd like a tour of the bathroom. Rivera has Usher syndrome, which means she has both hearing and vision disabilities and has trouble seeing in low light, especially when lights are dimmed on long-haul flights. "He led me down the aisle to show me where the bathroom was. He then oriented me to the bathroom itself: where the toilet was, the button to flush the toilet, the soap dispenser, the paper towels. As a person with only 5 percent of my vision remaining, figuring out new spaces can take me a while….The impact of this bathroom tour was huge for me." When she later asked if he'd be willing to guide her to the bathroom when the lights were dim, he was happy to oblige. Rivera adds, "A lot of inclusion is about simple human interactions like this one. It doesn't have to be complicated!"[9]

This is what I call the "self-actualization" of disabled people, where respect leads to positive outcomes, such as a boost in our self-esteem and confidence that can lead to an increased engagement in society. As Friedman says in the CQL research study, respecting people with disabilities not only counteracts discrimination but also helps disabled people to recognize our full personhood, to have opportunities to make choices and take risks, and to recognize disability as an identity and community.[10] In other words, treating disabled people with respect may start with addressing us (and not the people we're with) when you are speaking to us, but it must move beyond that toward breaking down ableist barriers and providing us with the tools to live life with dignity.

Dignity, which overlaps with respect, is defined by the Royal College of Nursing as "how people feel, think, and behave in relation to the worth or value of themselves and others." Treating someone with dignity means treating them "as being of worth, in a way that is respectful of them as valued individuals."[11]

When we are not treated with dignity, the message that we are not important or worthy is being sent. People with disabilities often overhear negative comments being made about us or receive such comments to our faces. It can be as overt as being dehumanized outright or as insidious as someone dismissing our opinions, fears, and concerns or even just ignoring us.

Conversely, being treated with dignity means being treated with respect, honor, integrity, and courtesy. It can mean small gestures in our interpersonal relationships, such as using respectful language and listening actively when disabled people share our opinions. But it can also mean big-picture and structural actions, such as ensuring that all disabled people have access to self-actualization, self-determination, social inclusion, and social justice.[12]

Take, for example, the simple issue of the clothes we wear. Some of us who have trouble dressing independently would benefit from clothes designed with Velcro or magnets rather than buttons or zippers. Let's come back to the Tommy Hilfiger adaptive fashion line as an example. In 2016, Hilfiger started designing this line in partnership with Runway of Dreams, a nonprofit working toward inclusion in the fashion industry, after seeing his autistic daughter experiencing challenges with getting dressed, and new collections are still being added.[13] In 2022, I was a model in a Tommy Hilfiger adaptive fashion runway show, wearing an oversized hot-pink blazer with magnets instead of buttons. I felt amazing because this outfit was an extension of my personality and made me feel that the way I dressed embodied who I was. After the show, all my friends, including my non-disabled friends, looked up the blazer because they wanted one, too! Having the option of adaptive clothing that is both functional and stylish gives us agency and can also make us feel and look good, a boost for our self-esteem.

Whether it's being given a choice in our wardrobe or other aspects of our lives—work, housing, hobbies, etc.—disabled people lead dignified lives when we have full autonomy. Dignity means that we have the power to make decisions for ourselves, the agency to participate in society the way we want to, and the ability to claim our universal human rights.

Dignity and respect are essential in our anti-ableist practice. Here are some strategies and practical actions you can take to treat disabled people with dignity and respect:

1. Respect disabled people in your interpersonal relationships.
    -   Interact with us in the same way you would anyone else. We are your family, friends, lovers, and colleagues.
    -   Talk to us directly, hold space for us to speak, and give us your attention. If you're talking to a person who is Deaf or hard of hearing, talk directly to them even if they are looking at their interpreters. Do not talk to aides, caregivers, or interpreters on their behalf.
    -   Use a regular or neutral tone when speaking. Don't talk down to us (we are not victims) or use a patronizing tone (we are not children), and certainly don't ignore us.
    -   Be aware of personal space. Don't pat us on the head or touch us without our consent. For example, if you're trying to help a wheelchair user or a blind person, don't push their wheelchair or grab their arm without asking first. If you're talking to a wheelchair user for a while, sit down so they don't have to strain their neck to look up at you.[14]
    -   Don't pet a disabled person's service animal. Their service animal is working to support them and shouldn't be distracted.
    -   Be sensitive to our different needs, and be ready to be flexible. For example, someone may find that direct eye contact makes them uncomfortable. If we have a limb difference and you want to shake our hand, let us lead. We may shake your hand with our other hand (that's what I do), or we may give you a nod in acknowledgment. Some of us need extra time to gather our thoughts, so be patient and let us set the pace of the conversation.[15] When in doubt, ask us how we prefer to communicate or if we need assistance in any way.

2. Allow disabled people to make dignified choices in every aspect of our lives.

- Include us in discussions about our care or other topics that concern us. Don't exclude us or make decisions on our behalf. We have unique perspectives to contribute to larger conversations in society.
- Take our opinions and suggestions to heart and work with us to implement them as best you can. Don't minimize or ignore our concerns. Reminder: many of the anti-ableist accommodations that disabled people need can benefit non-disabled people, too, such as closed captioning and elevators.
- Check in with us to see what our access needs are in different situations, and help us to overcome barriers so we can participate fully.
- Fight for equal opportunities and disability-inclusive spaces and accommodations that will enable us to make autonomous decisions. These include areas like employment, housing, school, health care, voting, transportation, food, finances, fashion, and social activities.
- Help us attain positions of power and influence. If you're in a position of power, hire us to be your employees and managers so that we have more structural agency to make systemic contributions. Vote us into office so that we can make more impactful political change.

3. Continue to work on yourself to unlearn ableism.

- Educate yourself about disability issues and engage in conversations within your own social circles to raise awareness and challenge ableist assumptions.
- Revisit the accounts you followed from the exercise in Chapter 14: Diversify Your Feed, such as Alice Wong, Imani Barbarin, Catarina Rivera, Haben Girma, and Mia Mingus. Education can be found in every sphere and is a continuous practice.

Reflection Questions

1. What does being treated with dignity and respect mean to you? In what ways has being treated this way impacted your quality of life? How would you feel if you were not treated this way?

2. Have you ever witnessed disrespectful or patronizing behavior toward disabled individuals? Did you intervene? If not, what could you have done instead?

CHAPTER 23

Exist in the Contradictions

"If you've met one disabled person, then you've met one disabled person." Emily Ladau, activist and author of *Demystifying Disability*, uses this line to illustrate that there is no single story of the disabled experience.[1] As we learned in Chapter 1: What Is Disability?, disability is incredibly diverse. We are all unique, whether it is across different disabilities or even within the same type of disability. While one person's experience might inform another's, no singular experience represents the entire disability community. We have intersecting identities, unique needs, and varied ways of navigating our disabilities. We are not a monolith (been a while!), just like any other community of people out there.

Because of this, we sometimes disagree. For example, much of what you'll find in this book is general guidance that I've attempted to pool from different resources that matches my own experiences, preferences, and beliefs. However, not every disabled person will agree with me or share my perspectives, which is why I've mentioned that I hope my personal stories and advice can be a catalyst for you to do your own research.

One example of where we might diverge is our language preferences. While I've discussed using words like *disability* and *disabled people* to refer to us in order to reinforce the idea that disability is a neutral rather than a negative term, some people prefer alternatives. Snowboarder Amy Purdy is fine with calling herself an adaptive athlete or a three-time Paralympic medalist; however, she doesn't call herself disabled. "Although I never really considered myself 'disabled' because my legs have actually allowed me to do so much, I couldn't be more honored to represent such a diverse & creative community!" she wrote in a Facebook post.[2] While we should respect individual preferences, keep in mind that removing the shame and stigma around disability is still an important anti-ableist practice because shame and stigma hold people back from identifying as disabled and receiving the support and accommodations that we need.[3] People have different preferences in etiquette, too: some of us like to be proactively asked before being offered assistance, while others prefer not to be approached at all, with the mindset that if we need something, we'll request it ourselves.

It is one thing to respect the individual wishes of disabled people when it comes to preferred language and behavior. However, it is a whole other thing when there is a conflict in our ideals, values, and methods. At the end of the day, I believe that all people reading this book want to live in an anti-ableist society. However, the means and ways we use to get there might look different from community to community and person to person.

As we learned in Chapter 7: Disability Intersectionality, one of the principles under the framework of disability justice is anti-capitalism. The reason is that capitalism's hyperfocus on productivity—the capability of our bodies to keep on producing—is ableist, and non-disabled bodies are valued over disabled bodies because of how much more they can potentially produce to support the capitalist system. I have to acknowledge that we still exist in a capitalist society, and much of my advocacy work is focused on getting disabled people paid and finding ways for us to survive and thrive within that system, which might not be supported under the anti-capitalism principle. I've also been paid an advance to write this book. I'm grateful to be able to support my livelihood through my advocacy work and pay it forward by investing in disabled entrepreneurs, awarding disability microgrants, and helping disabled people get paid.

Another example of diverging opinions in the disability community is Tim Tebow's Night to Shine disability prom. Some disability advocates have been critical of the event because of the way it segregates disabled teens and doesn't address the underlying issue of how disabled people feel excluded from the prom at their own school that their non-disabled peers are attending.[4] I remember bringing up this feedback to a friend who volunteered at the event, and she told me that Night to Shine could be transformative and life-changing for disabled people who attended it because they didn't feel welcome at the prom at their own school.

After this conversation, I changed my perspective and realized that all of our initiatives were intended to work toward acceptance and inclusion. Disability-only spaces are sometimes needed, as they can create a sense of *access intimacy*, a term coined by disability justice activist Mia Mingus, which she describes as "that elusive, hard to describe feeling when someone else 'gets' your access needs."[5]

It feels uncomfortable when disagreements happen, especially when members of your own community are critical of you. But I've learned over the many years I've been doing this work that the world doesn't exist in a binary. We can and must hold space for the inevitable contradictions that come our way. Sometimes we don't all agree on certain things—and that's okay. I was struck by something that workplace culture and DEI expert Denise Hamilton wrote on Threads: "We have to learn to disagree without destruction."[6]

A key point for me in any instance of conflict is what we can learn from it. There are some things we can agree to disagree on and continue to coexist in community together, for example, if it is the small issue of personal preference over whether one identifies with the label "disabled." However, there are bigger issues that benefit from call-ins and further education to ensure that we can redress harm. It is okay to disagree with one another, but it is also important to open ourselves to feedback and commit to continued learning while being in compassionate conversation with each other.

When we use phrases like "Shame on you," or we threaten someone's livelihood, what is the intended effect? Is it to lock the person in a punitive cycle of shame so that nothing gets done, or is it to empower them to take action to do better? When I'm on the opposite end of an exchange like this, and I see an opportunity to educate, correct, or even criticize, I try to do so with care and respect because I hope to continue the conversation, not end it. I also try to use sensitivity and consideration because I recognize that individual experiences are valid, and there is no one way of doing or being. I'll address ways to take accountability in the next chapter.

Mingus says, "We are trying to understand how we can build organizing and community spaces that are mixed-ability, cultivating solidarity between people with different disabilities. We are working to move together, as disabled people, through a world that wants to divide us and keep us separate."[7] Ultimately, I believe we all share a common goal of disability inclusion, even if we have different ways of pursuing that goal. If we are to exist in these messy contradictions that are a natural part of any community, it is important for us to respect our differences while calling for accountability and making space for productive anger and mutual growth.

Here are some tips and strategies:

1. Talk to one another directly and engage in conversation. Instead of talking *at* someone or calling them out, call them in to open a communication channel so that we can all keep learning. Productive anger, when dealt with well, can be a way of deepening relationships.[8]
2. Agree on a resolution plan or path forward so that you can follow up on the conflict, whether it is to apologize, redress harm, or make space for one another's unique needs. In these scenarios, prioritize impact over intention.
3. Engage with care and respect, and recognize that each individual's experience is valid. If the contradictions are uncomfortable, learn to sit with them instead of being scared away.

Reflection Questions

1. How do you feel when someone disagrees with you?

2. What contradictions or conflicts have you observed within the disability community or other communities in which you participate? How can you support efforts to navigate and address them?

3. How can we align our efforts so that we are all working toward similar goals of disability inclusion and equity, even if we are doing it in different ways?

4. What would "disagreement without destruction" look like to you?

CHAPTER 24

Take Accountability for Ableist Harm

As we do important anti-ableist work, some of us may mistakenly think that we are above making any more mistakes or less likely to make them, or that we no longer need to be corrected. However, the hard truth is that none of us are perfect. As people who still live in an ableist world and who are on an ongoing journey toward disability justice, we will continue to make mistakes, and being allies does not make us immune to criticisms or call-ins from the people we are collaborating with. I know I'm still growing and learning in this work.

What matters is not whether we make any mistakes at all but *how* we choose to respond when the mistakes happen—because they will. "Allyship is actually more about the mistakes than the things that you do right," says Maybe Burke, artist, educator, and speaker. "It's about how you deal with those mistakes and move forward."[1]

Take Soogia for example, an AAPI TikTok content creator who uses the handle @soogia1. When she used the phrase "tone deaf, dumb, and blind" in a post to describe someone's offensive behavior, commenters jumped up to inform her that the phrase was ableist. Soogia's initial reaction was to become defensive, but what I liked about her response was how she followed up with a reflection process that eventually led to understanding why the original ableist phrase, as well as the defensive gut reaction, was problematic:

Of course, my defenses went up, and I was like, no, I wasn't being ableist....But somebody very gently educated me on why that phrase is triggering....So, what do you do in those situations? I took the video down, and I really thought about it. I genuinely feel horrible that I let that video go out and that I was defensive about it....I can see [that] what I've done was hurtful, and...I promise and vow to do better.[2]

Being accountable for any harm you create can look like Soogia's response: listening to disabled people when we point out ableist words or behavior, waiting until your defensive reaction subsides so you can reflect on our feedback, apologizing meaningfully for the harm you've done, and working on what you can do to be better in the future. As with everything you do as an ally, don't center yourself when you practice accountability. Accountability means showing up to the people around you to address and repair the harm rather than shifting the attention back to you and what you did or what you intended to do. This is especially important if you wish to build trust within the disability communities you are a part of or that you are advocating with, especially since you have just broken that trust.

When people say they are sorry, their apologies often come off as half-hearted or insincere if they say something like "I'm sorry you feel this way because I didn't mean to do this," or "I'm sorry, but I didn't intend to hurt anybody." Such apologies are unhelpful and meaningless because they focus on the intention rather than the impact of the harm. The hard truth is that your opinions don't matter in this case—the opinions of the person being harmed do. Motivational speaker and disability advocate Spencer West modeled this key lesson on intention versus impact when he apologized for creating an anti-Semitic image by superimposing a six-pointed yellow star on his body, reminiscent of the badges that Jews were forced to wear during the Holocaust: "I didn't intentionally use this symbol, but at the end of the day that doesn't really matter because it had an impact, and I want to sincerely apologize for the mistake and the harm that this caused....I'm someone [who] does my best to try to be inclusive and not to be harmful, but mistakes happen, and when those happen, I think it's important to acknowledge them, own them, and apologize."[3]

Practically, an apology can look like this: (A) naming your actions that caused the harm and its impact, (B) taking responsibility and saying that you are sorry (and meaning it), and (C) committing not to do the harm again and/or explaining reparative actions you may take. For example, "Yesterday, I said/did [X], and (A) it was an ableist microaggression that hurt many people I care about, (B) I own up to my mistake and I apologize, and (C) I promise to do the work so that I will not cause such harm in the future."

However, it is also important to remember that taking accountability is much more than apologizing. It is not enough just to say the right words in the moment, which can be performative if we don't commit to following through with our actions and behavior.

Transformative justice and disability justice writer and educator Mia Mingus clarifies, "Accountability is not merely confessing what you've done; it is a process that must be practiced...within relationship....True accountability, by its very nature, should push us to grow and change, to transform." Additionally, Mingus urges that accountability must be proactive: "It is not another person's job to hold you accountable—that is your job. People can support you to be accountable, but no one but you can do the hard work of taking accountability for yourself."[4]

On her website Leaving Evidence, Mingus shares four elements of accountability: self-reflection, apologizing, repair, and behavior change.

We've already talked about the importance of reflecting and apologizing in this chapter. Repair involves working together with the people who have been harmed to make amends, rebuild bridges, and reestablish trust, along with the commitment that you will not cause the hurt again. If the people who have been harmed do not have a desire for repair, you still have to do the work on your own.

Then, changing your behavior starts with recognizing that harmful actions have roots in larger behavioral patterns or beliefs. Thus, behavioral change will not only help us to keep our promise to others not to harm again but also transform us and our society for the better.[5]

Taking accountability for my actions is something I'm still learning to do better in my anti-ableist practice. But that's why it's called a practice. As Mingus says, "We are aiming for practice, not perfection....We are human and we live in an incredibly violent and harmful world. The point is to learn how to be accountable *when we inevitably mess up*, so that we know what to do."[6]

No one has all the answers, and we're not going to get it right all the time. But I take hope from the fact that we have to make mistakes in order to grow and that growth will occur if we continue to educate ourselves and do this important work.

Reflection Questions

1. How do you feel when you make mistakes? How can you embrace these feelings more openly and vulnerably? What role does your ego play in all of this, and what are some strategies you can use to set it aside?

2. Review the apologies highlighted in this chapter and see how they line up with the accountability framework we've discussed.

3. Reflect on a situation where your impact did not align with your intention. How did you handle it? Did you apologize? What did you learn from that experience? What could you do differently in the future to more effectively be accountable?

4. Reflect on a genuine apology that you've received in the past. Was the person proactive and sincere to demonstrate a commitment to change? What key words or actions did they use that you might adopt? How did you feel after the apology was made?

5. What steps can you take to minimize the likelihood of repeating harmful actions in the future?

PART 3

ANTI-ABLEISM AND SOCIETAL CHANGE

CHAPTER 25

Lower the Disability Tax

Growing up, I always found the kitchen a little intimidating. So in 2020, during a period when many of us were sheltering at home, I decided to learn how to cook. I was already able to make basic meals like pasta, salad, and sandwiches, but working in finance meant I often ate out or turned to easily microwavable meals.

To prepare, I purchased kitchen staples, including a knife and cutting board. Of course, I bought a one-handed cutting board. It was a sturdy piece of plastic with suction cups on the bottom. On top, there were two features to help stabilize what I was cutting: sharp spokes that stuck out on one side and a clamp on the other side. It came with a "rocker knife," which I later learned was inspired by the Inuit ulu.

The catch: the board retailed for $75. (As of this writing, you can get it at Walmart for $64.85.[1])

For people who can use both hands, kitchen knives are available for $3 to $10 and cutting boards for $5 to $20. But to participate in the same activity—say, cutting a tomato—would cost me $75 over someone else's $30. Why did I have to pay over 100 percent more to do something as essential as cooking in my own kitchen?

The reality is that it is expensive to be disabled. Research shows that disabled people need at least 28 percent more income, at least $17,690 per year, to achieve a standard of living similar to that of non-disabled people.[2] Working-age disabled adults are less likely to be employed than our non-disabled peers and have lower wages on average.[3] Furthermore, caregivers often take time off work to support disabled family members, further reducing the overall household income.[4]

This is what many of us in the disability community call the *disability tax*—it costs us more to simply live. And it isn't just medical expenses, which is a common misconception. Becca Lory Hector describes the disability tax as "the additional effort, energy, finances, and time it takes us to regularly match what our peers and colleagues do on a daily basis."[5] So, while the disability tax includes financial costs like medical needs, adding accommodations to our homes or vehicles, grocery delivery, or buying one-handed cutting boards, it also includes costs like the extra time we need to get ready and leave the house, the mental energy needed to sort through complicated paperwork to request the disability benefits that are meant for us (which can result in reduced working hours), a slower pace of progress, and poor job performance. "Things like showering, getting dressed, preparing meals, and getting where we need to go can often cost us so much 'disability tax' that by the time we get to our jobs, we have already spent beyond our budget, and that can make keeping a job unsustainable," says Hector.[6] This is where the spoon theory and limited spoons also come into play: it takes more energy for us to exist and perform daily tasks when we might already have limited energy to start with.

The disability tax also affects disabled entrepreneurs and leaders, not just employees. "The next time someone says I don't look autistic, I might invite them to look at my bank statement," says social entrepreneur Sara-Louise Ackrill, referring to the money she's spent on consultants to help her with her autism, ADHD, cPTSD, anxiety, and OCD so that she can show up as the business owner of her company Wired Differently, a creative hub for neurodivergent professionals and students.[7] For neurodivergent individuals or people with mental health disabilities, the disability tax can also look like buying first-class tickets on trains or airplanes if we are easily overstimulated, renting one-bedroom apartments so we won't have to deal with roommates, and accessing therapy. For others, it can mean opting to take rideshare or a taxi over public transit that might be inaccessible and doesn't offer door-to-door service. In addition to my $75 cutting board, I often pay to check in my luggage on flights because I'm unable to put my carry-on luggage in the overhead compartment on my own.

Costs associated with the disability tax can be categorized as direct and indirect costs, according to the National Disability Institute. Direct costs are expenditures such as health care—with out-of-pocket costs more than twice as high for disabled people as those for people without disabilities[8]—personal assistance services, service animals, food for special diets, or accessible housing or housing accommodations, to name but a few. Indirect costs include forgone income when disabled people have to take time off work, when we face workplace barriers like employment discrimination, or when family members have to take lower-paying jobs in order to have the job flexibility they need to take care of a disabled person.[9]

A person's financial stability depends on the relationship between their income and expenditure. However, most means-tested US public assistance programs consider only a person's assets and income as a way to determine eligibility for a benefit: if your assets or earnings are above a certain limit, you will not qualify. These public policies do not factor expenses—not even the significant expenses disabled people often have to take on—into the equation.[10]

What ends up happening is that many of us are denied public assistance based on our savings and income levels, even though our extra disability-related expenditures mean we are not actually financially stable. To overcome this impossible hurdle, disabled people who depend on benefits might choose to keep their income and savings low, trapping them in a vicious cycle of poverty.

The Social Security Administration has two disability programs: SSI and Social Security Disability Insurance (SSDI). In 2024, the earnings threshold is $1,971 per month for those on SSI,[11] and for those on SSDI, it is $1,550 per month for a non-blind person and $2,590 per month for a blind person.[12] In some places, these thresholds are so low that it would make it hard to afford rent. A disabled person can lose their SSI benefits by having too much income, and they can lose their SSDI benefits by going back to work and surpassing the earnings threshold. They can also lose SSI benefits by being married. In this way, the government essentially controls the lives of disabled people on benefits, penalizing them for their successes, which doesn't erase the fact that they still need different types of support (such as a personal care attendant).

Neil Hughes, a fifty-three-year-old autistic and paralyzed worker who was placed on SSDI after a roofing accident, shares, "When moving to Utah from California in 2007, the state required divorce for me to keep Medicaid. I refused, so they required a Medicaid spend-down of 50 percent of all wages. The state worker didn't understand why I would work to then have half of the money taken." Since the roofing accident, Hughes has raised three kids while handling hospice for three family members, one of whom was his first wife, Willow, who died of stiff-person syndrome in 2014.[13]

When you're stuck in poverty, direct costs are further aggravated.[14] For example, living in low-income neighborhoods and food deserts means paying more to access food, and lacking savings or access to credit means relying on payday loans or check-cashing services. It's called the poverty trap for a reason.

Financial stress is a dangerous mix of both financial and mental or psychological burdens. "Being disabled is like having a second job," says artist and writer Rachel Litchman. "The hours spent on phone calls, filling out paperwork, and collecting medical records just to 'prove' deservingness for services we need can add up to hours lost from the day and lost income. While these administrative burdens are literally taxing, one of the worst consequences is the psychological costs."[15] Litchman calls this "navigation anxiety," the anxiety that comes from dealing with hostile systems and people that sometimes even traumatize disabled people, like the public benefits system, health care, or disability accommodation services. Because of navigation anxiety, many disabled people avoid engaging in tasks such as filling out forms or making decisions, even if for something we need. "Ironically, the navigation anxiety that emerges from having to navigate systems because of my disability is in itself disabling," says Litchman.[16]

There have been some recent steps in the right direction. In 2014, Congress passed the Achieving a Better Life Experience (ABLE) Act, which allows people to save for disability-related expenses in a tax-advantaged account that does not count toward their assets when determining eligibility for public benefits. In 2018, I attended the launch of CalABLE, the implementation of the ABLE Act in California, which has a set limit of $100,000 in savings, and I noticed that there was still lingering distrust among disabled people in the system.[17] One remaining issue is that it's up to individual states to implement the act; another is the question of what counts as disability-related expenses.

Another piece of recent good news is that a bipartisan proposal was introduced in the Senate in September 2023, seeking to raise asset limits for SSI from $2,000—set thirty-four years ago in 1989, when the cost of living was much lower—to $10,000, a more realistic and much-needed update that would allow more disabled people to qualify for federal benefits. Disability rights activist Patrice Jetter describes what it means to be able to subsist on only $2,000 in savings: "I needed to get my car fixed, and in order for me to save up $500 for a car repair, I needed four consecutive weeks' pay....So, in order to save the money, I didn't cash any of my paychecks, and I had to walk to work...and not buy myself anything for the whole month."[18]

Although Jetter supports the recent move, she points out that while this asset limit works for SSI, it does not apply to other services that disabled people may use, such as Medicaid, the Low Income Home Energy Assistance Program (LIHEAP), and the Supplemental Nutrition Assistance Program (SNAP, also known as food stamps). In other words, saving $10,000 for SSI would disqualify people from other essential benefits, and "you're going to be right back at square one." The solution, Jetter suggests, would be for all other programs to get up to speed. The government should also adopt a more holistic approach, recognize that disabled people rely on various services, and take into account our saving needs.[19]

Lowering the disability tax is a function of economic justice and equity and a crucial part of our anti-ableism work. We can all do our part to help lower the "taxes" of the disabled people in our lives. How? According to Hector, normalize asking for accommodations so that disabled people feel safe and free to do so, offer flexible schedules and hybrid remote work to recognize the extra time we need to do things, and simply provide accessibility. "Accessibility is my favorite way to lower that tax," says Hector. "It reduces the work a disabled colleague has to do simply to attend, which means they can just show up and participate with all their energy intact."[20]

Reflection Questions

1. Look up an everyday item that you've recently purchased. Now, look up that same item adapted for someone with a disability. Is there a price difference? How big is it?

2. Have you personally experienced or observed the impact of the disability tax?

3. What steps can be taken at the societal and systemic levels to create a more equitable and financially accessible environment for individuals with disabilities? What are some recent policy changes that address the financial challenges faced by individuals with disabilities? (This could include health care reform, accessible housing, and employment opportunities.)

4. Take a look at your workplace's disability, access, and leave policies. Where might they benefit from being more anti-ableist?

5. How can you personally contribute to efforts or initiatives to lower the disability tax? Are there ways you can challenge the disability tax in your own communities?

CHAPTER 26

Inclusive Design Benefits Everyone

When Michael Pachovas and a few friends poured cement along a curb to create a makeshift ramp for their wheelchairs in the 1970s in Berkeley, California, little did they know that their act of political defiance would set in motion an accessibility revolution around the United States. Under pressure from these disabled activists, including the likes of Ed Roberts, who would later be considered the father of the independent living movement, the city of Berkeley finally installed its very first "curb cut"—where a slope is cut into the curb to allow mobility devices to move through—on Telegraph Avenue in 1972, which eventually paved the way, literally, for thousands of other curb cuts throughout the country. Today, in the wake of the passage of the ADA in 1990, curb cuts are required on new constructions, renovation, or street work.

While this was an accessibility win for the disability community, something else surprising happened: people found that the effects of the curb cut benefited everyone—not just wheelchair users but also parents pushing strollers, kids riding bikes and skateboards, and workers pushing carts. I know I have definitely benefited from curb cuts while transporting my rolling luggage around the world. In fact, a study in a shopping mall in Florida found that nine out of ten "unencumbered pedestrians" veered off course to use a curb cut.[1]

"There's an ingrained societal suspicion that intentionally supporting one group hurts another. That equity is a zero-sum game," says attorney, civil rights advocate, and founder of PolicyLink Angela Glover Blackwell. "[But] when we

create the circumstances that allow those who have been left behind to participate and contribute fully—everyone wins."[2]

This is what is now known as the curb-cut effect: the phenomenon where
design solutions initially created for people with disabilities end up benefiting
the larger diverse population. Do you use voice-activated technology to search
for something online or turn on the lights, closed captioning when you watch
videos, or a touch screen on your phone? How about a keyboard, electric toothbrush, or hot tub? All of these technologies and products were first designed with
disabled people in mind.

Voice-activated technology was designed to assist people with limited mobility or vision disabilities, but today, voice assistants like Siri or Alexa benefit everyone by providing hands-free interaction. Closed captioning subtitles, created for
Deaf and hard-of-hearing individuals, are used by many of us, whether we're
watching a video in a noisy environment or trying to learn a new language. In
the late 1990s, electrical engineering doctoral student Wayne Westerman developed the first touch-screen technologies to aid his studies when he developed
carpal tunnel syndrome, a repetitive stress injury. The tech was later bought by
Apple cofounder Steve Jobs.[3] Pellegrino Turri designed one of the earliest typing
machines in 1808 for his friend Carolina Fantoni da Fivizzano when he realized
the blind countess wasn't able to write letters to her friends. It was the precursor
to the QWERTY keyboard we use today.[4] In 1954, dentist Philippe-Guy Woog
invented the electric toothbrush for people with limited mobility and those who
wore braces. And after Candido Jacuzzi created a therapeutic hydropump to give
his son relief from his rheumatoid arthritis, the Jacuzzi family scaled and com-
mercialized the invention to bring hot tubs into people's homes.[5]

It was the same story with Sam Farber, who one day noticed his wife, Betsey, having trouble holding a peeler due to her arthritis. "This got Sam thinking: why do ordinary kitchen tools hurt your hands? Sam saw an opportunity
to create more thoughtful cooking tools that would benefit all people (with or
without arthritis) and promised Betsey he would make a better peeler."[6] In 1990,
Farber founded OXO, a manufacturer of kitchen supplies and housewares that
prioritizes universal design.

Dr. Amy Kenny, inaugural director of the Disability Cultural Center at
Georgetown University, says of designing with disability inclusion in mind,

Disabled people are uniquely creative because we live in a world not built for our bodyminds. Everything from texting to touch screens to the potato peeler was designed by and for disabled people. Whether [or not] you identify as disabled, you are likely already benefiting from the innovation of our disability communities. Disability is a creative force that imagines a new world where everyone can thrive.[7]

The curb-cut effect also demonstrates that when we prioritize inclusive design, we set off a ripple effect that creates accessibility, convenience, and even positive health and economic outcomes for society. An example of the curb-cut effect in practice, according to Blackwell, is when protected bike lanes were first created along streets. Despite criticism that bike lanes would create more congestion, what people actually saw was that the risk of serious injury for New York City cyclists dropped by 75 percent, while pedestrians, a much larger group who were not the intended target of bike lanes, experienced 22 percent fewer injuries because bikes now had their own dedicated space. Not only that, but travel times on the surrounding streets either remained the same or improved.[8] Additionally, shops along streets that had protected bike lanes saw an increase in retail sales because pedestrians felt more comfortable navigating sidewalks, with some shops doubling their numbers and outperforming citywide trends.[9] You can take this further by considering how an increase in bike lanes also promotes positive health outcomes, as more people have the option to cycle to work, and reduces greenhouse gas emissions with fewer cars on the road, which benefits the environment.

Designing for accessibility is an *opportunity* that leads to innovation and social advancement. Accessibility shouldn't be seen just as a problem to be solved when it is a competitive advantage. I like to say that when people fear becoming disabled, what they actually fear is the fact that we live in an inaccessible world that is hostile and obstructive to disabled people, not disability itself. What will happen if we all rewire our mindsets to treat accessibility as an opportunity for better and mutually beneficial design?

In October 2022, I was invited to be part of a focus group called an "equity codesign" for a company that was working on virtual reality (VR) headsets. When the time came for us to put on the headsets, I realized they required two hands because they had a soft strap. The facilitator looked at my paralyzed hand and said, "This probably isn't going to work for you." Overwhelmed and distracted, I sat out the rest of the session and couldn't participate in the activity in the same way as everyone else. So much for an equity codesign! Fast-forward to a year later, in October 2023, when I was invited back to the same company to participate in another "equity codesign" for their next VR headset. As I shared my experience from the previous year with the product team, I started to become emotional. I realized I hadn't been able to fully process what had happened in 2022. The whole experience had disempowered me and had essentially left me thinking the lie "This is not for me."

Often, disabled people have these thoughts about the many experiences that are not accessible to us in life, whether it's gaming, going to the gym, or even wearing jewelry. But why should that be? We exist everywhere, and disabled people want to game, work out, and wear jewelry like everyone else. The problem isn't our disability but the fact that the rest of the world does not think about us when they design products, spaces, or experiences.

Here's the thing: when I was told by the facilitator that the VR headset wasn't for me, he wasn't just speaking to me; he was speaking to the twenty-one million of us who have upper-extremity disabilities at any point in time.[10] This number includes permanent disabilities, temporary disabilities like a broken wrist, and even situational disabilities, such as a new parent who carries their child with one arm while they perform errands. A design that doesn't account for one-handed use of a product means that millions of us will not be buying that product. Talk about a missed market opportunity!

Fortunately, the company seemed to have made strides since our last encounter. During the 2023 focus group, I was able to try on different headsets that were helmet-based and had hard straps. I came away from the experience feeling hopeful, seen, and heard. One of the members of the product team even told me that he would make sure they used a one-handed test on all of their headsets going forward. I realized that my presence in the group would have a lasting impact on future inclusive design and would broaden the company's customer base to include the large and diverse population of people like me. This was ultimately why I had decided to return after the first experience: to help pave the way so others would not feel disempowered the way I had.

Take, for example, accessibility overlays on websites, which we will explore in more detail in a later chapter. Marketed as "quick fixes" to companies in order to provide ADA compliance and help them avoid lawsuits, accessibility overlays are temporary and often barrier-enhancing efforts because they reformat pages, ironically making it more difficult for screen-reader users to find headers and buttons.[11] According to accessibility experts, the better solution is for companies to hire and train full-time employees and test their products with disabled people so that they launch without needing modifications instead of relying on artificial intelligence (AI) software. Unfortunately, when we prioritize "quick fix" accessibility tools over investing in inclusive design from the start, the result can backfire.

Inclusive design accepts and embraces multiple design variations that are meant for different target audiences, so long as they achieve the desired outcome. For example, a sloped ramp is an example of inclusive design because it benefits wheelchair users, even though a ramp may not be as easy as stairs for someone who uses crutches to navigate. As the *Handbook on Ageing with Disability* says, "Design for one to design for all."[12] If a venue has all of these—stairs, a ramp, and an elevator—we are getting somewhere.

Another example: the watch company Eone makes beautiful tactile watches for anyone—whether sighted or blind—to tell the time through touch. However, its wrist straps are not designed for people who can use only one hand, like me. (Watches with elastic wristbands are best suited for me.) In this case, the desired outcome for Eone is enabling a blind person to wear a watch so that they can tell the time, which is great. That being said, this gap presents yet another opportunity—not a problem—for the company to explore in expanding its product line, such as a tactile watch with an elastic or bracelet wristband that can be put on with one hand.

A final takeaway is that inclusive design cannot happen independent of disabled people. As the curb-cut effect shows, the unique needs of disabled people highlight the gaps and holes in the way society is designed. Microsoft abides by these design principles in its Inclusive Design Toolkit, saying, "Designing with constraints in mind is simply designing well."[13] The company's Xbox Adaptive Controller is one example. Recognizing exclusion, according to Microsoft, is the first step toward inclusive user experience (UX), such as how designing for someone with a permanent upper-extremity disability is also designing for anyone who can use only one arm at a particular moment in time.

When we design for those of us who exist at the margins or who are historically underserved, the result is universally beneficial design. Inclusive design breaks down social barriers and creates products, spaces, and systems that foster a more diverse, empathetic, equitable, and inclusive society.

What can you do to create accessibility and build inclusive design into your daily life? Here are some tips:

1. Conduct an accessibility audit on your pre-existing spaces, products, and systems to see what can be adapted or improved. You can look for things like doorways, signage, lights, or chairs; media and communication options like sign language, large print, or braille; staff training in disability-inclusive practices; and your overall business culture, such as whether your employees or customers have flexible work schedules. You can also use resources like Equal Entry, Ablr, Inclusive Web, Intopia, TetraLogical, and Knowbility, which offer audits, trainings, and consulting to evaluate your current practices for digital accessibility.

2. Collaborate with and seek feedback from the disability community to include us in your design process to ensure that the results are effective and beneficial for everyone. Compensate us for our efforts. You can explore resources like Open Inclusion and Gamut Management for research and product testing.

3. If you are a designer, ensure that disabled voices are part of the company's inclusive design strategies from the get-go by giving disabled people a seat at the table or promoting us to leadership positions. Listen to us and invite our opinions. You may want to follow the work of the Inclusive Design Research Centre (IDRC), which provides a framework for inclusive design:
   - "Recognize, respect, and design [for] human uniqueness and variability.

- "Use inclusive, open, [and] transparent processes, and co-design with people who have a diversity of perspectives, including people [who] can't use or have difficulty using the current designs.
- "Realize that you are designing in a complex adaptive system."[14]

4. Rewire your thinking and remind yourself that designing for disabled people is designing for the majority of humanity rather than for the minority.

Reflection Questions

1. Consider a feature that provides accessibility, such as captions on videos. What barrier is it solving? What potential benefits does it offer to a broader audience?

2. Can you identify everyday examples where disability-inclusive design has made a positive difference for you? Do you listen to audiobooks or use an electric toothbrush, for example?

3. Is there a way that you can incorporate inclusive design into your work? How can you make it a sustained effort rather than a onetime initiative? Consider incorporating inclusive design principles into your ongoing projects and practices.

4. If you're making or creating something, ask yourself, "Who has a seat at the table? Who is missing? And how can I bring them in?"

CHAPTER 27

Make Public Spaces Accessible (in Person and Digitally)

We must consider accessibility in everything we do. Whether we're working in a physical store serving customers or creating content for thousands of followers from the comfort of our homes; whether we're organizing an event in a public space or hosting an online gathering for a few people, we all have the power and responsibility to consider the access needs of disabled people and, by extension, all other members of our communities.

Disabled people are everywhere, and we are a vital part of society. If we want disabled people to be able to participate and contribute, our access needs—which disability rights advocate Keely Cat-Wells calls access *requirements*—must be considered.[1] These aren't just wishful or optional accommodations; they are requirements for disabled people to fully participate in a world that consistently erects barriers to entry. Ensuring that our public and online spaces are accessible means removing these barriers as well as creating new systems that enable the participation of all. Some require larger structural commitment. Some changes are easy once we overcome people's resistance to change. And we must get into the habit of reflexively confirming that we've made these spaces accessible as surely as we add a conference line to a virtual meeting.

We've also learned that fulfilling the access requirements of disabled people improves the lives of everyone at the end of the day. This is why disability advocates

185

Alice Wong, Mia Mingus, and Sandy Ho say, "Access should be a collective responsibility, instead of the sole responsibility of it being placed on just one or two individuals. It is all of our responsibility to...[center] access as a core part of the way that we want to live in the world together—as a core part of our liberation."[2]

Wong, Mingus, and Ho believe that accessibility should be seen as "an act of love" rather than "a burden or an after-thought," principles that they outline in their project Access Is Love.[3] As they say in their introduction, "Access [is] not only about logistics, but about deepening our shared humanity and dignity, growing access intimacy with each other, and an opportunity to create more justice and love in our world."[4]

The fact is that accessibility isn't just about building a ramp or making sure videos have captions. In the broader picture, accessibility goes beyond disability to highlight the various other inequities in an intersectional world where disabled people are also queer, people of color, poor and working class, parents, and more. This is why accessibility can also look like having a sliding scale for fees, flexible schedules for work, options for online participation, and venues that provide childcare and have gender-neutral bathrooms as well as being mindful of police presence and acknowledging Native communities and the land we work and live on.

Even beyond that, there's the notion of *access intimacy*, a term coined by Mingus as mentioned in Chapter 23: Exist in the Contradictions. "Access intimacy is not just the action of access or 'helping' someone. We have all experienced access that has left us feeling like a burden, violated, or just plain [expletive]. Many of us have experienced obligatory access where there is no intimacy." Instead, Mingus says, access intimacy is "the way your body relaxes and opens up with someone when all your access needs are being met...the closeness I would feel with people who[m] my disabled body just felt a little bit safer and at ease with."[5] It's when we know we're being seen, heard, and valued.

To me, access intimacy is being able to show up somewhere and not having to ask for help or permission to be there to fully participate. In 2022, I attended my first "camp" with the UBPN, a nonprofit that supports people with brachial plexus injuries. The UBPN hosts this event every couple of years, and that year it was at a YMCA in Estes Park, Colorado. On one of the days, we had the opportunity to sign up for different activities. I'm always up for trying new things in a supportive space, so I signed up for archery.

When I arrived, I was welcomed by a few of my new friends. My friend and fellow TikTok creator Sara Groves filmed the interaction:

YMCA staff member: "Do you want me to hold [the bow] and you want to pull?"

Me: "No, I'm going to try to pull it. What do I pull?"

Sara and friends: "You got it, you got it." "There you go." "Yeah! That was good!"

On the third try, my arrow struck the target! I felt really proud of myself, and even though I felt self-conscious throughout, here are a few things I appreciated about the experience: the YMCA staff member was proactive about offering assistance but gave me the option to try the activity myself. The group I was with was supportive, cheering me on the whole time. Everyone was patient and let me try a few times until I got it.

There have also been more times than I can count where I felt the friction of not having access intimacy, like a group of friends organizing an outing to take a pottery class. I asked the friend organizing it if the pottery studio would be able to accommodate my disability. They didn't know, so I reached out directly to the pottery studio, didn't hear back from them, and did not participate, even though I wanted to. Pottery is still something I'm excited to try, and I've been on the lookout for local studios where I'd be welcome in their space. Even in the example of the first VR headset "equity codesign" focus group, they had known that I was coming and understood the manifestation of my disability, yet I still felt disempowered because the facilitator had made assumptions and did not give me the opportunity to try.

Sometimes access intimacy is knowing that someone like me will be present at a gathering or someone anticipating our needs or working with us during an event to avoid that friction. For example, I attended a conference in Bentonville, Arkansas, a few years ago. Biking was one of the morning activities in the cyclist-friendly city, so I signed up and let the organizers know that I was coming. When I arrived and checked in, one of the event staff recognized my name and said, "Your bike is ready for you." They had already made adjustments to the bike, making sure the left-handed brake was for the back wheel, the seat was low enough for my height, and it was set in a gear I didn't need to change.

I'll share one final example. In 2021, I was invited to a pumpkin-carving event with a women's community in San Francisco. I had never carved a pumpkin before, and I honestly wasn't sure if I knew how, but the women's community was built on mutual support and vulnerability, so I stepped out of my comfort zone and showed up. One way that I've adapted to not being able to use both arms for most of my life is by using my feet instead! I let everyone know that I might be carving the pumpkin in my own way, then sat on a mat on the floor, stabilizing the pumpkin with my feet while I carved it. Everyone else was absorbed in carving their own pumpkins, and no one made me feel weird about it. I carved a cat into my pumpkin.

As we take these core principles to heart, we still have to start somewhere. "Accessibility is frequently portrayed as complicated by people who don't want to include it," says Sheri Byrne-Haber, an engineering, accessibility, and inclusion leader on LinkedIn. "But accessibility doesn't *need* to be complicated." Byrne-Haber's solution is simple: one step at a time. Drawing on the quote from American tennis legend Arthur Ashe, Byrne-Haber advises that you "start where you are, use what you have, and do what you can."[6]

Here is a list of practical suggestions we can all put into practice to make our physical and online spaces accessible for everyone and essentially build an accessibility-first culture. As we begin to create the type of world we wish to see, we can then dream bigger and expand our idea of what access looks like.

Physical Accessibility

1. When planning an event or choosing a space, consider as many accessibility requirements as you can. A good first question to ask yourself is whether a wheelchair user will be able to attend and fully participate in your event, from getting from the parking lot or public transportation to the main hall to using the public restrooms—are there accessible toilets and parking spots, ramps and working elevators, wide entryways, and suitable seating accommodations?[7] Next, do the same exercise for people with other access requirements, such as blind peo-

ple or those with low vision, Deaf or hard-of-hearing people, people with sensory sensitivities, people with learning disabilities, and people with chronic illnesses. Other logistical considerations include providing a quiet space for people who are overstimulated to rest, replacing bright fluorescent lighting with dimmer lights or lamps, ensuring that the environment is scent-free by using scent-free soap and refraining from wearing fragrances, and allowing service animals into the venue.

2. Where there are gaps in the infrastructure, search for and invest in services or supplementary material that can fulfill the missing accessibility requirements. For example, hire audio describers, ASL interpreters, or captioners for live events. Make sure that signage and other print materials are clear and available in sans serif font, OpenDyslexic font, large print, and braille. Consider providing on-site childcare support or medical support to serve the needs of different people. Serve food that meets everyone's dietary restrictions. You don't have to have every solution yourself, and you might want to hire an accessibility consultant to help with this.

3. Address different accessibility requirements within your event format or workday as well. For example, schedule breaks, or "biobreaks," so that people can leave to take medication, use the bathroom, or rest. Consider organizing a hybrid event that is a mix of in-person and virtual sessions or allow flexible work-from-home scenarios. Give people the option to use different modes of communication, such as email, text, or phone. Implement a mask requirement to ensure that immunocompromised people are able to participate.[8]

4. Don't isolate disabled people from the rest of our friends or community when making accommodations.[9] Give us the option to be flexible. For example, venues that do have accessible seating often require the people who use it to sit apart from our party or group. Remember: we have friends, too! At SoFi Stadium in Los Angeles, where I attended a Taylor Swift concert, I could swap my general admission ticket for an accessible ticket, and accessible seating was provided in every level and section instead of just in one area, which I deeply appreciated.

5. Include accessibility information on promotional materials to let the public know which types of accessibility requirements are being fulfilled

and which aren't,[10] e.g., "This performance is accompanied by ASL interpreters and audio describers." This will save disabled people a lot of time and energy, such as making the decision to inquire whether further accommodations could be made or not attending an event that cannot meet our access requirements instead of showing up none the wiser and realizing that we cannot participate. For example, Shane Burcaw, a YouTube creator and disability advocate who uses a wheelchair, shared an experience where he made a reservation at a restaurant because it had marked that it was wheelchair accessible on its Google business page; however, upon arrival, Burcaw and his family were greeted by three concrete steps to access the courtyard. There was no step-free access to the restaurant, and they had to find another place to eat. To prevent situations like this, be honest and transparent when you share what accessibility requirements can't be met, such as "This space is not wheelchair accessible" or "This is not a scent-free space."

6. Conduct access check-ins at every meeting, which means giving people the opportunity to share any access requirements we may have. This helps to create a space that "values access and disability" and that "destigmatize[s] it in an ableist culture that hides, shames and individualizes access."[11] Whenever I organize an event, I like to ask attendees during the RSVP or registration process if they have access requirements in addition to what we're already providing. Sometimes people are not comfortable sharing their access needs in public, but there are ways you can make it private, such as having them fill out a Google Form beforehand or during event registration or including an email address that people can use to reach out. Access requirements can look like this: "I would benefit from stepping out of the room from time to time to be in a quiet space," "I will need to go to the back of the room to do stretches while I listen," "I can't have my photo taken with flash photography," "I would like to sit closer to the front so I can see the screen," or "I would prefer that people speak into the microphone."

7. When interacting with a group, practice identifying yourself by name, describing yourself briefly, and providing your pronouns. This sets a model for other participants to follow. For example, "Hi, my name is

Tiffany Yu. My pronouns are she/her. I'm a disabled Taiwanese American woman in my midthirties with shoulder-length black hair, wearing a blue jumpsuit. I may need some assistance when we are grabbing our food and would appreciate it if someone can hold my plate." (Or "My access needs are currently being met.")

8. Hire or engage disabled consultants or accessibility experts when planning and designing events so we can lead the process.[12] Value our expertise, and follow through by implementing suitable advice. Also, remember that we all have unique perspectives. Include us not just as specialty consultants but also as regular employees, customers, and attendees, and invite and respect our input. You can also put together an "access committee" made up of disabled people when you plan an event,[13] though make sure to compensate us for our time.

9. Train staff to interact respectfully and competently with people with different types of disabilities who are your customers, clients, collaborators, or event participants. You can also designate specially trained staff members whose only responsibility is to address accessibility needs. This might also be helpful for speakers or presenters who prefer a lot of interactivity during their sessions, such as adjusting statements like "Please stand *if you are physically capable of standing/if you are able to/if that is accessible for you.*" Deaf or hard-of-hearing people might prefer to keep their eyes open if you have an activity where you ask participants to "close your eyes."

10. Include a line for accessibility in your event budgets. By allocating spending for accessibility from the get-go, you will be less likely to treat it as a last resort, both financially and mentally. This also ensures that you will dedicate resources to constantly improving accessibility over time. Remember, accessibility is not a one-fix issue. Also, do not make disabled people bear the costs you have incurred from providing accessibility, which is your legal responsibility per Title III of the ADA in the United States (Public Accommodations and Commercial Facilities).[14] Disabled people are your customers and target audience, too.

I was impressed when attending the *Barbie* world premiere in Los Angeles in 2023. 1IN4 Coalition, a nonprofit focused on increasing disability employment and representation in Hollywood, shared some examples of what it had done to make the premiere accessible, including finding a barrier-free venue (plus step-free access to the red carpet); training staff in how to assist disabled attendees; inviting disabled talent even though the film was not about disability; and providing signage and communication around access, open captions and audio description during the screening, and ASL interpreters onstage during the opening remarks.[15]

On another occasion, upon arriving at the Belasco Theatre in New York City to see *How to Dance in Ohio* on Broadway, I was handed a *Playbill* with an insert sharing accessibility resources, including cooldown spaces around the theater if people had sensory sensitivities. Sensory kits, which included headphones and sunglasses for people who are more sensitive to light and sound, could be borrowed.[16]

While we can celebrate the wins, there is always more work to be done. Besides ensuring our physical spaces are accessible, we also have to turn our attention to digital spaces.

Digital Accessibility

1. Provide image descriptions and alternative text descriptions for social media posts and other online content. This simple practice of describing any visuals that accompany your posts is quick and doesn't cost any money. Image descriptions are added to the content of a post, usually at the bottom or pinned as the first comment, while alt text is manually entered into an app's advanced settings. Alt text is useful because it appears when a picture fails to load, and it can help a page's search engine optimization. However, not all people use screen readers, so having both alt text and image descriptions is preferable. Alt text can be short and sweet, but image descriptions should be longer and provide more details.[17]

2. Provide accurate captions or transcripts for video or audio content. Many social media platforms like TikTok, YouTube, Instagram, and Facebook have auto-captioning services; however, these notoriously dubbed "craptions" are often nonsensical and unusable.[18] Fortunately, you can manually review and correct these auto-captions, or you can use live captioners instead, which are about 20 percent more accurate than these services.[19] You can also use platforms like Otter.ai or Descript to upload audio in return for a transcript. Transcripts are helpful not just for those who are Deaf or hard of hearing but also for people who are learning English, who have difficulty processing audio-only information, who can't access or listen to audio content at the moment, or who need transcripts for note-taking purposes later.[20]

3. Craft text content with accessibility best practices in mind. For example, avoid using all caps, and provide blank lines between paragraphs to improve readability. Try not to overuse emojis, as screen readers will describe every emoji that appears. If you are creating graphics with text on them, ensure that the color contrast is high enough so that the text is readable. Check out the Coolors Color Contrast Checker as a resource. Capitalize every word in hashtags, such as #DisabilityPride and #AntiAbleistBook, as capitalization allows screen readers to interpret hashtags.[21]

4. Put a content warning (CW) or content notice (CN) at the top of posts that contain emotionally triggering or traumatizing content. This practice prioritizes users' consent since it gives people the power and agency to decide whether to engage with a particular topic at a certain time. Examples of CNs are "CW: ableism and medicalized violence" or "CN: suicide and addiction."[22]

Remember, a list like this is just a starter guide. You will likely encounter a whole range of situations, different people, and diverse needs over the course of your anti-ableist journey, so you need to be flexible, open, and attentive to the needs of others; to take initiative to meet those needs; and to do so with respect, care, and love.

Improving accessibility is a work in progress. Even it if feels overwhelming, we all started somewhere, and wherever you are is a great place to start.[23] Just take things one step at a time, make space for one another, give each other grace to make mistakes along the way, and stay committed to the journey.

Reflection Questions

1. At the next event you RSVP to, check whether access information is provided. If not, reach out to the organizer to suggest that they add access information. Even "This space is not wheelchair accessible" is helpful.

2. At the next event you attend, keep track of all the details that might cause barriers for someone with a disability. Did you have to walk a long way to get to the venue from a car park or public transportation? How was the lighting inside the venue? Were there ASL interpreters or audio describers?

3. If you are an event organizer, consider what practical changes you can implement right now to make your next event more accessible. What are you not able to do this time, and can you plan and budget for it during the following event?

4. If you are a speaker or presenter with physical activities in your presentation, such as asking people to stand up or close their eyes, what are some ways to make those suggestions inclusive for people who have different disabilities?

5. At the next opportunity you have to introduce yourself, commit to sharing your name, pronouns, and access requirements. How would you visually describe yourself? How did this go over? Did it change the tenor of the meeting?

6. If you create content on social media, commit to adding image descriptions and capitalizing the first letter of each word in your hashtags for your next post. Note that you can even ask your community to chime in on the comments to help with adding an image description if you don't have the energy/spoons to do so. Observe the response. How does engagement change?

CHAPTER 28

Hire Disabled People

I believe we all have a right to work. Work is how we support ourselves—our interests and our general lifestyle—and can be a way for us to contribute to society. When the ADA was passed in 1990, it laid out four goals for the disability community: full participation, equal opportunity, independent living, and economic self-sufficiency. Twenty-eight years later, in 2018, Senator Tom Harkin, one of the chief architects of the ADA, said in a speech, "We have made significant progress on these [first three] goals, but when it comes to economic self-sufficiency, we still have a good deal of work to do."[1]

I define economic self-sufficiency as whether we can make enough money to cover our basic needs in life—in other words, our ability to afford food on the table and a roof over our heads. Many of us achieve economic self-sufficiency through the money we make at our jobs. Unfortunately, in 2022, thirty-two years after the ADA, the employment rate of people with disabilities in the United States was still only 21.3 percent, compared to 65.4 percent of people without disabilities, while the unemployment rate for disabled people was twice that of our non-disabled peers.[2] Disabled people are also "last hired, first fired" in many workplaces.[3] All of these are clear indications to researchers and activists that we still have a long way to go to remove disability bias in hiring.

In 2023, the employment rate of disabled people rose only slightly, to 22.4 percent, and alarmingly, this is considered a record high:[4] it factors in the new numbers of already employed people who acquired long-haul COVID over the preceding few years; an increasing demand for jobs in the labor market, where roles for disabled people have been concentrated in retail, food prep, and cleaning;[5] and employees' new access to remote work, a reasonable accommodation that disabled people were advocating for long before the pandemic.[6]

In short, we face a huge disability employment gap. Are disabled people not hired because we can't do the work? Or is the problem that companies won't hire disabled people in the first place due to ableist assumptions?

Disability bias in hiring practices has been well recorded. According to a study conducted by the Society of Human Resource Managers (SHRM), 35 percent of HR managers believed that the work couldn't be done by employees who have a physical or intellectual disability, while 42 percent believed that the work couldn't be done by employees with a learning or attention disability. Additionally, 23 percent cited discomfort and unfamiliarity around people with disabilities. Despite these assumptions that led to a reluctance to hire disabled people, the survey found that 97 percent of managers who were aware that one or more of their employees had a disability said those individuals performed the same as or better than their peers without disabilities. In other words, the lack of disability hires is not due to actual performance but rather hiring managers' inaccurate assumptions.

Not only are these assumptions by HR managers detrimental to disabled people seeking to be hired, but the company also loses out when potentially valuable employees are passed over and never given the chance to show what we're capable of. This leads some disabled candidates to "hide" our disabilities for fear that knowledge of our disability status will impact our ability to be hired.

How do we dispel and counter this myth? "What happens when you hire a person with disabilities is you see how we do our jobs," says Kathleen Martinez, who was the assistant secretary of labor for the Office of Disability Employment Policy with the Obama administration. "And then the mystery is over, and we're not special anymore. We've become a part of the fabric of the work culture."[7] It's that simple.

So when people ask me, "Tiffany, what needs to happen to close the disability employment gap?," I tell them the solution is right in front of them: hire disabled people, period. That's the only way we'll be able to meaningfully see those unemployment numbers change and you'll get to see what we're capable of. All employees, disabled and non-disabled alike, are expected to do good work and prove that we are capable. The only difference is that disabled people aren't even given a chance to interview or are dismissed at the interview stage due to hiring managers' ableist assumptions. A 2021 study investigating hiring discrimination against wheelchair users found that wheelchair users were 48 percent less likely to be invited to job interviews than non-disabled applicants.[8] That's why I often say that policy plus attitudes will create change.

At Diversability, we have always made a point of hiring directly from our disability community because we want to show that disability employment works. We bring on team members in a contract capacity for a three-month paid trial period first to see if the role is a good fit. Our team is remote, our work is project-based and asynchronous, and we know this isn't for everyone. Some don't make it past the trial period, and that's okay, while others have stayed with us for years and gone on to receive scholarships, awards, and their dream jobs.

Sometimes I get a follow-up remark: "But I don't want my employees to feel like they're a token hire." My answer to that is, well, even if we are, we still have to do well and be subjected to performance reviews like everyone else. I've been in jobs where I've excelled. But that doesn't mean disabled people should be expected to succeed or be good at everything, which is another unfair burden that society expects us to carry. I was also fired from a sales job at a real estate startup. Just like everyone else, there will be roles that we're good at and ones that we're not, specific to each of our skills and interests, and it's important that hiring managers and companies recognize that.

Sometimes the problem isn't just with employers who think that disabled people aren't capable. Disabled people, too, can internalize ableism and believe we can't do the job. According to a survey conducted by the Bureau of Labor Statistics, 78.9 percent of disabled people who were unemployed reported that we faced barriers due to our own disability—meaning we thought our disability rather than the lack of accommodations was the reason we could not do the job—a number significantly higher than those for other cited barriers, such as lack of training, poor transportation, and the need for special accommodations in the workplace.[9] In this case, I would dig deeper than these numbers, which are based on people's perceptions, and argue that ableism (setting the expectations low for disabled people) and a lack of accessibility and accommodations, rather than a person's own disability, are the real barriers to employment.

Here's the truth in numbers: there is a business case for disability inclusion. Research has found that disabled employees not only perform well in our jobs but even help organizations make more money. In 2018, a report from Accenture found that if more people with disabilities joined the labor force, the US GDP could increase by $25 billion.[10] A more recent Accenture report in 2023 showed that companies leading in disability inclusion generated 1.6 times more revenue, 2.6 times more net income, and 2 times more economic profit, with the likelihood of outperforming their industry peers by 25 percent in productivity.[11]

Hiring disabled people is not just about compliance; there are real benefits. "People with disabilities are a tremendous source of talent and innovation, as well as market share," says Jill Houghton, president and CEO of Disability:IN.[12] According to a 2016 study, 75 percent of disabled employees said we had an idea that we believed would provide value to our companies.[13] Additionally, some of us have unique capabilities due to our disabilities that make us good fits for specific job scopes. For example, managers at Auticon, an IT consulting company, report that autistic consultants are "especially adept at recognizing patterns, which makes them better than others at seeing correlations and interdependencies in large amounts of data."[14]

Additionally, disabled employees have been shown to be more motivated, productive, and loyal, precisely because it is often difficult for us to find employment in the first place. Research shows that many disabled employees demonstrate a desire to perform well, along with low absenteeism, high retention, and low turnover rates.[15] In an interesting case study, a Walgreens distribution center that had 30 percent disabled employees was found to have 20 percent more efficiency, half the turnover rate, and one-third fewer accidents than similar facilities with non-disabled workers.[16]

"For too long, people with disabilities, individuals who are perfectly qualified and overwhelmingly will work, faced enormous barriers to being offered a job," says disability rights attorney and former state senator Ted Kennedy Jr. "[There is] compelling evidence that disability inclusion actually accelerates business performance, brand loyalty, and shareholder returns."[17]

Hiring disabled employees can also contribute to a more collaborative and empathetic work culture. When interacting with disabled peers, other coworkers learn to develop cooperative and supportive behaviors, leading to greater team cohesion. In a survey, 88 percent of HR professionals agreed that hiring disabled employees caused a significant improvement in the work culture.[18] The benefits go beyond the company to affect consumers, too. When customers interact with disabled employees in customer service roles, the company is often viewed as being more socially responsible, which enhances their reputation and increases brand loyalty from customers.[19]

If you are in a position to hire as a manager or business leader, here are some practices you can use to close the disability employment gap:

1. Make sure your job descriptions use language that does not exclude candidates with disabilities. This means focusing on essential functions that are required to perform the job, as opposed to marginal or unnecessary functions.[20] For example, here are four examples of typical job "requirements" that employers should avoid, according to global disability ERG lead Jamie Shields: "must be able to work in a fast-paced environment," "must have strong verbal communication skills," "must hold a degree," and "must hold a driver's license."[21] Not all disabled people can work quickly due to pre-existing barriers, but that doesn't mean we can't work accurately and well. People who are Deaf, autistic, or neurodivergent may not be able to communicate by speaking, but they can communicate through other means with the aid of assistive technologies. Many disabled people do not have the same privileges as non-disabled people to secure an education, but that doesn't mean we will be less competent. Finally, "unless I'm applying to be a race car driver," says Shields, "please stop excluding Disabled folks who are unable to legally drive," especially if the requirement is for an office job.[22] Similarly, I've come across job descriptions that require candidates to be able to lift twenty-five pounds. Unless the job scope involves package delivery or moving heavy equipment, this is an unnecessary and marginal requirement that would exclude capable disabled candidates from your pool.

2. Include language in your job postings that encourages people with disabilities to apply, even if we do not meet all the listed qualifications. Most of us are familiar with the Hewlett-Packard statistic, "Men apply for a job when they meet only 60 percent of the qualifications, but women apply only if they meet 100 percent of them,"[23] and this phenomenon can be extended to many people in other minoritized communities, including disabled people. To bust the myth that requirements are set in stone, be transparent about your hiring procedures and guidelines. For example, you can write, "If you think you can do this job but don't meet every qualification, we encourage you to still apply. We would love to have a conversation with you." You can also state explicitly, "People with disabilities are strongly encouraged to apply."

3. Ensure that your job application processes are inclusive of people with disabilities. This can mean making application forms digitally accessible in different ways or being flexible with the in-person or remote interview process. Train interviewers in ADA compliance and how to ask appropriate questions.[24] You can also add language to the job posting such as "If you require a disability-related accommodation to submit your application, please email us." For example, Row House Publishing included this statement at the top of its Jobs page: "Note on accessibility: We at Row House believe that every person—no matter their background, identity, or disability—should have equal opportunity to pursue gainful and fulfilling employment. If any of our application guidelines do not meet your access needs, please email us here and let us know how we can assist you in applying for your desired position."[25]

4. When conducting the interview and making decisions, be careful that hiring for "company fit" does not become a way to exclude disabled candidates. Inclusive design and product equity strategist Chang Liu shared in a LinkedIn post that she did not get a job because the interviewers found it "uncomfortable" and "odd" that she had included music at the start of her presentation and two photo slides to break things up, practices that accommodate some neurodivergent individuals.[26] A good hiring practice is to recognize each candidate's diverse and unique perspectives and what they can bring to the table that others

can't. Hiring for "company fit" can backfire if it leaves you with a pool of employees who all think, look, and sound alike.

5. Intentionally seek out disabled candidates and recruit from platforms like LinkedIn, suggests DEI workplace consultant Kim Crowder. LinkedIn boasts a strong community of disabled professionals who talk openly about our disabilities and advocate for disability inclusion in the workplace.[27] Inclusively, Chronically Capable, and Mentra are a few other marketplace platforms for employers to hire disabled candidates.

6. If you find yourself struggling with your own disability bias when it comes to hiring disabled people, experiment with a trial period contract position—as we do at Diversability—or a paid internship or apprenticeship to start, sometimes known as temp-to-perm (temporary positions that can lead to a permanent role). However, do this only if you can commit to doing so for all your hires, not just your disabled hires.

7. Connect with research organizations that are working to close the disability employment gap, for example, Disability:IN, the Valuable 500, Lime Connect, and the Harkin Institute, and collaborate to see how you can implement disability-inclusive hiring practices in your institutions to attract disabled employees. Engage disabled DEI consultants who can provide advice.

8. In addition to focusing on hiring processes, you should allocate resources and invest in making your workplace a more accessible and disability-inclusive environment in general. These big-picture goals will automatically and naturally attract valuable disabled candidates who want to work with you. A friend recently shared that she had seen a job posting from Chani, a tech company on a mission to make astrology accessible, and that the benefits offered were really supportive for her as a chronically ill woman. They included an $80,000 salary floor, a four-day workweek, a flexible work-from-home policy, and unlimited menstrual leave along with the statement "Folks who are queer, trans, non-binary, Black, Indigenous, people of color, disabled, parents, are/have been system-impacted, immigrants, and anyone who has

experienced systemic oppression and/or gender-based violence are encouraged to apply."[28] Guess what? She applied.

Reflection Questions

1. Have you ever encountered a job listing that felt unwelcoming or inaccessible? What language in particular felt unwelcoming?

2. Check out a job listing from your current workplace or from another employer. Is there wording in the listing or application process that excludes people with disabilities? How might you change it?

3. If you are in a position to hire, have you noticed any biases related to disability when interviewing a disabled candidate? How can you recognize and challenge your own disability bias during the hiring process?

4. What steps can you take to advocate for hiring disabled people in your workplace as employees, consultants, or speakers? What role can you play in supporting disabled people through the hiring process? Are you open to hosting informational interviews, reviewing résumés, or interview prep?

5. Review the list of benefits of hiring disabled people. Are there ones you had not thought of before? Feel free to refer to the research if you receive pushback when you advocate for prioritizing hiring disabled people. Are there other benefits you might add, based on what you've read so far or your own interactions with disabled people? Do you regularly interact with disabled colleagues?

CHAPTER 29

Rethink Accommodations

When I was starting my career at Goldman Sachs, the bank had recently transitioned to an open-floor layout, and all new hires could get an ergonomic assessment of our workstation. The ergonomic specialist had me sit at my workstation so that she could determine what improvements would benefit me. While my colleagues and I received many of the same enhancements, including a second monitor and a keyboard wrist pad, I got a few extra items. First, I received a left-handed mouse since I'm left-handed, and because I'm five feet tall, I also got a footstool so that my feet would not hang off my chair.

When the specialist noticed that I type with one hand, she asked if I would benefit from speech-to-text technology, which I had frankly never heard of before. Today, I use a free tool with paid features called Otter.ai, which records my audio and puts together a rough transcript and even an outline, with a shareable link. I think this program is skilled enough to be used—for free!—by regular businesses. (And no, they don't pay me to say that.) I have many friends who use speech-to-text technology when sending text messages, and I still frequently use this technology to write large amounts of text (like this book), to get rough transcripts of my podcast episodes, or to help generate meeting notes.

I grew up with the assumption that accommodations for my disability were "special treatment" and that I should never ask for them. But what I saw with the ergonomic specialist was how she proactively offered me, as well as my non-disabled colleagues, many options without ever making me feel that my needs were special, extraordinary, or inconvenient. As Aubrey Blanche-Sarellano, a technology executive and workplace equity expert whose work focuses on anti-racism and disability inclusion, reminds us, "So often, as disabled people, we accept the bare minimum of kindness, accommodation, [and] understanding, especially at work."[1]

What I've come to learn is that accommodations promote equity. Accommodations are not a "nice to have" option or an "unnecessary cost." They exist so that disabled people can participate in the same way as everyone else and so that all of us can participate equitably. When not distracted by barriers to our participation, we focus and perform our roles more efficiently and with better results.

"Accommodations are almost always considered 'unreasonable' until they're actualized, at which point almost everyone, regardless of disability, appreciates them," says author Rebekah Taussig, referencing the curb-cut effect in a piece she wrote for *Time* magazine about the disempowering experience of flying commercially with a wheelchair.[2] "What if accommodations weren't reserved for extraordinary circumstances? What if we took this moment of rebuilding to listen to the ones on the edges experiencing the brunt of our inadequate systems and used their insights to make those systems work better for all of us?"

If we plan to offer accommodations, we need to think beyond the binary. Long before the pandemic, disabled employees were already advocating for remote work and telehealth, but their requests were often shut down by employers and medical establishments who said that those were unreasonable accommodations or couldn't be done. It took COVID for the world to realize that remote work was possible for everyone and that telehealth could be efficient and keep people safe and healthy without their having to lose a whole or half day of work to travel to a doctor's office. "The excuse we had always heard [was] like, 'Oh, we can't do that, because that would require us to have all these accommodations, and everyone has to be in the office from 9 to 5.' Now we know all that stuff is baloney," says Matthew Shapiro, founder of 6 Wheels Consulting.[3] As many employers expand return-to-office mandates, let's remember to embrace the pandemic-era flexibility in how we worked and not reimpose barriers that pushed many of us out of the workplace. Surveys have shown that working remotely doesn't interfere with employee productivity and that productivity actually increases.[4]

There is also a misconception that accommodations are cost-prohibitive and high-tech. While that may be true for some, like ASL interpreters, the majority of accommodations can be free for the employer,[5] such as speech-to-text technology like Otter.ai, turning on auto-captions during Zoom meetings, providing written materials in accessible formats like large print, and allowing remote work and flexible schedules.

Employers agree. In a study conducted by the Job Accommodation Network (JAN), 56 percent of surveyed employers reported that their accommodations cost zero dollars to implement. For those who invested in a onetime cost, such as access modifications to doors, bathrooms, and entrances; braille signage; or tech devices or software, the median expenditure was only $300. Furthermore, the employers reported that the benefits from making accommodations far outweighed the costs, including retaining valuable employees (85 percent), increasing productivity (53 percent), increasing attendance (48 percent), increasing safety (31 percent), and increasing company morale (30 percent).[6] This is in comparison to the average of $200,000 that companies spend to defend against discrimination lawsuits if they fall out of ADA compliance.[7] Simply put, accommodations are worth it.

What are some examples of accommodations that you can make for your employees? Because disability is so diverse and we have a vast range of experiences and needs, there is no definitive list. But you can start by taking stock of your situation, naming the disability if it has been disclosed (reminder: it is not necessary for employees to disclose our disability for you to make our requested accommodations), identifying the access barrier the employee faces, and searching for the right accommodation that can help us overcome the barrier and meet our access needs. Here are some examples:

Disability	Access Barrier	Access Needs Met
Low vision	Reading text in print or on a screen	• Audio transcripts of meetings • Large-print font on public notices • Anti-glare guard for computer monitor • Screen-magnification software • Frequent breaks to rest eyes • Additional or adaptive workstation lighting

Disability	Access Barrier	Access Needs Met
ADHD	Attentiveness and concentration	• Structured breaks during the workday • Quiet workspace • Tasks given as to-do lists • Time-management apps • On-site coach or mentor
Chronic pain	Relief from pain	• Ergonomic chairs • Flexible work schedules to take medication or take medical leave • Work-from-home option • Speech-to-text software • Reallocating lifting or other physically demanding duties to coworkers • Unlimited sick days
Hard of hearing	Participation in group discussions	• Written transcripts of meetings • Option for email instead of in-person discussion • Whiteboards or notepads • Closed captions or communication access realtime translation (CART) services
Autism	Communication with coworkers and managers	• Staffwide training on interacting with neurodivergent people • Written task list or agenda • One-on-one communication • Direct communication with opportunities for questions • On-site coach or mentor

Disability	Access Barrier	Access Needs Met
PTSD	Stress-free environment	• Apps for handling anxiety and stress • Counseling and therapy • Support animal • Flexible breaks • Remote work
Immunocompromised	Healthy and safe environment	• Mandatory mask requirement for workspace • Private area away from high traffic areas • Teleconferencing into meetings • Remote work • Flexible breaks
Wheelchair user	Navigating physical spaces	• Adjustable desks and workstations • Step-free entrance • Accessible bathroom and meeting rooms

I've found that the Job Accommodation Network (JAN) is an excellent free online database for employers to look up accommodation ideas for different types of disabilities or requirements, listed from A to Z.[8] For example, I can look up information by disability, such as typing in "PTSD," or by what JAN calls "limitation," such as "Attentiveness/Concentration." The latter is useful in cases where a disability is not disclosed. It also reminds us that the problem we're solving for is a lack of attentiveness or concentration, which can impact any employee, disabled or not.

The JAN website has a comprehensive list of accommodation ideas sorted by limitation or work-related function, and it provides real-life case studies from employees who have benefited from specific accommodations. For example, when a schoolteacher with PTSD experienced anxiety and flashbacks that prevented her from controlling her classroom, JAN suggested giving her special training on behavioral management techniques, supplying administrative support for student disciplinary actions, and providing her with a radio to get classroom assistance quickly if she needed it.[9]

As you start to invest in accommodations in your workplaces, here are a few tips and tricks to keep in mind:

1. Get to know your disabled employees better, and ask them what accommodations they need. Do your research, using online tools like JAN, to identify what accommodations you can start to implement. Familiarize yourself with your employees' strengths and areas of improvement as well as the value they bring to the company. A common trait among effective managers and leaders is to consistently ask themselves, "What do my employees need in order to thrive and perform well?"

2. Do not force employees to disclose their disability in order to grant them an accommodation. Instead, ask what barriers they face and what accessibility requirements they need without the pressure of disclosing. Take the initiative to meet employees where they are, and, if possible, reduce the labor or paperwork that employees have to go through in order to request an accommodation. Be mindful of "accommodation discrimination," as law professor Kat Macfarlane calls it,[10] which is when the deluge of paperwork required to obtain accommodations becomes a way for employers or coworkers to discriminate against the people who need them.

3. Provide a variety of accommodations. Don't just invest in one and consider your work done. Instead, think about how you can improve an employee's work performance using a combination of these different accommodations. You can sort accommodations into four categories: presentation, response, setting, and scheduling.[11] *Presentation accommodations* refers to the way information is presented, such as a presentation slideshow or printed information; *response accommodations* refers to how the employee is required to respond, such as work reports, emails, or group participation; *setting accommodations* refers to factors in the work environment,

---

such as lighting and noise level; and *scheduling accommodations* refers to how the workday is organized, such as midday breaks and timelines for assignments. Autistic author and journalist Eric Garcia shares, "If I'm interviewing people back-to-back...for a story, I need to take a sensory break for at least fifteen minutes, if not thirty minutes, just from the social burnout of talking and masking and unmasking."[12] Creating space for employees to obtain these accommodations without pushback can go a long way.

4. Give employees a trial period when using the accommodations, and make sure they have the opportunity to provide feedback on how effective they are. Not all accommodations will work as well for different employees, so you should collaborate to find the right fit.

5. If an accommodation doesn't work, consider that you might need to adapt or modify the task or job scope. For example, if an employee with PTSD is having trouble participating in large group discussions, assign them a brand-new task, for example, taking meeting notes or writing up the agenda. If an employee with mobility issues has trouble carrying heavy files or papers to the printer-copier, allocate that task to someone else instead.

Finally, while providing accommodations has to be our starting point, they are just the first step toward the final goal of inclusion and an accessibility-first culture. Disabled people need accommodations because our spaces are currently inaccessible. But once a space is accessible, we will no longer need those accommodations.

Though some of us might use the terms interchangeably, there is a difference between accommodations and accessibility. Accommodations are a reactive way to promote equity. According to Katie Rose Guest Pryal, JD, PhD, a speaker and expert on mental health and neurodiversity, they are special exceptions people make to pre-existing spaces in order to accommodate disabled people to ensure that we can participate. In contrast, accessibility is a proactive way to promote equity because it means creating spaces that are designed and built to be welcoming, inclusive, and functional for disabled people from the get-go so that we won't require extra accommodations, just like everyone else.[13]

Often, unlike my experience with the ergonomic specialist at Goldman, accommodations require that disabled people navigate privacy invasions and tedious paperwork. Imagine an open-plan workspace, says Pryal. Although designed to build community, it is challenging for neurodivergent employees to concentrate in such spaces because they can be loud and distracting without cubicle walls to break up the noise. In order to do their best work, a neurodivergent worker might need to wear noise-canceling headphones. However, what happens if headphones are against office policy because they inhibit community building? The employee will have to jump through hoops and over hurdles to submit an accommodation request to HR, which may also mean disclosing their disability or submitting medical records. Even if their request is successful, they may still experience judgment from coworkers who assume they've received "special treatment."[14]

If a workspace is truly accessible, there will be no burden for disabled people to prove that we deserve what we need because "accessibility presumes that disabled people are [already] part of a community....In an accessible space,...the door is open."[15] Marisa Hamamoto, a disability inclusion changemaker, speaker, dancer, and founder of Infinite Flow dance company, adds, "It's worth navigating methods and practices that foster a sense of community and safety. We do our best work in a culture of belonging, after all."[16]

Reflection Questions

1. How have you previously viewed or heard others describe accommodations? Reflect on how accommodations are tools for equity rather than "special treatment." How would you define accommodations now?

2. Explore the JAN web page. Are there accommodations you might personally benefit from?

3. Think about your employees or team members. What barriers do they currently experience in their work, and how do these

barriers affect their performance? What accommodations can you implement now to reduce or remove those barriers? How willing are you to adapt or modify tasks to better suit the needs of your disabled employees? How might you offer access/information to coworkers who need medical accommodations?

4. How can you follow through on these accommodations to ensure that they are working effectively for the employee?

5. Reflect on the difference between accommodations and accessibility. What are some steps you can take to commit to moving from making accommodations to providing true and inclusive accessibility?

CHAPTER 30

Build a Disability-Inclusive Work Culture

Work is where we spend most of our time and efforts. For those of us who work full time, that's at least forty hours a week. Through our jobs, we earn a living, chart a career path, and often contribute to society; it's also where we connect socially to a community of peers through our colleagues and team members. It's only natural to want to feel safe, valued, and seen at work.

Unfortunately, this is not the case for many disabled people. A 2023 DEI report found that only 4.6 percent of employees reveal their disability status to their employers.[1] According to a 2020 Accenture report, 76 percent of disabled employees and 80 percent of disabled leaders are not fully transparent about their disability at work, citing reasons like a lack of trust and a fear of prejudice or persecution. Additionally, 60 percent of disabled employees are more likely than non-disabled employees to feel excluded in the workplace.[2]

These statistics are temperature gauges for the level of psychological safety that disabled employees feel at work. In other words, four out of five disabled employees don't feel comfortable enough to disclose their disability for fear of reprisal or discrimination, such as coworkers judging their capabilities or a manager writing a biased evaluation or passing them over for promotion. "People are not disclosing their disabilities because the risk of employment discrimination is so real, and they're rightly afraid," says disability rights lawyer Haben Girma.

"This is particularly relevant for people with non-apparent disabilities."[3] Due to this stigma, many disabled employees feel like they can't ask for the accommodations they need and deserve to do their job well; therefore, they underperform. They then worry about asking for assistance from a disadvantaged position and can't explain to others why their performance is suffering and what they'd truly benefit from (accommodations), feeding a culture of secrecy and cycle of shame.

Because of the silence that surrounds this topic, there is, unsurprisingly, a perception gap between how employees feel in the workplace and how leaders think they are doing in terms of providing a healthy and supportive working environment. More than 80 percent of leaders believe that their employees feel safe talking about their disabilities or expressing work concerns, while only slightly more than 60 percent of employees agree.[4] This gap in the data leads to ignorance and a lack of urgency when it comes to making change. When leaders don't know what employees truly think, and the culture already promotes trepidation and silence, it is hard to recognize what needs to be done.

Luckily, this is not an impossible chicken-and-egg scenario. There's a simple answer to escaping the cycle: from the start, organizations must build a disability-inclusive culture that includes trustworthy systems for reporting and advocacy. When employees feel supported at work and believe that their needs and voices matter, it will start a chain reaction that leads to more transparency and communication.

"The more we talk about disability, the more we create awareness and an open, inclusive work environment," says Meg O'Connell, president of Global Disability Inclusion. "Studies show that if you feel supported and can bring your 'whole self' to work, you're going to be more productive and engaged."[5]

When employees can unlock their full potential, the company always benefits. We've learned that there is a strong business case for a disability-inclusive work culture: organizations that focused on disability engagement grew sales 2.9 times faster and profits 4.1 times faster than their counterparts that did not do so.[6] Additionally, fostering a disability-inclusive culture doesn't just benefit people who are already employed—it also helps to attract talented disabled candidates to the pool.

Disabled people have so much to offer the companies we work for. We have our own professional goals, unique talents, and skills honed from living with our disabilities that have made us more creative, compassionate, and determined. Yarelbys Túa is a disability and inclusion advocate and model who was diagnosed with cancer at age fourteen. After receiving treatment, she acquired a spinal cord injury, leaving her with a physical disability in her right leg. Regarding how her disability has pushed her to be more adaptive and creative, she says, "When we adapt our mind, we start to see opportunity where once was a problem. My disability shifted my mindset from complaints to solutions. I started spending more time and energy on 'how can I make this work?'"[7] If Túa can shift her mindset in her personal life, imagine what someone with those skills can bring to a work culture. To do our best work, we deserve to thrive in an environment where we feel free to express our authentic selves, knowing we won't be judged, silenced, or ignored.

Now it is up to our employers to meet us in the middle to provide accommodations, accessibility, and inclusivity so that we can further develop our confidence and advance our careers.

How should organizations begin to foster a disability-inclusive culture in the workplace? In addition to making physical and digital spaces accessible (see Chapter 27) and rethinking accommodations (see Chapter 29), here are nine other factors, taken from a 2020 Accenture report[8] and a 2023 Valuable 500 report:[9]

1. **Workplace Representation and Role Models:** You can't be what you can't see. Hire disabled employees at all levels of your organization to foster a thriving disability community. Having disabled leaders can also show others in the company what's possible and help to create an open and empathetic culture. At Microsoft, when leaders like Dona Sarkar and Craig Cincotta shared their disabilities publicly, they noticed more connection and openness, especially when other team members responded to say that they shared similar experiences. "By [disclosing as a leader], you make a far safer space for employees to open up about their disabilities," says Sarkar.[10]

Cincotta adds, "Anytime you have a more inclusive environment, you're able to see fresher ideas, broaden your perspective and get the best version of people."[11]

For me, having leaders throughout Goldman sharing about their disabilities helped put me at ease when it came to advocating for my own disability. While we're striving for a company culture that encourages transparency, remember that choosing to disclose one's disability should still be a choice, especially if we're not there yet.

2. **Flexible Work:** Most disability-related accommodations are seen as inconvenient until they're actualized, and remote work is one example. Due to the pandemic, we've seen companies move swiftly toward flexible work-from-home schedules. The *Los Angeles Times* reported that workplace politics and discrimination sometimes made being in the office undesirable for minoritized employees. At home, these employees didn't have to experience microaggressions, and they were able to focus better, accomplish more in their own space, and improve their quality of life.[12] Be open to your employees' unique working preferences and encourage honest communication about what schedules or working scenarios are best for them, whether it is take-what-you-need paid time off or hybrid remote and in-person arrangements.

Arthur Gwynne heads the operations of Recording Artists and Music Professionals with Disabilities (RAMPD) and is a full-time manager for Lachi, a blind singer-songwriter and disability advocate. Gwynne identifies as neurodivergent and explains how remote work during COVID enabled both him and Lachi to perform at their professional best:

When COVID hit...Lachi was in a uniquely prepared position. Artists were scrambling as studios shut down [but] with a studio set up [at home] that fit her needs, Lachi was writing and producing twice as fast and with far more confidence than she had been when she was renting studios. I also found myself thriving during the shutdown. With the office moving to remote work—no commute, no draining small talk—I found myself awash with boundless energy. And with an improved mood and a self-built home office of my own, my productivity skyrocketed.[13]

This flexibility allowed them both to show up as their fullest selves:

[Lachi's] brewing success manifested into self-confidence and acceptance of her disabilities and neurodivergences. She began speaking up about it and the lack of disability representation in the music industry....My difference and lived experiences are an asset, and when I'm accommodated right, I am a [expletive] wizard....This is just one of the many examples of how prioritizing accessibility and honoring accommodations really allow people in all walks of life and stages in their careers to flourish and truly contribute to the betterment of our world in the way only they (and the mind and body with which they came) can. A life of navigating a world that was not built for us made us both creative, innovative, and driven, powerful traits we were able to explore once our access needs were met.[14]

3. **ERGs:** These groups bring employees with common interests and backgrounds together, often with the goal of building inclusive initiatives in the workplace. ERGs can become trusted internal resources that push employees to see the power, strength, and influence of the disability community; they also help employees to realize that they're not alone as they advocate for their needs.

My involvement in Goldman's disability ERG, the Disability Interest Forum, led me to later become one of the cofounders of Bloomberg L.P.'s disability ERG. Ultimately, my experience with ERGs became the inspiration for relaunching Diversability—creating a community of disabled people with a shared mission to achieve disability justice and liberation. Being part of an ERG also allowed me to network and connect with like-minded individuals and senior leaders like Rich Donovan, who founded Lime Connect and would go on to create Return on Disability, a disability-focused consulting and design company. I am still connected with some of the people I met through these ERGs, cheering them on as they progress in their careers. That being said, it is not the responsibility of people in those ERGs, nor should companies rely on them, to advocate for change across the entire company; that change should be championed by company leaders, not employees.

4. **Fair Pay:** A disability-inclusive culture is not complete without economic justice, which means equitable pay. Despite the strides made by the ADA, it is still legal to pay disabled people below the minimum wage—and it's important to remember that most disabled people bear additional costs, whether it's medical expenses or retrofitting their homes to make them accessible. I feel extremely privileged to have been able to start my career in investment banking, where analysts were all paid the same base rate, but many disabled people don't share my experience. Over time, companies like Salesforce and Adobe have taken a step forward in their public commitment to fair pay across gender and ethnicity, and some states like Colorado, California, New York, and Washington now have pay transparency laws that require pay information to be included in job listings.[15] We must keep moving forward. To get started, organizations can conduct fair pay assessments and redesign bonus plans. For example, some companies now include a disability representation metric in their annual bonus plans, redesigning bonuses based on increasing the percentage of employees who identify as having a disability.[16]

5. **Family-Support Policies:** Prioritizing such policies helps not only disabled employees but also caregivers, whether it's the parent of a disabled child or someone caring for their parents. The fact is that when companies support employees outside work, they are helping them to show up better in the office. Family leave can look like time off for new parents or caregivers, while family-support policies can look like providing additional training for employees who have disabled family members. For example, Intuit offers its employees four weeks of support time to care for a family member with a chronic condition as well

as a remote learning platform that teaches parents how to care for children with developmental disabilities.[17]

6. **Freedom to Innovate:** Disabled people are some of the most creative, innovative people out there because we've learned how to be flexible and to adapt in an environment that wasn't built for us. Angela Mills, a manager at Microsoft, explains of her quick problem-solving skills, "Every person with a disability has honed skills to work around the limitations that their disability brings. I cannot imagine having been more successful in my career if I didn't have the disability."[18] When employees are free to lean in to their strengths to innovate, they will perform well individually and can also share their strengths with the rest of the company. Organizations should give disabled employees a seat at the table so that the 75 percent of them who say they have an idea that would benefit the company[19] can be heard. Foster an encouraging, instead of a judgmental, culture that values diversity and disabled employees' expertise. Organizations can also support innovation by paying for skills training and other professional development opportunities. During my time at Bloomberg, the company prided itself on internal mobility and offered opportunities to shadow and network with employees in different departments to learn more about their roles.[20]

7. **Mental Well-Being Policies:** Disabled people have five times more mentally unwell days than our non-disabled peers.[21] Existing in an ableist world as a disabled person is distressing! For disabled employees, being able to talk to their supervisors and peers about their mental health is important, as is having access to therapy and other mental health support. When companies invest in employees' mental wellness, that not only helps them do their job better but also allows them to feel seen and supported, which builds trust. Accenture offers employees a resource called Thriving Mind that teaches them how to use recharge strategies in the face of stress. They also have an in-house mental health ally program, with five thousand trained employees who volunteer to provide support, a listening ear, and additional resources to their peers.[22]

8. **Disability Inclusion Training:** Organizations should provide this type of training for all employees, with the larger goal of raising awareness of ableism and educating employees on how to do better, whether they're interacting with their disabled colleagues, clients, and customers or participating in society in general. For example, at Lemon Tree Hotels, a company committed to hiring people with a range of disabilities in every department, employees are trained in how to work well with their disabled peers, such as not making last-minute changes to schedules, and how to communicate in sign language.[23] Training also includes teaching leaders how to manage disabled employees, whether it's responding to an accommodation request or building a healthy relationship in which the employee feels safe enough to express their authentic self. Disability inclusion training should be developed in partnership with the disability community so that the lessons accurately reflect the lived experiences and perspectives of people with disabilities.

9. **Organizational Goals:** Set a clear intention of and commitment to disability inclusion in your organizational goals to stay focused on what needs to be done. Goals are a public statement that allows the organization to be accountable to its employees and others outside the company in the long term. Practically, having these goals also reminds you to make plans for accommodations and accessibility in annual initiatives and budgeting. Keep data reports on companywide disability-inclusive initiatives to track patterns and help to close the disability data gap.

Jessica Lopez, Diversability's former social media manager, says about how working with us helped expand her career aspirations, "[At Diversability,] I was given the opportunity to grow in a way I would've never been able to anywhere else. I was given the mentorship to learn on-the-job, and that experience led me to build career goals that I never would've considered."[24] At the end of the day, having a disability-inclusive culture shows employees that they're valued as people, that they can be open about who they are, and that their contributions will benefit the company.

Reflection Questions

1. How does your current workplace approach disability inclusion? How would you like to see your company's leaders demonstrate their commitment to disability inclusion?

2. Do you feel that there is a sense of psychological safety at your workplace for people to be transparent about their disabilities? Keep in mind the perception gap noted in the 2020 Accenture report. How can you actively contribute to improving the representation of disabled individuals in your workplace?

3. Of the nine factors previously listed, which do you feel your workplace is doing well? Which could be improved?

4. What steps can you personally take to contribute to a more disability-inclusive culture (such as cofounding your company's disability ERG, serving as its executive sponsor, or supporting it in another capacity)? What can you do within your team or department?

5. How can you support disabled employees in progressing in their roles at the company and stepping up into leadership positions?

6. Have you witnessed any positive impacts of a disability-inclusive workplace?

CHAPTER 31

Cater to Disabled Customers

In the fall of 2023, Victoria's Secret launched an adaptive line of intimate wear for which I got to be part of the wear test. I was excited. Growing up, my perception of what was sexy and attractive was defined by the models I saw in Victoria's Secret advertising, and they certainly didn't look like me. One of the products was an adaptive bra that clasped in the front. As I put on the bra, I thought about how many people with brachial plexus injuries or upper-extremity disabilities often resort to wearing sports bras because it's too difficult to clasp bras in the back with one hand. In that moment, it hit me how throughout history, businesses haven't really thought about us and intimate wear in this way, even something as simple as moving the clasp to the front.

Disabled people are your customers. Globally, with 1.85 billion disabled people in the world (larger than the population of China), and an additional 3.3 billion if you count our friends and family, the disability market controls over $13 trillion in disposable income.[1] In the United States, we have over $490 billion in disposable income, while the discretionary income—money available for non-essential items after basic living expenses have been met—of working-age disabled adults is $21 billion, more than the $16 billion of the Hispanic community and $3 billion of the African American community combined.[2] With these numbers, shouldn't businesses be catering to us as well?

Disabled people are viable customers with purchasing power and economic influence. We want to buy fashionable clothes, shoes, and jewelry. We want the latest gadgets, phones, and technology. We travel, we watch movies and plays, we buy household wares. We eat in restaurants. It is a significant economic move for businesses to acknowledge us as a demographic and to cater to us, which can help attract new customers, earn customer loyalty, and gain market share. Conversely, if businesses don't make their services and products accessible, it is a clear indication that disabled people should not patronize or support them. We will simply spend our money elsewhere.

Take what happened to content creator Taylor Lindsay-Noel, who conducts accessibility reviews as a wheelchair user. Despite checking online, calling, and calling again the day of the event to double-check whether a restaurant booking for a friend's thirtieth birthday was wheelchair accessible, Lindsay-Noel arrived to find only steps to enter the restaurant. When she requested a portable ramp, the restaurant staff told her they didn't have one because it would be "illegal" and suggested lifting her 350-pound wheelchair into the restaurant. Lindsay-Noel had to show the manager proof of her discussions with two other staff members who had said the restaurant was accessible, as well as the Google listing, but the night was already "ruined."[3] Lindsay-Noel and her friends acted quickly and found another restaurant on short notice. The restaurant later apologized for the misinformation and, on Lindsay-Noel's advice, continued to work with her to provide new accessibility improvements, such as ordering a portable ramp, implementing better staff training, and even having a braille menu and an audio menu.[4] In response to a supportive commenter on her TikTok post who remarked that the restaurant having better accessibility would elevate the experience for all customers, Lindsay-Noel added, "Exactly what I think! It'll only help their restaurant's reach in the future."[5]

Lindsay-Noel's experience teaches us a few things: that disabled people are customers, too; that misinformation or a lack of accessibility has the potential to lose the business customers; and that working to improve accessibility would open the door to a brand-new market.

Beginning November 10, 2023, retail giant Walmart announced that it would implement sensory-friendly hours from 8 to 10 a.m. every day. This includes turning off the radio, dimming the lights, and showing static instead of moving images on televisions. Sensory-friendly accommodations cater to customers who have sensory-processing disorders, which is common among people with autism,

ADHD, and PTSD, just to name a few. To create the best experience, Walmart invited the expertise of disabled customers and launched a pilot program within selected stores on Saturdays, which was an overwhelming success, before expanding to all outlets in the United States and Puerto Rico. According to Walmart, the new initiative was driven by a desire to create a culture of belonging. "These changes may have seemed small to some, but for others, they transformed the shopping experience," says a Walmart press release.[6] Sometimes considering the needs of disabled customers involves simple solutions—whether it's establishing sensory hours or moving bra clasps to the front—with great impact.

Providing accessibility goes beyond physical accommodations in a space; it should also be built into product design, customer service, and overall business attitudes. "Thirty-two years [after the ADA], accessibility still too often feels like an afterthought," says disability writer Andrew Pulrang in an article for *Forbes*. "Accessibility is still treated like some kind of premium feature rather than a civic responsibility for businesses, or a civil right for customers."[7] As customers, we all want to feel seen and appreciated, we want to have freedom and agency, and we want our products to fulfill our needs. That includes disabled customers, too.

Pulrang points out that catering to disabled customers is more urgent than ever as the population ages and the number of disabled people rises during the ongoing COVID-19 pandemic. Additionally, with more accessible options available these days, such as online shopping and delivery services, disabled customers have more power and choice to reject inaccessible brick-and-mortar businesses. As Pulrang says, "Accessibility...may soon become a genuine and significant competitive necessity, as it has always promised to be."[8]

Businesses change to keep up with shifting consumer expectations. This happened in the beauty industry in 2017, when Fenty Beauty launched forty shades of foundation to serve customers with different complexions when other beauty companies didn't. Suddenly, forty shades became the new standard for customers. In order not to lose their market share, other beauty brands had to make their product lines more inclusive to keep up. *Forbes* contributor Sonia Thompson writes, "Once [customers] see a brand that makes a point of catering to their needs, their bar for their standard of excellence changes. They see what's possible, and subsequently expect brands that want their business to be intentional about serving their needs as well."[9]

Customers should be the ones driving and determining business trends, and businesses would do well to be proactively inclusive instead of waiting to make changes only once they realize they're losing out. "[Customers] remember the [brands] who took the time to see them first when nobody else did," Thompson adds.[10] In other words, intentionally catering to disabled customers builds customer loyalty and enhances a brand's overall reputation, not just with disabled people but also with our friends, family, and loved ones.

Disability inclusion and accessibility advocate Meryl K. Evans, who is deaf, shares,

> Smart businesses provide multiple ways to communicate and [multiple] contact options. I needed to get some coffee for an event. I looked up a major chain's contact information. There was only an address and a phone number. I contacted the company's accessibility team and suggested they provide another contact option like email, texting, and online chat....Meanwhile, I contacted another coffee shop. They provided an email and a phone number. Guess who got my business? Accessibility brings in money for businesses.[11]

If you are part of a business, what else can you do to keep disabled customers in mind? Here are a few strategies:

1. Make your public and digital retail spaces accessible—see more in Chapter 27: Make Public Spaces Accessible (in Person and Digitally). This could include ensuring that your aisles are wide enough for shoppers and customers who are wheelchair users and having a way to access items on a shelf that might be out of reach for people at different heights.

2. Use inclusive design practices to create new products—see more in Chapter 26: Inclusive Design Benefits Everyone—or add modifications or adaptations to existing products. Test these products with disabled consumers and listen to and implement our feedback.

---

3. Advertise and promote to the target market by hiring disabled models and actors. Representation in marketing efforts helps get disabled customers into physical or digital stores once we see for ourselves that we are included and valued. Inclusive marketing strategies also help enhance brand image among the public and set new standards in terms of both media representation and accessible products.

4. Price your products and services fairly and competitively. Disabled customers have the same expectations as everyone else, and we should not be made to bear additional costs for products or services that have been designed for us. This is known as the "disability tax" or the "crip tax," as addressed in Chapter 25: Lower the Disability Tax.

5. Train staff in customer service roles to serve disabled customers. The first rule to remember is that disabled customers are just customers, and while staff may have to do things a little differently, the heart of the interaction—providing a service—should be the same.[12] Be respectful and courteous, take the initiative to help as you would with anyone else, be patient, and if you're not sure what to do in a particular scenario, ask, "How may I help you?" and listen to our answer, or be proactive and say, "I'm here if you need any assistance or support."

6. Recognize that the disability market is diverse, and one size does not fit all.[13] Like Walmart, you can undertake pilot programs to test products or services so that you can go back to the drawing board to improve on them if necessary. Create communication channels so that your customers can provide feedback.

7. Define how disabled consumers fit into your business's pre-existing or new goals. Plan and budget for the disability market, and keep data so that you can take note of trends and keep improving.

Reflection Questions

1. What are some brands you have noticed that cater to the disability community? What specific things are they doing to attract disabled customers with their products, services, or marketing?

2. If you are disabled, have you personally encountered challenges as a disabled consumer, and how did those experiences impact your perception of the business?

3. If you are a business owner, what are some barriers that people with different disabilities might encounter when interacting with your business? What improvements can be made to better serve disabled customers? How is your business engaging with the disability community? In what ways can businesses showcase their commitment to disability inclusion?

4. Reflect on the last time you shopped in person. What barriers might have existed for people who have different disabilities? What about the last time you shopped online?

5. What influence do you have in making businesses more accessible to disabled consumers (in both physical and digital spaces)? What role can consumers play in advocating for disability inclusion within businesses, and how can they make their voices heard?

CHAPTER 32

Support Disability Entrepreneurship

You could say disabled people have a knack for entrepreneurship, that our experience and skills uniquely qualify us for this role. Keely Cat-Wells, founder of C Talent and Making Space, writes, "I would never [have] become an entrepreneur if I didn't become disabled. As disabled people, we are often very entrepreneurial in our day-to-day lives navigating a world that was not built with us in mind."[1] Cat-Wells also lists the general skills of a disabled person—"delegation skills, resilience, leadership, time management, inherent ability to adapt, problem-solving"—and observes that they overlap with the general skills of an entrepreneur.[2]

Add skills like innovation, flexibility, sensitivity, quick and critical thinking, determination, and resourcefulness—and the fact that disabled people are at the forefront of pioneering accessibility and coming up with new and better ways of living—and you have a formidable entrepreneur.

Diego Mariscal is the founder, CEO, and chief disabled officer of 2Gether-International, the leading startup accelerator run by and for disabled entrepreneurs. He tells me,

I oftentimes say that disability is a competitive advantage for business....
The story that I often use is: when I was a kid, I fell off a horse, and the coach was really surprised that I got back on it right away...for me, falling

231

off a horse was just like every other fall that I had…apparently that's very rare; usually people don't want to get right back on the horse. But I feel like that's an analogy of my life, particularly as somebody with cerebral palsy. But what people don't know…or it's not often discussed, is that, yes, even though we're resilient and creative, there are systematic barriers that affect…people with disabilities.[3]

Many of us are part-time or full-time entrepreneurs. In the United States, disabled people are twice as likely as non-disabled people to be self-employed.[4] However, we often find our way into self-employment or entrepreneurship because we're forced to or don't have a choice. "Disabled people have to become entrepreneurs because capitalism won't give them flexible schedules, work from home, [or] accommodations that make them feel safe," says disability awareness consultant Andrew Gurza.[5] When the current ableist work system isn't set up to support people like us because of inaccessible workplaces and infrastructure, not to mention biased and discriminatory attitudes, it's no wonder many of us resort to taking charge of our own work in order to survive.

This happened to me. I was fired from a job at a real estate startup in March 2017. At the time, I was already working on Diversability as a side hustle and was even doing speaking gigs on the topic of the side-hustle generation and how it was a good pathway into entrepreneurship. But I had never envisioned that it would become my full-time hustle. After I was fired, as I was receiving unemployment benefits, I told myself that I would work on Diversability while I applied for jobs. During that period, I had to be creative in terms of supporting myself because Diversability wasn't generating enough income. I listed my apartment on a short-term rental site and sold a lot of my furniture on Craigslist and eBay. During those first couple of years, I was the epitome of a scrappy entrepreneur. To attend conferences, I tried to get sponsor tickets or a scholarship, and I stayed with friends and used points to book my flights. While I was privileged to have access to savings during this time, this level of instability does not work for many disabled people, who may become unhoused and lose access to health care without consistent income.

In 2020, Diversability was accepted into Meta's Community Accelerator Program. We received over $50,000, which we used to launch a membership community and bring in more partners. I also started to do more paid speaking engagements, and I made more content on social media to expand my advocacy. Soon I was bringing in brand partnerships, doing one-off consulting gigs, and participating in creator programs. Since its incorporation in 2015, Diversability has grown to ten team members at its largest, and we have been able to support our disabled team members' livelihoods and also pay members of our community through speaking engagements and other paid opportunities.

Today, I'm proud to call myself a creative entrepreneur. I've even started doing some angel investing as a disabled investor in startups founded by underestimated entrepreneurs. While my journey into entrepreneurship wasn't planned, I'm honored to have been able to support the disability community in meaningful ways. But it certainly wasn't an easy road.

Cory Lee runs the accessible travel blog *Curb Free with Cory Lee* and has spinal muscular atrophy, type 2. While he is now on a mission to make traveling easier for wheelchair users around the world, he reports a similarly rocky trip to entrepreneurship. After graduating from college, he applied to hundreds of jobs in his field, disclosing his disability in each application in the hope of presenting his truest self. Months into the process, he tells me, he'd received "exactly zero responses, despite being fully qualified." He says, "At that point, I started thinking that maybe disclosing my disability upfront was hurting me." That all seemed to change when he got a call to fly to Pittsburgh for an interview. "Confidently, I rolled into the office, locked eyes with the hiring manager, and without hesitation, he looked at me and said, 'Um, this job involves traveling, so you're definitely not the best fit.' As if I didn't travel to get there! I was turned down before I was even given a chance to interview...once again."[6] Around the same time, he was preparing for a vacation to Australia to celebrate his graduation and found a gap in the market: very little accessibility information existed online for destinations outside the United States.

> The day after realizing [there was] a lack of accessible travel information, and just two weeks after the doomed trip to Pittsburgh, I launched my travel blog....Since then, I've traveled to over forty countries and all seven continents, launched annual group trips in exciting destinations, and started a nonprofit. It's been more than I could've ever dreamed of, and now, I'm grateful that I didn't get the job....In the end, everything worked

out for me, but unbelievable job discrimination still heavily exists against the disabled community, and that needs to change.[7]

Even after most of us have been forced out of traditional employment, disabled entrepreneurs continue to face our own unique set of barriers. According to Access2Funding, a study conducted in the UK, disabled entrepreneurs are four hundred times less likely to receive funding[8] and hold just 0.1 percent share of voice (SOV)—meaning media mentions—despite being the largest minority group in the world.[9] Eighty-four percent of disabled entrepreneurs said they don't have equal access to the same investment opportunities and resources as their non-disabled peers (the remaining 16 percent responded, "Maybe"), and only 17 percent said they were treated equally in terms of investment opportunities. Some of the reasons cited for this gap were a lack of participation opportunities and support, inaccessible systems and processes, stereotypes or lack of awareness, and risk management misconceptions.[10]

Celia Chartres-Aris, cofounder of Access2Funding, explains why this might be the case: the misconception of seeing disability-owned businesses through the lens of charity rather than recognizing their commercial value. "There remains this pervasive mentality that if it's anything to do with disability, and helping disabled people, it can't be a for-profit business."[11] Her cofounder, Joseph Williams, adds that the typically risk-averse venture capitalist ecosystem is a closed shop that limits itself to historical formulas it is used to, such as funding Oxford and Cambridge graduates (who receive 70 percent of all investments in the UK), even if it doesn't prove worthwhile. "The default social narrative around disability continues to be one of support and pity. As disabled people, we deserve an excellence conversation as well," says Williams.[12]

Despite these misconceptions, the facts speak the truth. Disability-owned businesses in the UK, which make up one-quarter of all small businesses, contribute almost 10 percent to the country's GDP. Based on estimations, these findings equate to a missed funding opportunity of £500 million annually.[13] In the United States, self-identified disability-owned businesses have a total of $32.4 billion in economic impact. The number is underreported due to a gap in the data, but Disability:IN estimates that if one-quarter of all registered small businesses are disability-owned, a total of $5 trillion would be contributed to the economy.[14]

Once again, we see the same story of a vast but untapped pool of capable and competent disabled entrepreneurs who are excluded from the conversation due to ableism, which has both social and economic costs.

Unsurprisingly, it often falls to disabled investors to address this gap. Mariscal's 2Gether-International was the first of its kind to focus exclusively on disabled entrepreneurs. Over the past ten years, the accelerator has supported more than eighty high-growth, high-impact companies, including talent management company C Talent (acquired by Whalar) and software startup YellowBird (raised $6.25 million in funding), and generated more than $40 million in revenue and acquisitions, with plans to develop a model that will support three thousand founders per year. Underlying its goals is the recognition that entrepreneurship is a crucial pathway to shrinking the gaps in wealth and employment in the disability community.[15]

"Funding entrepreneurs with disabilities isn't an act of charity or just a DEI practice—it's an economic imperative," says Mariscal. "People need to see the unrealized potential of our underestimated community." According to Mariscal, one way we can do this is for local governments to provide funding directly to disability-owned businesses or accelerators that support disabled entrepreneurs rather than yet another job placement program. Nothing about us without us. "We, as disabled individuals, are in the best position to address our community's needs," he says.[16]

Disability-owned businesses deserve your confidence. And if you're not in a position to invest, you can still purchase our businesses' products and services. Here are some strategies for investing in, patronizing, and supporting disability-owned businesses:

1. Support disability-focused accelerator or business programs—for example, 2Gether-International, Remarkable, the Disability Entrepreneurship Institute at the Viscardi Center, and the Gallaudet Innovation and Entrepreneurship Institute—that reinvest funds in the disability community to support emerging disabled entrepreneurs. We know best how to help our community—but we do

need financial and economic support. You can also invest directly in disability-owned businesses. A recent success story is Wheel the World, a travel startup focused on disability tourism, which raised $6 million in a pre–Series A investment round. The funds will be used for customer retention and new user acquisition, with features like guaranteed accessibility for hotel rooms booked on the site and a price-match offer.[17]

2. Provide disabled entrepreneurs with access to startup capital and investors as well as resources, training, and mentors to support us on our journey. This information should be widely available and made accessible to as many people as possible. For example, the Viscardi Center in collaboration with Iona University organizes the IdeaSpark program, which selects twenty disabled participants over the summer—at no charge—and provides training, mentorship (Iona students engage as peer mentors), and a chance to pitch their ideas to win a cash grant of $7,500.[18] Remarkable runs accelerator programs in Australia and the United States for tech startups that positively impact disabled people, providing seed funding and support. Enable Ventures, launched in 2022, is the first venture capital fund dedicated to closing the disability wealth gap. The JAN provides individualized, case-by-case assistance for disabled people looking to start a business.[19] Small Business Hub, powered by the National Disability Institute, also provides resources, training, and assistance.[20] Various public grants are available for aspiring disabled entrepreneurs, including the Social Security Administration's Plan to Achieve Self-Support (PASS).[21]

3. Acquire disability-owned companies. In 2017, Accomable, a London-based startup that provided disability-friendly travel listings, was bought by Airbnb for an undisclosed price. The Accomable team joined Airbnb to expand home listings for disabled people,[22] and its CEO, Srin Madipalli, became the head of accessibility at Airbnb through 2020. Keely Cat-Wells's first company, C Talent, which represents disabled artists and creators, was acquired by the creator and talent management company Whalar in 2022, marking one of the largest investments ever made in disabled talent within the creative industry.[23] Examples

like these demonstrate that disability-focused businesses work and can thrive in our economy, and every acquisition will hopefully pave the way for similar success stories down the road.

4. Patronize disability-owned small businesses. You can check out adaptive fashion marketplaces like Patti + Ricky and gift guides like Emily Ladau and Kate Caldwell's "2023 Disability Holiday Gift Guide"[24] to research small businesses and entrepreneurs to support. These businesses feature products like accessories, art and prints, stationery, apparel, and self-care products. On our Diversability Instagram, during Small Business Saturday in 2023, we requested that followers tag disability-owned small businesses in the comments to improve discovery and share resources.[25] There are even informal Google Sheets floating around that can be collaboratively updated as new businesses are introduced. Do your own research to find out what other disability-owned small businesses are out there, try their products, and advocate for them among your family and friends. Remember, inclusively designed products, even if created by and for disabled people, are for everyone.

5. Engage the services of disabled consultants, experts, and speakers to fulfill your own business needs, such as your organization's accessibility requirements. In fact, don't stop there: work with disability-owned businesses at all levels and in all industries, whether in manufacturing, media, or other services. "By elevating supply-chain diversity, you're supporting disabled businesses and increasing the quality of your business," says disability inclusion leader Jessica Lopez.[26]

6. Advocate for policies that will facilitate and aid disabled professionals who are self-employed. This includes policies that encourage self-employed people to become more entrepreneurial. For example, advocacy is needed to make adjustments to disability and unemployment benefits so disabled people can feel more comfortable taking business risks rather than fearing losing their benefits.[27] Self-employment and entrepreneurship are strategies to close the gaps in wealth and unemployment in the disabled community, and they can incentivize disabled people to enter the market.

7. Increase data collection to combat the disability data gap and track the growth of disability entrepreneurial trends. If you are a disabled entrepreneur with a for-profit company that is at least 51 percent owned or managed by someone with a disability, get certified as a disability-owned business enterprise (DOBE) with Disability:IN. Not only will you help to contribute to the data, but certified DOBEs are also given access to business development training and corporate networks.[28]

Reflection Questions

1. Have you consciously supported disability-owned businesses in the past? Are there any potential biases you may have about disability-owned businesses?

2. What are some items you frequently buy? Is there a way you can incorporate disability-owned businesses into your shopping habits? Feel free to search for things like "disability-owned restaurant," "disability-owned bookstore," or "disability-owned candle company" based on businesses that you would frequent and support.

3. How can you help disabled entrepreneurs to overcome barriers? For example, can you invest, offer mentorship and guidance, or buy from their businesses?

4. How might your purchasing and investing decisions contribute to challenging ableism in your circles? How can you help your community to create a supportive environment for disabled entrepreneurs?

CHAPTER 33

Advocate with Disabled People

A big goal we've set throughout this book is to learn how to be a better ally to the disability community. Being an ally is not a self-proclaimed identity; instead, it is about the choices you make and actions you take on a moment-by-moment basis.

Unfortunately, certain types of allyship end up being performative, with people taking on the superficial label of an "ally" to feel better about themselves or to gain social standing. They may use only their words, thoughts, or intentions to virtue signal without taking any proactive steps toward action, or they may put on a show of being an ally when it is convenient for them but fail to show up in critical moments that carry more risk. Other times, allies center themselves by speaking over or on behalf of disabled people without actually listening to us. These instances occur when allyship is one-sided and defined only by the ally instead of by disabled people, with the disabled person being seen as inferior or a charity case.[1]

Because of this, I like to distinguish between the roles of an ally (sometimes called a co-conspirator) and an advocate. While allyship might refer to the type of support where an ally provides assistance to the cause of an underrepresented or marginalized group, advocacy refers to active participation in a larger cultural, political, or social movement.[2] An advocate is someone who uses their privilege to call out injustice and who fights alongside a community to effect change. In addition to challenging and dismantling ableist attitudes and structures, non-disabled advocates with the disability community proactively work to rebuild their environments and culture with the larger goal of disability justice.

The sustained, dedicated, and careful practice of this type of advocacy ultimately leads to activism.[3] You do not have to be disabled to be a disability advocate.

Like everything else, being an advocate comes with nuances. An advocate helps to amplify disabled voices and give us a platform; they do not replace or drown out our voices. In your advocacy work, you must always remember who came before you and what cause you are doing this for—disabled people and our liberation in an ableist world and, on a larger scale, the liberation of all people.

There is a saying we often use: "Nothing about us without us." It originates from the Latin phrase *Nihil de nobis, sine nobis*, which started as a motto for people who wanted a say in how they were governed. This led to the political slogan "No taxation without representation" during the American Revolution. In the 1990s, writer and disability rights activist James Charlton applied the concept to the disability rights movement; it was also the title of his book published in 2000.[4] One example of the failure to apply "Nothing about us without us" is when non-disabled people fight for "cures" for disabilities under the assumption that disabled people would have an easier life without the disability. This is harmful because it reinforces the belief that disability is a problem to be fixed when that energy could be redirected toward advocating for accessibility. Not every disabled person wants a cure, and the treatments are often framed as miracles when they might provide only marginal benefits, if any. Not to mention, they may be expensive. I spent many years after becoming disabled going to doctors' appointments and acupuncture sessions and meeting with neurosurgeons in an attempt to "fix" my arm. But a brachial plexus injury is known to be a lifelong injury.

In 2018, I was at a conference where the CEO of a tech company told me that deafness would soon cease to exist because of cochlear implants. Well-intended people incorrectly assume that cochlear implants "cure" hearing loss, without a thought for the fact that many Deaf people use ASL and proudly embrace Deaf culture and the Deaf community. Additionally, the cost of cochlear implants can range from $50,000 to $100,000, and the surgery may still be financially inaccessible even if it is partially covered by health insurance.[5]

There are also examples of well-intended inventions that were created for disabled people without our input. One was a toothbrush meant for blind people that featured a wider handle and two brush heads that came together at a 90-degree angle so that the person using it could reach every part of their teeth.

However, most of us don't need to see our teeth in order to brush them![6] Another invention was shoes meant for blind people that had magnets mounted at the instep so that the wearer of the shoes could align them in the right direction and know which was the left shoe and right shoe. But a blind person would know that anyway once they put on their shoes by feeling how each one fit on their foot.[7]

A more recent example of these misguided inventions is web accessibility overlays. Accessibility overlays are AI-powered tools marketed as a "quick fix" for accessibility problems, such as small text size and low color contrast, on pre-existing websites. When you visit a website, you may notice a round "accessibility" icon in one of the corners that, when you click on it, opens a menu of different options that are supposed to make websites more accessible. However, disabled users disagree. "I've not yet found a single [overlay] that makes my life better. I spend more time working around these overlays than I actually do navigating the website," Patrick Perdue said in an interview with the *New York Times* about navigating websites as a blind user.[8]

Web accessibility overlay companies have risen in popularity because of their claim that their widgets will enable companies to comply with the ADA and avoid lawsuits. Some of these companies are publicly traded, with revenues in the millions, and others have raised millions of dollars in funding. Yet in 2023, more than nine hundred companies with an accessibility widget or overlay on their website were sued over accessibility, up from six hundred in 2022.[9] In addition, more than seven hundred accessibility advocates and web developers have signed an open letter calling for people not to install these tools on their websites.[10] These overlay companies have since hired some disabled people, but they have not addressed the root of the problem, which is that they ironically make it harder for disabled people who use screen readers to access websites that use these overlays.

Instead of using overlays, Accessibility.Works suggests a three-step process: auditing the site, remediation, and verification.[11] You can also follow design best practices known as the Web Content Accessibility Guidelines (WCAG) 2 and work with accessibility experts certified by the International Association of Accessibility Professionals (IAAP). If you're not able to hire someone to conduct an audit of your site, you can check out an automated audit such as Google Lighthouse and the WAVE Evaluation Tool to start.

As disability rights activist Imani Barbarin says, "The authorities on disabled people are disabled people."[12] Nothing about us without us. Disabled people are already regularly silenced, ignored, and invisibilized when society does not listen to us or take our concerns seriously, and it is especially disappointing when this happens in advocacy spaces. In a post on her website *Crutches & Spice*, Barbarin describes how the voices of disabled people are often overridden by those of non-disabled allies when it comes to creating inclusive policies or spaces, a phenomenon she equates with the all-male panels that discuss women's inclusion in the corporate world: "To be true to the mission of disability inclusion, it requires that you [as a non-disabled advocate] think of yourself as a vessel to pass along what those in the disabled community [have] expressed rather than being our voice. Taking up space in advocacy for a marginalized group is a privilege, one that you can wield to make the public sphere more inclusive or one you can use to center yourself."[13]

Instead, Barbarin suggests that non-disabled allies and advocates simply "pass the mic." Writer and disability blogger Holly Tuke shares similar advice: "Listen to us and take our lead....Remember that disabled people know best—we are the ones living with our disabilities and chronic illnesses every single day. When you listen to us, take note of what we're saying, and if you can, act on it."[14] Writer Andrew Pulrang adds, "We're not even looking for advocacy, if it means non-disabled people speaking *for* us, defending *their* perception of *our* rights without our full participation or consent....It's even more important to discover and center disabled people's concerns, priorities, and preferences, even if you don't always understand or agree with them."[15]

Ryan Prior is a journalist and author in Washington, DC, who lives with myalgic encephalomyelitis/chronic fatigue syndrome, which is mostly in remission. During the height of the COVID-19 pandemic, when he was covering health and science stories, he developed a "laser focus" on what would become known as long COVID—about which he has also published a book called *The Long Haul*. He tells me,

> As a reporter, my training is to look for the world's top experts on any topic and to interview them. For long COVID, I formed relationships with the Patient Led Research Collaborative for COVID. Few of the members of this collective were formal scientists, but [the rest were just patients.] Yet they banded together across continents and often from their beds, where they were severely ill with fatigue and brain fog. The group published the first research on long COVID by early June 2020. And over the next several

years, their expertise would frequently be called on by the US Congress, the CDC, and the World Health Organization. Several of their research papers were the most highly read and cited science across the globe....Perhaps the most important insight that I'm taking with me from the last few years of reporting, advocacy, and scholarship is the value of "proximate leadership." This is the idea that lived experience and boots-on-the-ground insight is by far the most useful way for us to solve the world's most pressing problems.[16]

If you notice a problem, research solutions from disability-specific sources. You don't have to come up with a unique solution. Odds are, disability activists already have, as we are the experts. Here's what I mean: don't speak for us. *But* I also hope you will resolve to fight with us. We are stronger together, and as Drew Dakessian writes for World Institute on Disability, "The allyship [and advocacy] of those who don't have disabilities is essential for the liberation of those who do."[17] We all have a role to play in dismantling ableism.

I hope this book will not only teach you to be a better and genuine ally but also inspire and push you to be a proactive advocate for disability inclusion as you listen to disabled people.

You don't have to be disabled to advocate for disability rights, but you do need to follow our lead. Here are some ways you can do so, using the acronym PAPUSD (Platform, Amplify, Partner, Use your privilege, Share your story, Decenter yourself):

1. **Platform:** Give the voices of disabled people a platform by inviting us to the table in decision-making processes or voting us into positions of power. You can also amplify our concerns by repeating our requests in person if they aren't generating a response or sharing or liking our posts on social media. If you are invited to speak at an event and you notice that the conversation would benefit from a disabled perspective, consider "passing the mic" and suggesting to the event organizers that they add a disabled voice to the conversation.

2. **Amplify:** Share, consume, and disseminate work or content created by disabled people to educate yourself and others on your advocacy journey.

3. **Partner:** Engage in formal partnerships with disability-led organizations in your advocacy work, or build friendships with disabled people so that you can hear what we have to say and understand our lived experiences. Continue to sustain these community relationships so you can always be accountable.[18] Organizations you can check out and partner with could include the Arc, Centers for Independent Living (there are many of these located throughout the country), and the AAPD. Attending disability commission meetings in your hometown or municipal district is also a great way to learn more about local issues.

4. **Use Your Privilege:** When you have done your homework and consulted with disabled people, leverage your privilege to remove access barriers, create equitable opportunities, promote awareness, and ensure accessibility in your community. You may want to use your privilege to advocate for accessibility in the workplace overall, especially if your disabled colleagues don't feel safe doing that for themselves. For example, take the initiative to make sure that the organizations you're part of, the places you visit, and the content you create are accessible to everyone, even if you don't directly benefit from this accessibility. As an advocate, you don't need to wait for a personal reason or a triggering event to make spaces and content accessible; remember that you're constantly working to make systemic change in the larger culture.

5. **Share Your Story:** If you are a non-disabled ally or advocate who is a family member or caretaker of a person with disabilities, share your story and personal experience with disability to advocate for accessibility and disability rights. However, make sure to tell your story from your point of view, and do not confuse your story with your disabled loved one's story—they are related but different. Advocate with us, not for us.[19]

6. **Decenter Yourself:** Respect the limits of your knowledge and what you can do, and decenter yourself in your advocacy work. Acknowledge that you're not the expert and that many have come before you.[20]

Reflection Questions

1. Think about times you've benefited from an ableist system. (It can be as simple as taking the stairs to class and realizing there was no elevator to get there.) How can you start your own advocacy work to address this access barrier in consultation with the disability community?

2. How can you actively involve disabled voices in decision-making processes within your community, such as the board of your religious congregation, school, or museum? At work? Within the local government?

3. As you advocate, are you centering your own experience as a non-disabled person or the experiences of disabled people? How can you share your story without conflating it with the experiences of disabled individuals or overshadowing them?

4. Reflect on disability organizations you support. How can you contribute to and support their advocacy efforts? What are some ways that you can stay educated on disability issues?

5. Are there ways you can remove access barriers in your community? For example, is there a local business that you love but that might not have step-free access? Can you mention that to the owners without shaming them? Could you explore helping them acquire a ramp? The StopGap Foundation is a Canadian nonprofit that has created over two thousand brightly painted ramps for businesses. Is there a local organization that you could partner with?

CHAPTER 34

Get Civically Engaged

In 2016, I met with Victor Calise, the commissioner for the New York City Mayor's Office for People with Disabilities. I was living in New York City at the time, and it had been almost a year since Diversability's relaunch event in April 2015, which Calise had attended.

"As you know, I'm building a disability community through the events we're hosting at Diversability," I told him. "If there's anything we can do to support or amplify the work that you're doing, let me know."

"I think what you're doing is great," he responded, "but I need you to start showing up at City Hall. We won't know what issues you care about unless you make a public comment."

He was right; I wasn't showing up. I actually didn't even know where City Hall was.

It would take a move across the country before I started showing up at City Hall—in San Francisco in 2017. I was new to the city and was trying to figure out how to plug into the local disability community. When I saw that there was an advisory body called the San Francisco Mayor's Disability Council, I started showing up at meetings.

Around this time, electric scooter companies had descended upon San Francisco, and the sidewalks were littered with scooters that were not parked correctly. During one meeting, I made a public comment on the need for sidewalk safety for disabled San Franciscans. Shortly afterward, I noticed that these electric scooters had been removed from the sidewalks, and San Francisco soon implemented a permanent permit process for scooter companies if they wanted to operate in the city. It was one example of the local government moving quickly and a clear sign of how public and civic engagement had the capacity to make change.

After a few meetings, a council member asked if I would be interested in joining the Mayor's Disability Council. I was sworn in by Mayor London Breed in September 2019, and I served through the summer of 2022.

During my time, I led the call for a mayoral proclamation of July as Disability Pride Month, organized a digital exhibition featuring Bay Area disability leaders, curated events that were shared on San Francisco's ADA30 website in honor of the thirtieth anniversary of the ADA, and put in a request that would end up lighting San Francisco City Hall multiple years in a row to recognize the ADA's anniversary on July 26.

Fun fact: my request to light up City Hall consisted of a simple email. After they said yes, I posted about my efforts on LinkedIn in the hopes of empowering other people across the country to make similar requests to light up landmarks in their home cities. At least two commenters replied to say they'd had success in Tampa and Buffalo, illustrating how easy a request can be as well as the power of the ripple effect.[1]

In March 2023, when the US government was making moves to ban Tik-Tok, I was invited to Washington, DC, to talk with members of Congress about why TikTok was so important to me as an advocate—how it empowered an entire group of disability advocates to find our voice, expand our audience, and build our career.[2] These days, I attend meetings of the City of Los Angeles and County of Los Angeles Commissions on Disability, and I serve on the LA28 Olympic and Paralympic Games Working Group on Local Hire and Workforce Development in preparation for the 2028 Summer Olympics and Paralympics. I'm proud and excited about the legacy this work will leave for disability inclusion.

By sharing my journey, I hope to give you a sense of what's possible, especially when you're first starting out. The first steps toward getting civically engaged don't need to be difficult or intimidating—sometimes it's just about showing up to a commission meeting so you can understand what's going on or getting over the mental barrier and telling yourself that as one person, you *can* make change. More important, once you're in it, is building your knowledge of the changing political landscape around you, plugging in to your local communities or organizations to do the work, and having a continued commitment to showing up and persevering even when things get hard.

Here's a story of a recent win in terms of how sustained civic engagement can create ripple effects that lead to systemic change for disability rights. In 2017, Mayor Jim Kenney created the Philadelphia Office for People with Disabilities through an executive order to ensure that the city complied with accessibility laws; however, the executive order meant the office could be dismantled at any time. Despite Philadelphia having the highest population of disabled people of the top-ten largest US cities, it still failed many of its residents over the years with broken sidewalks and missing curb ramps—among other inaccessibilities—leading to a 2019 lawsuit and a 2022 settlement to install and fix ten thousand curb ramps.

With the continued efforts of disability advocates, in November 2023, 86 percent of Philadelphians voted to codify the Philadelphia Office for People with Disabilities in city law, effectively making it permanent.[3] And as of December 2023, Philadelphia became the first sensory-inclusive city, as certified by KultureCity, a nonprofit organization that trains and certifies venues with sensory-inclusive modifications. Over sixteen thousand city employees, contractors, and volunteers have been trained in sensory-inclusive practices with the help of a grant and are better prepared to assist residents, guests, and employees with sensory sensitivities.

"Engagement is for everyone," says Nico Meyering, the chair of the Mayor's Commission on People with Disabilities.[4] "Philadelphians realize Disability rights are human rights."[5]

Getting civically engaged is one of the most direct ways to create systemic change. In 2021, I interviewed Dr. Anne Marie Murphy, a molecular geneticist and the executive director of Equal Hope, an organization in Illinois that works to save lives by eliminating health disparities across women's cancers. In 2007, Equal Hope started publishing work showing that Chicago had a large disparity in mortality between Black and white women with breast cancer, suggesting that these gaps were not a biological issue but rather a systemic issue due in part to limited health-care access and structural racism. As a result of Equal Hope's work, as of 2013, Chicago has gone from having some of the most pronounced breast cancer disparities to being a leader in the United States in reducing breast cancer deaths among Black women.[6]

Murphy's work demonstrates systemic change in action. "Health disparities are manmade, and they can be mankind-solved," Murphy tells me. "To make change, you need to get to systemic change. Learning about the political system is important because so many aspects of structural racism are politically determined."[7] It's the same with disability—intersectionality, once again.

Civic engagement doesn't even have to start at the local government level. Isabel Mavrides-Calderón is a nineteen-year-old Latina disability justice activist and White House speaker on accessibility who lives with a physical disability and chronic illness. She wrote to me recently about how disabled students are typically not accommodated or considered in school emergency drills and how it is the parents and faculty who shape their potential fates. In one instance, a student "was left behind in a burning building" because nobody spared a thought for her needs:

[This] story is indicative of the wider experience of disabled students during emergencies....As school shooting drills have become the norm in schools across the country, the United States Department of Homeland Security advises students to follow these three steps in the case of an actual school shooting: "run, hide, and fight." But for the students who can't do any of those things, they are often seen as unworthy and left behind to die....From the process of creating an emergency plan, to creating accessible buildings and exits, to policy decisions, disabled people are constantly left out of the decisions that impact their lives the most.[8]

This is exactly the work to which Mavrides-Calderón has dedicated her life. She added,

At the end of the day, the fault of this issue does not lie with scared parents or teachers [who] do not know how they can help their students in a situation that is not part of their job description. It is an issue that we must all come together as a society to solve, by first placing more value on disabled people's lives. We must advocate for stronger legal protections for disabled students. It should not be their burden to bear, yet disabled students and families must think about this issue before the consequences are too late. Parents and students can start by asking to include emergency preparedness as part of their 504 plan[s]. Administrators, make sure to include disabled people in the emergency planning process. Every student has individual needs, [so] make discussing an emergency plan a regular part of the school planning process.[9]

There are other ways to make change as well. In 2018, Jenny Sichel, a Paralympic silver medalist from Rio 2016, partnered with Link20, a social network of disability rights advocates, to lead a campaign on the pay gap for US Paralympic medalists using the hashtag #EqualMedalPay. At the time, Paralympic gold medalists received $7,500 for each medal, but if an athlete was on the Olympic team, they received $37,500.[10]

"We believe that the medal payout policy sends a disturbing message to our Paralympic athletes, and the rest of the world, that some athletes are inferior to others merely because they happen to have a disability," Link20 wrote in a letter to Lawrence Probst, the chair of the US Olympic Committee Board. "We believe a message of equality, reflected in equal payouts for both Olympic and Paralympic athletes who win medals, is far more fitting with the ideals of the Olympic movement."[11]

On September 21, 2018, the US Olympic Committee Board voted to pay Olympians and Paralympians equally, including retroactive payments for all medals won starting in 2018, totaling $1.2 million and marking a 400 percent raise for thousands of Paralympic athletes.[12]

We all have a part to play, and this is where you come in.

"While we celebrate the achievements and how far we have come, there is still so much to do," says disability rights advocate Keely Cat-Wells.[13] *As of this writing,*

1. It is still legal to pay disabled people below minimum wage in thirty-eight states (an additional five states are in the process of phasing out sub–minimum wage).
2. Disabled people still face dehumanizing and unsafe experiences when they fly. More than thirty-one wheelchairs and mobility devices are damaged per day during air travel in the United States, robbing wheelchair users of their mobility and dignity.[14] If you wish to learn more

about this issue, check out the #JustPlaneWrong campaign from Paralyzed Veterans of America (PVA) and #RightsOnFlights from Sophie
Morgan. As of July 26, 2023, PVA advocacy had successfully called for
new single-aisle aircraft to make lavatories big enough for a disabled
passenger and their attendant.[15]

3. Getting married is financially and medically impractical or impossible for millions of disabled people. For example, if a disabled person
   receives SSI or Medicaid, their benefits can be reduced or revoked
   upon marriage if their non-SSI spouse earns $925 or more per month
   based on 2022 benefit levels.[16] The SSI Savings Penalty Elimination
   Act was introduced in September 2023 by US senators Sherrod Brown
   (D-OH) and Bill Cassidy (R-LA) and would increase the asset cap
   to $10,000 for individuals and $20,000 for married couples. The current asset caps are $2,000 and $3,000, respectively, and have not been
   changed since 1984.[17]

4. Disabled people still undergo forced sterilization. In many states, doctors, family members, guardians, and judges have the power to sterilize
   disabled people against their will.

5. There is still a lack of anti-discrimination policies in 193 member
   states of the UN. Studies show that only 45 countries have anti-
   discrimination or other disability-specific laws.[18]

To create systemic change, we need to keep showing up and maintaining the
momentum that disability advocates have put in motion for decades while keeping
our eyes on the shifting political and social landscape. Javier Robles, a professor
and director of the Center for Disability Sports, Health, and Wellness at Rutgers
University, explains, "It was an amazing day when the ADA became law....But
a law like the ADA doesn't magically fix things." Citing the example of COVID,
Robles describes how the ADA failed to fully protect people with disabilities when
the pandemic caused competition for scarce resources like ventilators, leaving disabled people to be openly discriminated against and left to die. "There's work to
be done to improve access and change attitudes. Change will come when we teach
disability history and empower younger people with disabilities."[19]

So what can you do to get civically engaged to make systemic change?

1. Identify a topic that you care about, and go from there. Familiarize yourself with pre-existing legislation and what types of reform are needed. For example, I first started attending City Hall meetings in order to learn what people cared and talked about. You can also get inspired by work that other advocates have done elsewhere. Someone in my network recently made a public statement requesting masked mornings at museums, a precedent set by another city, to provide immunocompromised people with safe access.

2. Show up. It is not enough to be aware or in the know—change requires action. Start with small steps by showing up in your own circles; in your local communities; and then on the city, county, state, and national levels. Showing up can look like sharing a social media post (though this shouldn't be your only action!); signing a petition; volunteering for a cause; attending City Hall meetings; participating in marches; or emailing, calling, or writing letters to your representatives. Change can consist of both symbolic and practical actions. I remember once saying that the work I did around the mayoral proclamation for July's Disability Pride Month wasn't anything groundbreaking, but Black, biracial, queer disability justice educator Alex Locust was quick to tell me not to minimize it: "The success that you achieved in getting that proclamation is inherently really amazing. And the beauty of that is that we don't know what change that will cause. Having that Disability Pride Month explicitly named could touch someone a month from now. They could be the person who—because you were demonstrating that pride and that authenticity—can work on the housing issue or financial inequities for disabled people."[20]

3. Let your representatives or decision-makers know what you are calling for. There are many old campaigns out there that provide helpful templates for social media posts and language for reaching out to representatives—for example, #NoBodyIsDisposable was a 2020 campaign launched during the pandemic's hospital bed triage to call for an

end to care rationing.[21] You just have to adapt it to the topic at hand. Here's a general template for letters or emails you can use:

- Introduce yourself and your connection to the geographic area and issue. For example, "My name is Tiffany Yu, and I was appointed to the San Francisco Mayor's Disability Council (MDC) in 2019."
- Highlight the specific ask: "On behalf of the MDC, we are requesting that you proclaim July 2020 'Disability Pride Month' in honor of the thirtieth anniversary of the ADA."
- Provide context for why this matters and why it is important to the geographic area: "This proclamation will follow other major cities that have declared 'Disability Pride Month,' including New York City in 2015 and Los Angeles in 2016. The passage of the ADA in 1990 signified a turning point for the civil rights of disabled people. By designating July as Disability Pride Month, the city also recognizes the important role the Bay Area played in launching the modern disability rights and independent living movement…[and] honors its identity as a city that fights for equality for all disenfranchised communities."
- If possible, mention specific steps that can be taken to achieve this request. For example, in addition to requesting a formal proclamation of July as Disability Pride Month, we requested that the city host and promote a master calendar of Disability Pride Month events, light up various city landmarks in blue and white (at the time, we chose the colors of the wheelchair access symbol, though I later learned that purple is the international color for disability, and we would change the request in later years), and host a virtual roundtable consisting of elected officials and disability rights activists to discuss concerns about employment and housing.

4. Engage in different levels of political action. Political actions can include influencing policymakers to consult with and consider disabled people when making policies, lobbying lawmakers to create laws that support

our rights, pressuring public officials to enforce existing laws and policies that protect us, and interacting with community service providers like social workers, medical professionals, and service staff to ensure that they respect our needs.[22]

5. Listen to disability rights advocates and help to create platforms for, amplify, or support our pre-existing work. We've been doing this for a long time, and we know how best to help ourselves—you know it by now: nothing about us without us. "Centering [our] experiences promotes a more authentic understanding of disability rights issues and challenges," writes DEI educator Keri Gray.[23] You can keep supporting disabled activists by sharing our social media posts; creating or ensuring opportunities for us to speak at events or media outlets; and partnering and collaborating with disability rights movements, organizations, or collectives to work toward common goals.

6. Systemic change requires a combination of policy change and attitudinal change. Continue to educate yourself about ableism, and conduct frequent accessibility checks in the spaces you're in. Attend conferences and seminars, read books, follow disabled advocates on social media, and talk to disabled friends and family members to keep unlearning ableism so you can be a better ally, activist, and advocate.

7. Stay committed. If you meet an obstacle or a wall, don't be discouraged. Advocacy work can be an uphill battle, and it's important to remain resilient and focused if something doesn't pan out the first time. Once, while I was still serving on the San Francisco Mayor's Disability Council, on behalf of the council, I wrote a letter to the city about implementing mandatory masks on public transit so that disabled people could travel safely. Unfortunately, I didn't make much progress there, but I've known over my many years in advocacy that not everything happens at the pace you would like it to. It is helpful to set short-term goals while keeping your eye on long-term outcomes. Remind yourself of the bigger picture and recognize that systemic change will eventually occur after accumulated and sustained pressure.

Finally, remember that the systemic changes that we're fighting for should be the floor, not the ceiling, of the type of world that we want to build together: one where disabled people aren't just surviving within the thresholds but instead have the opportunity to thrive, flourish, and bloom in the room.

Reflection Questions

1. How are you currently staying up-to-date on disability issues? You can follow sites like Disability Scoop or subscribe to newsletters from organizations like the AAPD. You can also subscribe to the *Disability Debrief* newsletter and *Crip News* on Substack, as mentioned in Chapter 14: Diversify Your Feed.

2. What are some disability issues that resonate with you, and how can you champion these ideas within your personal and professional spheres? Examples are economic empowerment, housing, health care, education, and climate change.

3. What are some of the grassroots initiatives and campaigns that disability rights organizations are leading? How can you partner or collaborate with them or amplify their message? What levels of political action can you engage in to influence policymakers? In what ways can you get involved to help influence systemic change in your community?

4. In what ways can you commit to taking action to support disability rights and disability justice? How can you contribute to shaping a future where disability is celebrated?

CONCLUSION

The Anti-Ableist Manifesto

In 2022, I went to a camp hosted by the UBPN that brought together people who have brachial plexus injuries, our families, and our doctors. On the first night, during a roller-skating event hosted at the YMCA, a person came up to me.

"Hi, I'm a pediatric hand surgeon. I watched your TEDx talk," he said. In it, I had talked about how chronic exclusion was a microaggression that I had experienced throughout my adolescence and how it still impacted the way I navigated life with a disability in an ableist world. I also talked about how underlying my physical disability was my PTSD and the mental health aspect of not having had the space to grieve what I had lost.

People who have brachial plexus injuries often interact with a whole slew of medical professionals—sometimes it's a hand surgeon, sometimes a surgeon who specializes in elbows and shoulders, sometimes a neurosurgeon. That is in addition to ongoing physical therapy and occupational therapy. Many people who have brachial plexus injuries are also children due to medical malpractice during childbirth where the arm is forcibly pulled, a form of trauma to the body, and no one really thinks about providing mental health support alongside those other medical procedures and surgeries. Certainly no one had thought about it when I had come in with a paralyzed arm as a nine-year-old. I underwent many doctor's appointments and invasive pre-tests for a surgery that never happened on top of fresh trauma and grief from the car accident.

"Thank you so much," I told the doctor. "Actually, to be frank, I have a difficult relationship with medical professionals due to my own medical trauma."

The doctor took this in stride. "I just wanted to say that watching your talk inspired me to add a mental health professional to my team."

What this doctor was doing was a welcome surprise—an unintended positive impact of my talk—and something I had never thought would happen when I first decided to share my story. His work would be life-changing for future kids with brachial plexus injuries. We may never know fully who will be impacted by our words and actions, but that day, I learned the power of using my voice.

I share this story with the hope that this book will be that catalyst for you. After putting this book down, some of you may make simple, immediate changes like replacing the phrase *paralyzed by fear* with a different description on your website, blogs, and posts or in your conversations. Some of you might move to provide children with physical disabilities with access to mental health support as they go through medical procedures. Whatever the resulting actions look like, I hope this book has ignited a spark within you, urging you to be an active participant in this movement for change, where disability is no longer viewed as a hindrance or shameful but rather as a source of strength, innovation, and diversity, deserving of celebration.

Before you turn these final pages, use this opportunity to reflect on the transformative journey we have taken together. A big reason I've used the "Me, We, Us" framework for *The Anti-Ableist Manifesto* is to communicate this important lesson: individual action leads to collective change. We started with personal actions, such as growing our knowledge and dismantling stereotypes; then worked to combat ableist microaggressions in our relationships; and finally moved to wider systemic changes, such as using inclusive design, prioritizing accessibility, and fighting for policy change. *Inclusivity* isn't just a buzzword or a trend; it's integral to our shared values. When we grow our awareness and change individual attitudes and behaviors, these changes will ripple out into our relationships and expand to shape our community and systems as a whole. This collective effort is what moves the needle and propels all of us forward beyond simply accommodation and toward an equitable, accessibility-first, disability-inclusive society.

As I have witnessed over the past couple of years, there is a hunger for more knowledge, understanding, and change in the disability space. It's the reason you've picked up this book. So I hope you can take what you've learned, the insights and strategies you've gained, and the empathy you've cultivated and channel it all into real-world change. I hope you can nourish that original hunger and use it to unite all of us so that we can build connections, coalitions, and partnerships to continue to do this work together as allies, co-conspirators, and advocates.

It will be an ongoing journey with some missteps along the way. But through it all, we must be gentle, keep ourselves accountable, and cheer one another on. All of these steps and missteps, taken together, will bring us closer to a world where every person is celebrated. Through these connections and mutual support, we're strengthening the threads that weave all of our communities together in our collective fight for justice and liberation.

As Australian aboriginal activist Lilla Watson is credited with saying, "If you have come to help me, you are wasting your time. If you have come because your liberation is bound up with mine, then let us work together."[1]

As we close, remind yourself that this is a call to action. Finishing this book is not the end of your journey but the beginning. It's a call to question norms, challenge the status quo of ableism, and craft and co-create the future we envision for everyone.

Here it is, *The Anti-Ableist Manifesto*, followed by a piece of art by Afro-Latina disabled art activist Jennifer White-Johnson.

The Anti-Ableist Manifesto

1. Disability is not a bad word or a bad thing.
2. Educate yourself.
3. Not all disabilities are apparent.
4. Don't erase history.
5. Learn about the models of disability.
6. Disability is intersectional.
7. We matter.
8. Use your privilege.
9. Turn guilt into action.
10. Representation matters.
11. Diversify your feed.

12. Halt microaggressions.

13. Don't make assumptions.

14. Don't give unsolicited advice.

15. Believe us.

16. We are not your inspiration.

17. Break the cycle of social isolation.

18. Be curious, but respect boundaries.

19. Treat us with respect.

20. We are not a monolith.

21. Embrace imperfection.

22. Challenge the disability tax.

23. Design inclusively.

24. Hire us.

25. Accommodations and accessibility promote equity.

26. Build a disability-inclusive culture.

27. We have consumer power.

28. Invest in disabled entrepreneurs.

29. Nothing about us without us.

30. Advocate proactively.

31. Be an ally.

32. Confront ableism.

33. Be anti-ableist.

Image description: Twenty-seven of the thirty-three aforementioned statements, which loosely reference themes from each of the thirty-four chapters, are creatively displayed in different fonts in a poster designed by Jennifer White-Johnson titled *The Anti-Ableist Manifesto*.

THE ANTI-ABLEIST MANIFESTO

DISABILITY IS NOT A BAD WORD. OR A BAD THING. ♿

DISABILITY IS INTERSECTIONAL.

BREAK THE CYCLE OF SOCIAL ISOLATION.

BE CURIOUS, BUT RESPECT BOUNDARIES.

 DON'T ERASE HISTORY.

DIVERSIFY YOUR FEED.

ACCOMMODATIONS AND ACCESSIBILITY = PROMOTE EQUITY.

BELIEVE US. DESIGN INCLUSIVELY. BE AN ALLY.

WE ARE <u>NOT</u> YOUR INSPIRATION.
WE ARE <u>NOT</u> A MONOLITH.

TREAT US WITH RESPECT.

HALT ⊘ MICROAGGRESSIONS.

DON'T GIVE UNSOLICITED **ADVICE.**

REPRESENTATION MATTERS.
ADVOCATE PROACTIVELY.

EDUCATE YOURSELF. LEARN ABOUT THE MODELS OF DISABILITY.

USE YOUR PRIVILEGE.

NOTHING ABOUT US WITHOUT US.

INVEST IN DISABLED ENTREPRENEURS. HIRE US.

TURN GUILT INTO ACTION. CHALLENGE THE DISABILITY TAX.

CONFRONT ABLEISM.   BE ANTI-ABLEIST.

ACKNOWLEDGMENTS

In some ways, I still can't believe that I wrote a whole book. I often talk about how none of this work exists in a vacuum. It takes a village.

First, to the Diversability community, the broader disability community, and everyone who has engaged with me and my work, I am only here because of all of you. I am so grateful and proud to be in community with and learning alongside you. Thank you for sharing your stories, insights, and perspectives that are featured throughout this book. I hope that this continues to uplift and amplify all our voices.

To my family: my mom, my late dad, and three siblings. November 29, 1997, changed all of our lives. It hasn't been easy but thank you for making it possible so that I could do this work.

To my incredible agent, Charles Kim, thank you for championing me from the beginning when I wasn't sure if I had a book in me. From a high school dream that sat on the proverbial shelf gathering dust for decades, this book came into existence because of you. You believed in me, my voice, and my message when I didn't yet believe in myself. Thank you to Regina Brooks and the entire team at Serendipity Literary Agency for your continued support and advocacy throughout the process.

To Alison Dalafave at Hachette Go, for trusting that this was a book that needed to be a Hachette Go book and out in the world. To Mollie Weisenfeld, my editor, for picking up where Alison left off and being an incredible partner throughout the process. And to the entire team at Hachette Go, thank you for all the work you did behind the scenes to make this book a reality.

To Kimberley Lim, my collaborative writer and editor, thank you for your patience and your partnership on this project. You were able to take transcripts, calls, and ramblings and help turn them into something I'm so proud of. To say that this book would not exist without you is an understatement.

To Lauren Freedman, thank you for joining my book team at the last minute and your support in getting to the final manuscript. I'm grateful for your friendship.

To my designer Jennifer White-Johnson, I have been looking for something that we could work on together! Thank you for taking my vision of *The Anti-Ableist Manifesto* art and turning it into a reality. There is already so much excitement about it because of your design.

To my beta readers Dr. Amy Kenny and Aubrey Blanche-Sarellano, thank you for being the best cheerleaders and taking the time to review the early drafts and provide your feedback. This book is better because of you and I'm grateful to be in community with you.

To the Changemaker Authors Cohort from Narrative Initiative and Unicorn Authors Club, thank you for being a core part of my support system in helping me get my manuscript to the finish line. To my book coaches, Minal Hajratwala and Camila Márquez, thank you for making space for my tears, frustration, and overwhelm and for "getting it" the only way that other authors would. To my fellow Changemaker Authors, I can't wait to see your books out in the world.

There are likely others I haven't named that will come to me later—partners, supporters, mentors, and friends—who have been instrumental to this journey, thank you for everything.

Finally, to you, for reading this book. I am so grateful for your support and your interest in disability equity and inclusion and becoming anti-ableist. You all give me hope for the future.

NOTES

Introduction

1. Brené Brown, *The Gifts of Imperfection: Let Go of Who You Think You're Supposed to Be and Embrace Who You Are* (Center City, MN: Hazelden Publishing, 2010).

2. Tiffany Yu, "039: Making the Disability Experience Accessible ft. Emily Ladau, Author of Demystifying Disability," *Tiffany & Yu* podcast, August 24, 2021, https://www.tiffanyyu .com/podcast/039.

3. Elisabeth Rosenthal, "College Entrance in China: 'No' to the Handicapped," *New York Times*, May 23, 2001, https://www.nytimes.com/2001/05/23/world/college-entrance -in-china-no-to-the-handicapped.html.

4. Kimberlé W. Crenshaw, "Demarginalizing the Intersection of Race and Sex: A Black Feminist Critique of Antidiscrimination Doctrine, Feminist Theory and Antiracist Politics," *University of Chicago Legal Forum* 139 (1989): 149.

5. UN Women, @UNWomen, Instagram, July 3, 2020, https://www.instagram.com/p /CCNZ8e1jBze/.

6. "What Is Public Narrative and How Can We Use It?," Narrative Arts, https://narra tivearts.org/article/public-narrative/.

Chapter 1: What Is Disability?

1. "Disability," Merriam-Webster, https://www.merriam-webster.com/dictionary/disability.

2. "Impair," Merriam-Webster, https://www.merriam-webster.com/dictionary/impair.

3. Fabiola Cineas, "Merriam-Webster Has a New Definition of 'Racism,'" *Vox*, June 10, 2020, https://www.vox.com/identities/2020/6/10/21286656/merriam-webster-racism -definition.

4. "Disability," World Health Organization, https://www.who.int/health-topics/disability.

5. Catarina Rivera, LinkedIn, December 20, 2023, https://www.linkedin.com/posts /catarinarivera_disability-disabilityadvocacy-disabilityawareness-activity-7142913983480537088 -bKlI/.

6. World Health Organization, "Disability," March 7, 2023, https://www.who.int/news -room/fact-sheets/detail/disability-and-health.

7. Catherine A. Okoro, NaTasha D. Hollis, Alissa C. Cyrus, and Shannon Griffin-Blake, "Prevalence of Disabilities and Health Care Access by Disability Status and Type Among Adults—United States, 2016," *Morbidity and Mortality Weekly Report* 67, no. 32 (August 2018): 882–887, http://dx.doi.org/10.15585/mmwr.mm6732a3.

8. Dr. Amy Kenny, email interview with the author, January 29, 2024.

Chapter 2: Not All Disabilities Are Apparent

1. Disability:IN, "'Non-apparent Disability' vs. 'Hidden' or 'Invisible Disability'—Which Term Is Correct?," January 5, 2022, https://disabilityin.org/mental-health/non-apparent-disability-vs-hidden-or-invisible-disability-which-term-is-correct/.

2. Invisible Disabilities Association, "Invisible Disability," https://invisibledisabilities.org/what-is-an-invisible-disability/.

3. Coqual, "Key Findings: Disabilities and Inclusion," 2017, https://coqual.org/wp-content/uploads/2020/09/CoqualDisabilitiesInclusion_KeyFindings090720.pdf.

4. Angie Collins-Burke and Suzanne Cronkwright, "The Challenges of Living with an Invisible Illness," *Psychology Today*, April 17, 2021, https://www.psychologytoday.com/us/blog/stroke-awareness/202104/the-challenges-living-invisible-illness.

5. Jocelyn Apodaca Schlossberg, "Confronting Mental Health Barriers in the Asian American and Pacific Islander Community," UCLA Health, May 9, 2023, https://www.uclahealth.org/news/confronting-mental-health-barriers-asian-american-and-2.

6. Sasha Hamdani, @ThePsychDoctorMD, Instagram, November 15, 2021, https://www.instagram.com/p/CWTtmjMsRx4/.

7. Nancy Becher, LinkedIn, May 2023, https://www.linkedin.com/posts/flyingpigwrangler_disability-invisibledisability-chronicillness-activity-7062087755761098752-oWj8.

8. Paul Farhi, "A Rochelle Walensky Interview Sparked Outrage. But the CDC Says ABC Omitted Crucial Context," *Washington Post*, January 12, 2022, https://www.washingtonpost.com/lifestyle/media/walensky-abc-interview/2022/01/12/b5744ad4-73be-11ec-bc13-18891499c514_story.html.

9. Becca Lory Hector, LinkedIn, June 2023, https://www.linkedin.com/posts/beccalory hector_neurodiversity-neurodivergent-autisticadults-activity-7073992649828941824-i3-w.

10. Yoana Cholteeva, "Half of Workers with Invisible Disabilities Say Difficulty Getting Support at Work Makes It Not Worth It, Research Shows," People Management, May 9, 2023, https://www.peoplemanagement.co.uk/article/1822122/half-workers-invisible-disabilities-say-difficulty-getting-support-work-makes-not-worth-it-research-shows.

11. Eric Garcia, email interview with the author, January 17, 2024.

12. Fran Kritz, "Selena Gomez Opens Up About Her Experience with Psychosis: What Experts Want You to Know," Everyday Health, November 10, 2022, https://www.everydayhealth.com/bipolar-disorder/selena-gomez-opens-up-about-her-experience-with-psychosis/.

13. Kelsey Garcia, "Selena Gomez Launches Wondermind Mental Health Platform, Says 'It's OK to Not Be OK,'" *Popsugar*, April 4, 2022, https://www.popsugar.com/fitness/selena-gomez-wondermind-mental-health-company-details-48611084.

14. Cathy Applefeld Olson, "Selena Gomez Joins 'White House Conversation on Mental Health' Hosted by MTV," *Forbes*, May 18, 2022, https://www.forbes.com/sites/cathy olson/2022/05/18/selena-gomez-joins-white-house-conversation-on-youth-mental-health -hosted-by-mtv/.

15. Andrew Kaufman and J. H. Cullum Clark, "Gary Cohn—Overcoming Obstacles, Taking Risks, and Growing from Failure," *The Strategerist Podcast*, George W. Bush Presidential Center, May 13, 2022, https://www.bushcenter.org/publications/strategerist -s5-ep05-gary-cohn.

16. Becca Lory Hector, LinkedIn, June 2023, https://www.linkedin.com/posts/becca-loryhector_neurodiversity-neurodivergent-autisticadults-activity-7073992649828941824-i3-w.

Chapter 3: Disability Is Not a Bad Word

1. Paul Simmons, "The Origins of 'Disability' and Its Application Under the ADA," Rocky Mountain ADA Center, November 14, 2019, https://rockymountainada.org/news /blog/origins-disability-and-its-application-under-ada.

2. "'Distinguished and Disabled' with Lachi and Rebecca Howell," *The Heumann Perspective* podcast, March 24, 2021, https://judithheumann.com/1768-2/.

3. Meriah Nichols, "3 Reasons to Say 'Disability' Instead of 'Special Needs,'" March 1, 2017, https://www.meriahnichols.com/3-reasons-say-disability-instead-special-needs/.

4. Leon Jakobovits, "Effects of Repeated Stimulation on Cognitive Aspects of Behavior: Some Experiments on the Phenomenon of Semantic Satiation," McGill University, April 1962, https://escholarship.mcgill.ca/concern/theses/c821gp587.

5. Sharon Wooldridge, "Writing Respectfully: Person-First and Identity-First Language," National Institutes of Health, April 12, 2023, https://www.nih.gov/about-nih /what-we-do/science-health-public-trust/perspectiveswriting-respectfully-person-first -identity-first-language.

6. Minnesota Governor's Council on Developmental Disabilities, "Speak About People First Language," interview with Kathie Snow, 2013, https://mn.gov/mnddc/kathie-snow /kathie-snow-15.html.

7. Anjali Forber-Pratt, "Say the Word," Public Health Post, February 19, 2020, https:// www.publichealthpost.org/research/say-the-word/.

8. Tiffany Yu, @ImTiffanyYu, Instagram, February 15, 2022, https://www.instagram .com/reel/CaA8ykYgN9W/.

9. National Center on Disability and Journalism, "Disability Language Style Guide," August 2021, https://ncdj.org/style-guide/.

10. Andrew Pulrang, "It's Time to Stop Even Casually Misusing Disability Words," *Forbes*, February 20, 2021, https://www.forbes.com/sites/andrewpulrang/2021/02/20/its-time -to-stop-even-casually-misusing-disability-words/.

11. Aubrey Blanche-Sarellano, LinkedIn, 2023, https://www.linkedin.com/posts /adblanche_disabled-ableism-lateralableism-activity-7020510397807960064-IdRV.

Chapter 4: Disability Is Not a Bad Thing

1. Julie Harris, LinkedIn, 2023, https://www.linkedin.com/posts/julie-a-harris_disability inclusion-disabilityawareness-autism-activity-7079126360136278019-6gvt/.

2. Linguistic Society of America, "Guidelines for Inclusive Language," https://www.lin guisticsociety.org/resource/guidelines-inclusive-language.

3. Sophie Morgan, *Driving Forwards: A Journey of Resilience and Empowerment After Life-Changing Injury* (New York: Little, Brown, 2023).

4. Catarina Rivera, @BlindishLatina, "Let's Get Rid of 'the Blind Leading the Blind,'" Instagram, June 6, 2023, https://www.instagram.com/p/CtJs3V7Pyi2/.

5. Leigh Weingus, "50 Glennon Doyle Quotes That Will Remind You That You Can Do Hard Things," Silk and Sonder, December 27, 2022, https://www.silkandsonder.com/blogs /news/glennon-doyle-quotes.

Chapter 5: A Brief History of the Disability Rights Movement

1. Carl Sagan, *Cosmos* (New York: Random House, 1980).

2. Southern Adirondack Independent Living, "A Brief Timeline of the History of Disabilities: The Shameful Treatment of People with Disabilities," *Sail On* blog, July 1, 2018, https://sailhelps.org/a-brief-timeline-of-the-history-of-disabilities-the-shameful-treat ment-of-people-with-disabilities/.

3. Paul Chambers, "Bethlem Royal Hospital: Why Did the Infamous Bedlam Asylum Have Such a Fearsome Reputation?," History Extra, 2020, https://www.historyextra.com /period/victorian/bethlem-royal-hospital-history-why-called-bedlam-lunatic-asylum/.

4. Historic England, "From Bethlehem to Bedlam—England's First Mental Institution," https://historicengland.org.uk/research/inclusive-heritage/disability-history/1050-1485 /from-bethlehem-to-bedlam/.

5. Jacob Waltuck, "Disabilities and Witch Trials," 14th Street Y, October 19, 2022, https://www.14streety.org/2022/10/19/disabilities-and-witch-trials/.

6. Southern Adirondack Independent Living, "A Brief Timeline of the History of Disabilities: The Shameful Treatment of People with Disabilities."

7. Minnesota Governor's Council on Developmental Disabilities, "Understanding and Progress," Parallels in Time: A History of Developmental Disabilities, https://mn.gov /mnddc/parallels/four/4a/1.html.

8. John Van Cleve and Barry Crouch, *A Place of Their Own: Creating the Deaf Community in America* (Washington, DC: Gallaudet University Press, 1989).

9. Minnesota Governor's Council on Developmental Disabilities, "Make the Deviant Undeviant," Parallels in Time: A History of Developmental Disabilities, https://mn .gov/mnddc/parallels/four/4b/1.html.

10. Jessica Lopez, "The History of Disabled People," How We Got to Now, July 20, 2021, https://www.howwegottonow.com/post/disability.

11. Susan M. Schweik, *The Ugly Laws: Disability in Public* (New York: New York University Press, 2009), https://www.english.upenn.edu/sites/www.english.upenn.edu/files/Schweik-Susan_Ugly-Laws_Law-Language.pdf.

12. Paul Longmore and Lauri Umansky, *The New Disability History: American Perspectives* (New York: New York University Press, 2001).

13. Charles Davenport, *Heredity in Relation to Eugenics* (New York: Henry Holt and Company, 1911), https://catalog.hathitrust.org/Record/001492130.

14. "The Supreme Court Ruling That Led to 70,000 Forced Sterilizations," *Fresh Air*, NPR, March 7, 2016, https://www.npr.org/sections/health-shots/2016/03/07/469478098/the-supreme-court-ruling-that-led-to-70-000-forced-sterilizations.

15. BP Perry, "Aktion T4: The Nazi Euthanasia Programme That Killed 300,000," History Channel, https://www.history.co.uk/article/aktion-t4-the-nazi-euthanasia-programme-that-killed-300000.

16. ADL Education, "A Brief History of the Disability Rights Movement," Anti-Defamation League, March 5, 2017, https://www.adl.org/resources/backgrounder/brief-history-disability-rights-movement.

17. Wage and Hour Division, "Fact Sheet #39: The Employment of Workers with Disabilities at Subminimum Wages," US Department of Labor, revised July 2008, https://www.dol.gov/agencies/whd/fact-sheets/39-14c-subminimum-wage.

18. Lillie Heigl, Kimberly Knackstedt, and Elena Silva, "Pennies on the Dollar: The Use of Subminimum Wage for Disabled Workers Across the United States," New America, February 14, 2024, https://www.newamerica.org/education-policy/reports/the-use-of-subminimum-wage-for-disabled-workers-across-the-us/.

19. ADL Education, "A Brief History of the Disability Rights Movement."

20. Julia Carmel, "Before the A.D.A., There Was Section 504," *New York Times*, July 22, 2020, https://www.nytimes.com/2020/07/22/us/504-sit-in-disability-rights.html.

21. Carmel.

22. Britta Shoot, "The 1977 Disability Rights Protest That Broke Records and Changed Laws," Atlas Obscura, November 9, 2017, https://www.atlasobscura.com/articles/504-sit-in-san-francisco-1977-disability-rights-advocacy.

23. "Judy Heumann (1947–2023)," Judy Heumann, https://judithheumann.com/project/about/.

24. Emma Olson, "January 23 Is Ed Roberts Day," Access Living, January 23, 2020, https://www.accessliving.org/newsroom/blog/ed-roberts-a-pioneer-for-equality/; National Park Service, "Ed Roberts," https://www.nps.gov/people/ed-roberts.htm.

25. Ability Center, "Ed Roberts (1939–1995)," https://abilitycenter.org/ed-roberts-1939-1995/.

26. "Events Leading Up to DPN," Gallaudet University, https://gallaudet.edu/museum/history/the-deaf-president-now-dpn-protest/events-leading-up-to-dpn/.

27. Lopez, "The History of Disabled People."

28. Stephanie Woodward, "A Short History of Justin Dart, Jr., 'Father' of the ADA," Center for Disability Rights, 2010, https://cdrnys.org/blog/advocacy/a-short-history -of-justin-dart-jr-father-of-the-ada/.

29. Lopez, "The History of Disabled People."

30. "March 12, 1990: Disability Rights Activists Make 'Capitol Crawl' for the ADA," Zinn Education Project, https://www.zinnedproject.org/news/tdih/capitol-crawl-for-ADA/.

31. ADL Education, "A Brief History of the Disability Rights Movement."

32. ADL Education.

33. Matt Gonzales, "Record Number of Lawsuits Filed over Accessibility for People with Disabilities," Society for Human Resource Management, March 23, 2022, https://www .shrm.org/resourcesandtools/hr-topics/behavioral-competencies/global-and-cultural -effectiveness/pages/record-number-of-lawsuits-filed-over-accessibility-for-people -with-disabilities.aspx.

34. "Frequently Asked Questions Regarding the Convention on the Rights of Persons with Disabilities," United Nations Department of Economic and Social Affairs, https://www .un.org/development/desa/disabilities/convention-on-the-rights-of-persons-with-disabilities /frequently-asked-questions-regarding-the-convention-on-the-rights-of-persons-with -disabilities.html.

35. "Background of the Convention: Committee on the Rights of Persons with Disabilities," United Nations Human Rights Office of the High Commissioner, https://www.ohchr.org /en/treaty-bodies/crpd/background-convention.

36. "The Movement for Disability Rights and Justice," American Association of People with Disabilities, https://www.aapd.com/movement/.

37. "Frida Kahlo's 6 Disability Themed Paintings," Disability Rights Florida, July 6, 2022, https://disabilityrightsflorida.org/blog/entry/Frida_Khalos_6_Disability_Themed _Paintings.

38. "The Movement for Disability Rights and Justice."

39. Haben Girma, "Hey, Texas. Students Need to Learn About Helen Keller. Don't Remove Her," *Washington Post*, September 19, 2018, https://www.washingtonpost.com /opinions/hey-texas-students-need-to-learn-about-helen-keller-dont-remove-her /2018/09/19/e8b85d3a-bb76-11e8-bdc0-90f81cc58c5d_story.html.

Chapter 6: Models of Disability

1. Anitra Rowe Schulte, "Models of Disability," The Nora Project, July 21, 2022, https:// the noraproject.ngo/nora-notes-blog/models-of-disability-1.

2. Keagan Stoyles, "Models of Disability and How They Impact Teaching," Facing Canada, May 19, 2022, https://facingcanada.facinghistory.org/models-of-disability.

3. Accessible Education Center, "Medical and Social Models of Disability," University of Oregon, https://aec.uoregon.edu/content/medical-and-social-models-disability.

4. Susan Lacke, "The History and Evolution of Disability Models," Accessibility .com, January 15, 2021, https://www.accessibility.com/blog/the-history-and-evolution -of-disability-models.

5. Lacke.

6. Diversability, @Diversability, "Models of Disability," Instagram, January 29, 2022, https://www.instagram.com/p/CZVE8RcPl58/.

7. "Models of Disability: An Overview," Mobility International USA, https://www .miusa.org/resource/tip-sheets/disabilitymodels/.

8. "Models of Disability: Types and Definitions," Disabled World, September 10, 2010, https://www.disabled-world.com/definitions/disability-models.php.

9. "Spotlight on Resources—2024 Edition," Social Security Administration, 2024, https://www.ssa.gov/ssi/spotlights/spot-resources.htm.

10. "Models of Disability: Types and Definitions."

11. Puneet Singh Singhal, email interview with the author, January 24, 2024.

12. Dr. Amy Kenny, email interview with the author, January 29, 2024.

13. "What Are Models of Disability," Christian Blind Mission, https://participation.cbm .org/why/disability-participation/models-of-disability.

14. David Brindle, "Mike Oliver Obituary," *Guardian*, March 19, 2019, https://www .theguardian.com/society/2019/mar/19/mike-oliver-obituary.

15. "Social Model of Disability," Foundation for People with Learning Disabilities, https://www.learningdisabilities.org.uk/learning-disabilities/a-to-z/s/social-model-disability.

16. Lacke, "The History and Evolution of Disability Models."

17. "Convention on the Rights of Persons with Disabilities," United Nations, https:// www.un.org/development/desa/disabilities/convention-on-the-rights-of-persons-with -disabilities/convention-on-the-rights-of-persons-with-disabilities-2.html.

18. "Introducing the Human Rights Model of Disability," Disability Advocacy Resource Unit, https://www.daru.org.au/how-we-talk-about-disability-matters/introducing-the -human-rights-model-of-disability.

19. "Promoting the Rights of Persons with Disabilities," Bureau of Democracy, Human Rights, and Labor, US Department of State, January 20, 2021, https://www.state.gov/promo ting-the-rights-of-persons-with-disabilities/.

20. John Swain and Sally French, "Towards an Affirmation Model of Disability," *Disability & Society* 15, no. 4 (June 2000): 569–582, https://doi.org/10.1080/09687590050058189.

21. David Wasserman and Sean Aas, "Disability: Definitions and Models," *Stanford Encyclopedia of Philosophy*, December 16, 2011, https://plato.stanford.edu/entries /disability/.

22. Amy Carney, "6 Theoretical Models of Disability," *100 Days of A11y*, November 8, 2019, https://100daysofa11y.com/2019/11/08/theoretical-models-of-disability/.

23. Paul K. Longmore Institute on Disability, "San Francisco Disability Community Cultural Center: Final Report," San Francisco Department of Aging and Adult Services, May 2019,

https://www.sfhsa.org/sites/default/files/media/document/migrated/Report_Disability%20
Community%20Cultural%20Center%20Public%20Report_May%202019.pdf.

Chapter 7: Disability Intersectionality

1. Kimberlé W. Crenshaw, "Demarginalizing the Intersection of Race and Sex: A Black Feminist Critique of Antidiscrimination Doctrine, Feminist Theory and Antiracist Politics," *University of Chicago Legal Forum* 139 (1989): 149.

2. Microsoft Enable, "Disability Intersectionality: At a Glance," YouTube, 2022, https://www.youtube.com/watch?v=L9dCkPALlhQ&feature=youtu.be.

3. Grace Tsao, "Guest Blog Post: Growing Up Asian American with a Disability by Grace Tsao," *Disability Visibility Project*, February 21, 2016, https://disabilityvisibility project.com/2016/02/21/guest-blog-post-growing-up-asian-american-with-a-disability -by-grace-tsao/.

4. Koko Nishi, "Mental Health Among Asian-Americans," American Psychological Association, 2012, https://www.apa.org/pi/oema/resources/ethnicity-health/asian -american/article-mental-health.

5. "Why Asian Americans Don't Seek Help for Mental Illness," Mass General Brigham McLean, May 2, 2023, https://www.mcleanhospital.org/essential/why-asian-americans -dont-seek-help-mental-illness.

6. Wendy Lu, "What It's Like Being Disabled and Asian in America," *Huffington Post*, May 24, 2019, https://www.huffpost.com/entry/disability-asian-americans-immigrants -stigma_n_5cd1c2c7e4b0548b7360bf26.

7. Mia Ives-Rublee, July 17, 2020, Facebook, https://www.facebook.com/SeeMia Roll/posts/pfbid0Bdp87f263kK8mw8Gqa2BtjSfGA7UXK3rJWMqxArdEf9D9nrL6cLDWr BUXyrW1T4Gl.

8. "Understanding Disability in the LGBTQ+ Community," HRC Foundation, August 12, 2022, https://www.hrc.org/resources/understanding-disabled-lgbtq-people.

9. "LGBT People with Disabilities," Movement Advancement Project, Center for American Progress, National Center for Lesbian Rights, National LGBTQ Taskforce, https://www.lgbtmap.org/file/LGBT-People-With-Disabilities.pdf.

10. Yema Yang, email interview with the author, January 25, 2024.

11. Yang.

12. "Identity and Cultural Dimension: Hispanic/Latinx," National Alliance on Mental Illness, https://www.nami.org/Your-Journey/Identity-and-Cultural-DimensionsHispanic-Latinx.

13. Dior Vargas, email interview with the author, January 30, 2024.

14. "Adults with Disabilities: Ethnicity and Race," Centers for Disease Control and Prevention, last reviewed September 16, 2020, https://www.cdc.gov/ncbddd/disabilityand health/materials/infographic-disabilities-ethnicity-race.html.

15. Keri Gray, email interview with the author, January 29, 2024.

16. Gray.

17. Ronnie Cohen, "Young People with Disabilities More Likely to Be Arrested," Reuters, November 10, 2017, https://www.reuters.com/article/us-health-disabilities-law-enforce ment/young-people-with-disabilities-more-likely-to-be-arrested-idUSKBN1DA2SZ.

18. Dr. E. Faye Williams, "Autism Awareness Month—Remembering Elijah McClain," Seattle Medium, April 5, 2021, https://seattlemedium.com/autism-awareness-month-remem bering-elijah-mcclain/.

19. Vilissa Thompson, "Understanding the Policing of Black, Disabled Bodies," Center for American Progress, February 10, 2021, https://www.americanprogress.org/article /understanding-policing-black-disabled-bodies/.

20. Abigail Abrams, "Black, Disabled and at Risk: The Overlooked Problem of Police Violence Against Americans with Disabilities," Time, June 25, 2020, https://time.com /5857438/police-violence-black-disabled/.

21. Eric Harris, email interview with the author, January 18, 2024.

22. Patty Berne, "Disability Justice—a Working Draft by Patty Berne," Sins Invalid, June 10, 2015, https://www.sinsinvalid.org/blog/disability-justice-a-working-draft-by-patty-berne.

23. Tiffany Yu, "It's Time to Recognize Climate Change as a Disability Rights Issue," Rooted in Rights, December 11, 2017, https://rootedinrights.org/its-time-to-recognize-cli mate-change-as-a-disability-rights-issue/.

24. "Disability Justice Is Climate Justice," Sins Invalid, July 7, 2022, https://www.sinsin valid.org/news-1/2022/7/7/disability-justice-is-climate-justice.

Chapter 8: What Is Ableism?

1. Lisa Diedrich, "Reading Notes: Ableism (A Brief History of the Emergence of a Term)," February 6, 2023, https://lisadiedrich.org/2023/02/06/reading-notes-ableism-a-brief -history-of-the-emergence-of-a-term/.

2. Jamie Shields, LinkedIn, 2023, https://www.linkedin.com/posts/shieldsjamie_social saturday-saturdayvibes-diversityandinclusion-activity-7027651534863626240-VgoK/.

3. Jamie Shields, email interview with the author, January 29, 2024.

4. Shields.

5. "Ableism," Merriam-Webster, https://www.merriam-webster.com/dictionary/ableism.

6. Diedrich, "Reading Notes."

7. Diedrich.

8. Talila A. Lewis, "Working Definition of Ableism—January 2022 Update," January 1, 2022, https://www.talilalewis.com/blog/working-definition-of-ableism-january-2022-update.

9. "What Is Ableism?," Disability & Philanthropy Forum, https://disabilityphilanthropy .org/resource/what-is-ableism/.

10. Rebecca Finkelstein, "What You Need to Know About Ableism," Diversability, August 20, 2020, https://mydiversability.com/blog/2020/8/20/what-you-need-to-know-about-ableism.

11. Joseph Shapiro, "One Man's COVID-19 Death Raises the Worst Fears of Many People with Disabilities," NPR, July 31, 2020, https://www.npr.org/2020/07/31/896882268 /one-mans-covid-19-death-raises-the-worst-fears-of-many-people-with-disabilities.

12. Toria Barnhart, "Disability Activist Dies After United Airlines Destroyed Her Custom Wheelchair," *Newsweek*, November 4, 2021, https://www.newsweek.com /disability-activist-dies-after-united-airlines-destroyed-her-custom-wheelchair-1646198.

13. Andrew Limbong, "Microaggressions Are a Big Deal: How to Talk Them Out and When to Walk Away," NPR, June 9, 2020, https://www.npr.org/2020/06/08/872371063 /microaggressions-are-a-big-deal-how-to-talk-them-out-and-when-to-walk-away.

14. "What Are Microaggressions?," Cleveland Clinic, February 2, 2022, https://health .clevelandclinic.org/what-are-microaggressions-and-examples/.

15. "Examples of Workplace Microaggressions and How to Reduce Them," Baker College, February 23, 2021, https://www.baker.edu/about/get-to-know-us/blog /examples-of-workplace-microaggressions-and-how-to-reduce-them/#microassaults.

16. "Welcome to Casual Ableism," Casual Ableism, http://casualableism.com.

17. Eric Harris, email interview with the author, January 18, 2024.

18. Becca Lory Hector, email interview with the author, January 22, 2024.

19. Catarina Rivera, email interview with the author, January 22, 2024.

20. "Microaggressions—What Are They and How Do They Cause Harm?," disAbility Law Center of Virginia, February 28, 2023, https://www.dlcv.org/microaggressions.

21. "Internalized Oppression," Anti-Racism Daily, https://the-ard.com/glossary/interna lized-oppression/.

22. Andrew Pulrang, "5 New Year's Resolutions for People with Disabilities," *Forbes*, December 31, 2020, https://www.forbes.com/sites/andrewpulrang/2021/12/31/5 -new-years-resolutions-for-people-with-disabilities-1/.

23. Fannie Lou Hamer, "'Nobody's Free Until Everybody's Free': Speech Delivered at the Founding of the National Women's Political Caucus, Washington, D.C., July 10, 1971," in *The Speeches of Fannie Lou Hamer: To Tell It Like It Is*, ed. Maegan Parker Brooks and Davis W. Houck (Jackson: University Press of Mississippi, 2010).

Chapter 9: What Is Anti-Ableism?

1. Ibram X. Kendi, *How to Be an Antiracist* (New York: One World, 2019).

2. "Anti-Ableism," Salem State University, https://libguides.salemstate.edu/anti-oppres sion/anti-ableism.

3. Talila A. Lewis, "Working Definition of Ableism—January 2022 Update," January 1, 2022, https://www.talilalewis.com/blog/working-definition-of-ableism-january-2022-update.

4. Liz Jackson, "We Are the Original Lifehackers," *New York Times*, May 30, 2018, https://www.nytimes.com/2018/05/30/opinion/disability-design-lifehacks.html.

Notes

Chapter 10: Why You Should Care About Disability

1. Tiffany Yu, "Reimagine Georgetown: Diversability," November 17, 2009, https://ytiffa.wordpress.com/2009/11/17/reimagine-georgetown-diversability/.

2. Ardra Shephard, "How to Be Proud of What's Broken This Disability Pride," *Tripping on Air*, July 12, 2020, https://trippingonair.com/2020/07/how-to-be-proud-of-whats-broken-this-disability-pride.html.

3. "Mayor Breed Proclaims July Disability Pride Month in San Francisco," Mayor's Office of Disability, City and County of San Francisco, https://sfgov.org/mod/node/964.

4. "Mayor Breed Proclaims July Disability Pride Month in San Francisco."

5. "Disability," World Health Organization, March 7, 2023, https://www.who.int/news-room/fact-sheets/detail/disability-and-health.

6. Catherine A. Okoro, NaTasha D. Hollis, Alissa C. Cyrus, and Shannon Griffin-Blake, "Prevalence of Disabilities and Health Care Access by Disability Status and Type Among Adults—United States, 2016," *Morbidity and Mortality Weekly Report* 67, no. 32 (August 2018): 882–887, http://dx.doi.org/10.15585/mmwr.mm6732a3.

7. "Factsheet on Persons with Disabilities," United Nations, https://www.un.org/development/desa/disabilities/resources/factsheet-on-persons-with-disabilities.html.

8. "Disability Stats and Facts," Disability Funders Network, https://www.disabilityfunders.org/disability-stats-and-facts.

9. Kathy Katella, "What Happens When You Still Have Long COVID Symptoms?," Yale Medicine, June 7, 2023, https://www.yalemedicine.org/news/long-covid-symptoms.

10. USAFacts Team, "How Many People Have Long COVID?," December 4, 2023, USAFacts, https://usafacts.org/articles/how-many-people-have-long-covid/.

11. David A. Taylor, "She's Considered the Mother of Disability Rights—and She's a 'Badass,'" *Washington Post*, May 25, 2021, https://www.washingtonpost.com/lifestyle/magazine/judy-heuman-crip-camp-film-rights-pioneer/2021/05/21/d3ab3fa6-b278-11eb-a980-a60af976ed44_story.html.

12. Molly Burke, @MollyBurkeOfficial, "Reminder to Care About the Disabled Community Regardless If You Are Disabled or Not," TikTok, July 11, 2023, https://www.tiktok.com/@mollyburkeofficial/video/7254680395218701611.

13. The Try Guys, "Why Don't We Care About Disabled People?," YouTube, June 4, 2022, https://www.youtube.com/watch?v=k8QmBmcXetg.

14. Michelle MiJung Kim, LinkedIn, 2021, https://www.linkedin.com/posts/mjmichellekim_diversity-equity-inclusion-activity-6803753279194046464-061T.

Chapter 11: Recognize and Use Your Privilege

1. "Ableism and Non-disabled Privilege," Explore Access, University of Arkansas—Partners for Inclusive Communities, https://exploreaccess.org/disability-as-diversity-postsecondary/ableism-and-non-disabled-privilege/.

275

2. As/Is, "What Is Privilege?," YouTube, July 4, 2015, https://youtu.be/hD5f8GuNu GQ?si=5l2KYltDjdjpwPRP.

3. Lydia X. Z. Brown, "Autistic Hoya's Brief Abled Privilege Checklist," https://autist ichoya.files.wordpress.com/2016/03/brief-abled-privilege-checklist-mar-2016.pdf.

4. Arlan Hamilton, *It's About Damn Time: How to Turn Being Underestimated into Your Greatest Advantage* (New York: Currency, 2020).

5. Gina Crosley-Corcoran, "Explaining White Privilege to a Broke White Person...," Duke University School of Medicine, February 2022, https://medschool.duke.edu/sites /default/files/2022-02/explaining_white_privilege_to_a_broke_white_person.pdf.

6. "What Is Privilege?," United Way for Southeastern Michigan, 2021, https://unitedway sem.org/equity_challenge/day-3-what-is-privilege/.

7. Andrew Pulrang, "4 Ways People with Disabilities Can Have Privilege Too," *Forbes*, January 25, 2023, https://www.forbes.com/sites/andrewpulrang/2023/01/25/4 -ways-people-with-disabilities-can-have-privilege-too/.

8. Ijeoma Oluo, *So You Want to Talk About Race* (New York: Seal Press, 2018).

Chapter 12: Overcome Your Non-Disabled Guilt and Shame

1. "The Anatomy of White Guilt," Unitarian Universalist Association, https://www.uua .org/files/documents/gardinerwilliam/whiteness/anatomy_white_guilt.pdf.

2. Letty M. Russell, Kwok Pui-lan, Ada Maria Isasi-Diaz, and Katie Geneva Cannon, *Inheriting Our Mothers' Gardens: Feminist Theology in Third World Perspective* (Philadelphia: Westminster John Knox Press, 1988).

3. Ali Pattillo, "White Shame: How to Convert Guilt into Action," Inverse, June 17, 2020, https://www.inverse.com/mind-body/white-shame-anti-racism-efforts.

4. Pattillo.

5. Lily Zheng, LinkedIn, 2023, https://www.linkedin.com/posts/lilyzheng308_diversity -equity-inclusion-activity-7062468852797894656-NQHd.

6. Pattillo, "White Shame."

7. bell hooks and Amalia Mesa-Bains, *Homegrown: Engaged Cultural Criticism* (Boston: South End Press, 2006).

Chapter 13: Accurate Disability Representation Matters

1. "Disability Impacts All of Us," Centers for Disease Control and Prevention, https:// www.cdc.gov/ncbddd/disabilityandhealth/infographic-disability-impacts-all.html.

2. "Disability Inclusion," World Bank, https://www.worldbank.org/en/topic/disability.

3. Annenberg Inclusion Initiative, "Inequality in 1,300 Popular Films: Examining Portrayals of Gender, Race/Ethnicity, LGBTQ & Disability from 2007 to 2019," USC Annenberg, September 8, 2020, https://assets.uscannenberg.org/docs/aii-inequality_1300 _popular_films_09-08-2020.pdf.

4. "Seen on Screen: The Importance of Disability Representation," Nielsen, December 2022, https://www.nielsen.com/insights/2022/the-importance-of-disability-representation/.

5. Tanushree Kochar, "Out of Sight, Out of Mind: Why (Accurate) Disability Representation Matters," Young Leaders of Global Health, https://sites.duke.edu/ylghc /projects/newsletter/issue12-december-2021/out-of-sight-out-of-mind-why-accurate-disability -representation-matters/.

6. Cara Buckley, "Scary Is How You Act, Not Look, Disability Advocates Tell Filmmakers," *New York Times*, November 17, 2020, https://www.nytimes.com/2020/11/17/movies /witches-movie-disability.html.

7. Dr. Hanna Shaul Bar Nissim and RJ Mitte, "Authentic Representation in Television 2018," Ruderman Family Foundation, February 2020, https://rudermanfoundation.org /white_papers/the-ruderman-white-paper-on-authentic-representation-in-tv/.

8. William Heisel, "Time for Hollywood to Make Disabilities More Than Just Oscar Material," USC Annenberg, February 7, 2020, https://centerforhealthjournalism.org /our-work/insights/time-hollywood-make-disabilities-more-just-oscar-material.

9. Patrick Hayes, "The Inspiring Stories of the Only Three Disabled Actors to Have Won Oscars," Movie Web, February 15, 2023, https://movieweb.com/inspiring -stories-disabled-actors-oscars/.

10. McKinley Franklin, "Inevitable Foundation and WME Announce Partnership to Expand Opportunities for Disabled Writers," *Variety*, March 29, 2023, https://variety .com/2023/film/news/inevitable-foundation-wme-disabled-writers-1235567934/.

11. Vilissa Thompson, "'Nothing About Us Without Us'—Disability Representation in Media," Center for Disability Rights, https://cdrnys.org/blog/disability-dialogue/nothing -about-us-without-us-disability-representation-in-media/.

12. Matthew Von Der Ahe and Kennedy Garcia, email interview with the author, January 23, 2024.

13. Gabby Gonta, Shannon Hansen, Clair Fagin, and Jennevieve Fong, "Changing Media and Changing Minds: Media Exposure and Viewer Attitudes Toward Homosexuality," *Pepperdine Journal of Communication Research* 5, article 5 (2017), https://digitalcommons .pepperdine.edu/pjcr/vol5/iss1/5.

14. "Academy Establishes Representation and Inclusion Standards for Oscars Eligibility," Oscars, September 8, 2020, https://www.oscars.org/news/academy-establishes-repre sentation-and-inclusion-standards-oscarsr-eligibility.

15. Sebastian Cortez, "Degree Deodorant Launches #TrainersforHire Campaign to Challenge Fitness Industry After 81% of People with Disabilities Say They Do Not Feel Welcome in Fitness Spaces," Degree, September 20, 2021, https://www.prnewswire.com/news-releases /degree-deodorant-launches-trainersforhire-campaign-to-challenge-fitness-industry-after-81 -of-people-with-disabilities-say-they-do-not-feel-welcome-in-fitness-spaces-301380445.html.

16. Willyanne DeCormier Plosky, Ari Ne'eman, Benjamin C. Silverman, David H. Strauss, Leslie P. Francis, Michael A. Stein, and Barbara E. Bierer, "Excluding People with Disabilities from Clinical Research: Eligibility Criteria Lack Clarity and Justification,"

Health Affairs 41, no. 10 (October 2022), https://www.healthaffairs.org/doi/10.1377/hlt haff.2022.00520.

17. Frank Stephens, "I Am a Man with Down Syndrome and My Life Is Worth Living," Real Clear Politics, September 2017, https://www.realclearpolitics.com/video/2017/10/31 /frank_stephens_i_am_a_man_with_down_syndrome_and_my_life_is_worth_living.html.

18. Travis Reginal, "Providing Better Support to Students of Color: The Importance of School Climate, Belonging, and Well-Being," Urban Institute, February 11, 2021, https://www .urban.org/research/publication/providing-better-support-students-color-importance -school-climate-belonging-and-well-being.

19. Halle Kiefer, "*Oklahoma!*'s Ali Stroker Becomes First Wheelchair-Using Performer to Take Home a Tony," *Vulture*, June 10, 2019, https://www.vulture.com/2019/06/2019-tony -awards-ali-stroker-acceptance-speech.html.

20. Frank Rizzo, "'How to Dance in Ohio' Review: Musical About Autistic Young Adults Is a Touching Broadway First," *Variety*, December 10, 2023, https://variety.com/2023/legit /reviews/how-to-dance-in-ohio-review-broadway-musical-1235832602/.

21. "Where Is the Diversity in Publishing? The 2019 Diversity Baseline Survey Results," Lee & Low Books, January 28, 2020, https://blog.leeandlow.com/2020/01/28/2019diversity baselinesurvey/.

22. JoAnn Yao, "Q&A with Alice Wong, Disability Visibility: 17 First Person Stories for Today (Adapted for Young Adults)," We Need Diverse Books, October 26, 2021, https://diverse books.org/qa-with-alice-wong-disability-visibility/.

23. Currie Engle, "How a Community of TikTokers Is Debunking Disability, One Viral Video at a Time," *Women's Health*, July 26, 2022, https://www.womenshealthmag.com/life /a40541814/disability-tiktok-creators/.

24. Jared Duval, Ferran Altarriba Bertran, Siying Chen, Melissa Chu, Divya Subramo- nian, Austin Wang, Geoffrey Xiang, Sri Kurniawan, and Katherine Isbister, "Chasing Play on TikTok from Populations with Disabilities to Inspire Playful and Inclusive Technology Design," *Proceedings of the 2021 CHI Conference on Human Factors in Computing Systems* (May 2021), https://dl.acm.org/doi/abs/10.1145/3411764.3445303.

25. Tiffany Yu, @ImTiffanyYu, and Nicola Swann, @Made.With.Mud, "Part 228," Insta- gram, May 21, 2023, https://www.instagram.com/reel/Csh-6JSot4e/.

26. "With Limited Inclusive Content in Traditional Media, Brands and People with Disabilities Are Finding Representation on Social Media," Nielsen, July 2023, https://www .nielsen.com/insights/2023/with-limited-inclusive-content-in-traditional-media-brands -and-people-with-disabilities-are-finding-representation-on-social-media/.

27. "With Limited Inclusive Content in Traditional Media."

28. "Visibility of Disability: Portrayals of Disability in Advertising," Nielsen, August 2021, https://www.nielsen.com/insights/2021/visibility-of-disability-portrayals-of-disability -in-advertising/.

29. Gus Alexiou, "Advertising Industry Must Overcome Its Anxiety Around Disability Representation," *Forbes*, July 26, 2021, https://www.forbes.com/sites/gusalexiou/2021/07/26 /advertising-industry-must-overcome-its-anxiety-around-disability-representation/.

30. Maliha Shoaib, "The Year Fashion Backtracked on Diversity," *Vogue Business*, December 18, 2023, https://www.voguebusiness.com/story/fashion/the-year-fashion-back tracked-on-diversity-equity-inclusion.

31. Stephanie Thomas, email interview with the author, January 30, 2024.

32. "With Limited Inclusive Content in Traditional Media."

33. "With Limited Inclusive Content in Traditional Media."

34. "Insight from Nielsen: New Research Shows That Disability-Inclusive Content Is Smart Business," Geena Davis Institute on Gender in Media, September 5, 2023, https://see jane.org/spotlight/insight-from-nielsen-new-research-shows-that-disability-inclusive -content-is-smart-business/.

35. Alexiou, "Advertising Industry Must Overcome Its Anxiety Around Disability Representation."

36. "How Stories About Disability Help Create Empathy," We Need Diverse Books, August 28, 2019, https://diversebooks.org/how-stories-about-disability-help-create-empathy/.

Chapter 14: Diversify Your Feed

1. Siobhán Kangataran, "Diversify Your Feed," LinkedIn, March 15, 2022, https://www .linkedin.com/pulse/diversify-your-feed-siobh%C3%A1n-kangataran/.

2. Kendra Cherry, "Mere Exposure Effect: How Familiarity Breeds Attraction," Very-well Mind, April 26, 2023, https://www.verywellmind.com/mere-exposure-effect-7368184.

3. Pablo Barberá, John T. Jost, Jonathan Nagler, Joshua A. Tucker, and Richard Bon-neau, "Tweeting from Left to Right: Is Online Political Communication More Than an Echo Chamber?," *Association for Psychological Science* 26, no. 10 (August 21, 2015), https://doi.org /10.1177/0956797615594.

4. Jessica Sauge Rauchberg, "TikTok's Digital Eugenics: Challenging Ableism and Algo-rithm Erasure Through Disability Activism," *Flow*, September 28, 2020, https://www.flow journal.org/2020/09/tiktok-digital-eugenics/.

5. Rauchberg.

6. Lauren Freedman, email interview with the author, January 24, 2024.

Chapter 15: Interrupt Ableist Microaggressions and Harassment

1. "Understanding Microaggressions: 7 Examples and How to Reduce Them," Fierce, https://www.fierceinc.com/understanding-microaggressions-7-examples-and-how-to -reduce-them/.

2. Tiffany Yu, "The Power of Exclusion | Tiffany Yu | TEDxBethesda," YouTube, April 4, 2018, https://youtu.be/qVtDejw8ZBw?si=SnvCxNLT3eai8L9x.

3. Becca Lory Hector, LinkedIn, February 21, 2023, https://www.linkedin.com /posts/beccaloryhector_trulyinclusiveleadership-disabilityinclusion-activity-703378259 1971352576-g2nZ/.

4. Dr. Rebecca Eunmi Haslam, "Interrupting Bias: Calling Out vs. Calling In," Seed the Way, http://www.seedtheway.com/uploads/8/8/0/0/8800499/calling_in_calling_out__3_.pdf.

5. Haslam.

6. Laura Zornosa, "Anne Hathaway Apologizes for Her Character in 'The Witches,'" *Los Angeles Times*, November 6, 2020, https://www.latimes.com/entertainment-arts/mov ies/story/2020-11-06/anne-hathaway-apologizes-disability-community-the-witches -character.

7. Anne Hathaway, @AnneHathaway, Instagram, November 5, 2020, https://www.insta gram.com/tv/CHOGW7JlpRv/.

8. Danielle Connolly, email interview with the author, January 25, 2024.

9. Imani Barbarin, "The Pandemic Tried to Break Me, but I Know My Black Disabled Life Is Worthy," *Cosmopolitan*, March 11, 2022, https://www.cosmopolitan.com/enter tainment/a39355245/imani-barbarin-black-disabled-activist-self-love/.

10. "Letter from the Disability Community to CDC Director Rochelle Walensky," Disability Rights Education & Defense Fund, January 13, 2022, https://dredf.org/2022/01/13 /letter-from-the-disability-community-to-cdc-director-rochelle-walensky/.

11. Paul Farhi, "A Rochelle Walensky Interview Sparked Outrage. But the CDC Says ABC Omitted Crucial Context," *Washington Post*, January 12, 2020, https://www.washing tonpost.com/lifestyle/media/walensky-abc-interview/2022/01/12/b5744ad4-73be-11ec-bc 13-18891499c514_story.html.

12. Brian Anderson, LinkedIn, 2023, https://www.linkedin.com/posts/briananderson 80_allyship-dadlife-dei-activity-7047243588816015360-eVdX.

13. Emily May, "Bystander Intervention: A Promising New Trend in Addressing Workplace Harassment," Medium, May 25, 2021, https://emilymaynot.medium.com /bystander-intervention-a-promising-new-trend-in-addressing-workplace-harassment -b3f7102d5348.

14. United Brachial Plexus Network, @UBPN_Official, Instagram, October 16, 2022, https://www.instagram.com/p/CjyKu6st-Lz/.

15. Jennifer Chassman Browne, email interview with the author, January 29, 2024.

16. Better Allies, "Be a Better Ally with These Clever Responses to Microaggressions," Medium, May 3, 2019, https://betterallies.medium.com/be-a-better-ally-with-these-clever -responses-to-microaggressions-3f1ec3c1ee27.

17. Better Allies.

18. "Bystander Effect," *Psychology Today*, https://www.psychologytoday.com/us /basics/bystander-effect.

19. "Bystander Effect."

20. "Bystander Approaches—When You're a Witness to, or Know About, an Assault," University of New England, https://www.une.edu.au/connect/respect-now-always/helpful -or-hurtful-bystander.

21. "The 5Ds of Bystander Intervention," Right to Be, https://righttobe.org/guides /bystander-intervention-training/.

22. "Harm Reduction: 6D's of Bystander Intervention," Bass Coast, https://basscoast .ca/blogs/news/safe-coast-6-ds-of-bystander-intervention.

23. "Harm Reduction."

24. Sophia Graham, "Bystander Roles for Disability Access," *Toward Access*, https://towardsaccess.com/homepage/bystander/.

25. Graham.

26. Aubrey Blanche-Sarellano, email interview with the author, January 28, 2024.

Chapter 16: Stop Making Assumptions

1. Tiffany Yu, "The Power of Exclusion | Tiffany Yu | TEDxBethesda," YouTube, April 4, 2018, https://youtu.be/qVtDejw8ZBw?si=BUWXysuu2uctaljF.

2. "Myths and Facts About People with Disabilities," Easterseals, https://www.easterseals.com/support-and-education/facts-about-disability/myths-facts.html.

3. Tiffany Yu, "How to Help Employees with Disabilities Thrive," TED, April 2023, https://www.ted.com/talks/tiffany_yu_how_to_help_employees_with_disabilities_thrive.

4. Allie Funk, "Don't 'Assume Competence,' Instead 'Assume Personhood,'" Medium, June 1, 2022, https://medium.com/@alliedfunk/dont-assume-competence-instead-assume-personhood-7e69cffcd8fa.

5. Meryl K. Evans, email interview with the author, January 18, 2024.

6. Mike Luckett, @MikeTheQuad, and Tiffany Yu, @ImTiffanyYu, Instagram, October 26, 2023, https://www.instagram.com/reel/Cy3RMa4LFsf/.

7. Meryl Evans, CPACC (deaf), LinkedIn, 2024, https://www.linkedin.com/posts/meryl_merylmots-disability-accessibility-activity-7143299014535360512-F-dw.

8. Tiffany Yu, @ImTiffanyYu, "Part 198," Instagram, September 17, 2022, https://www.instagram.com/reel/Cinn5iDgGpF/.

9. "Disability Etiquette—a Starting Guide," Disability:IN, https://disabilityin.org/resource/disability-etiquette/.

Chapter 17: Don't Give Unsolicited Advice

1. Dr. Amy Kenny, email interview with the author, January 29, 2024.

2. Meryl K. Evans, email interview with the author, January 18, 2024.

3. Jason Graham, "Dealing with Unsolicited Advice," Invisible Disabilities Association, https://invisibledisabilities.org/coping-with-invisible-disabilities/relationshipsunsolicited-advice/.

4. E Krebs, @SaltySicky, Twitter, June 6, 2021, https://twitter.com/saltysicky/status/1401399637563514883.

5. Russell Lehmann, @russl.co, and Tiffany Yu, @ImTiffanyYu, Instagram, September 23, 2023, https://www.instagram.com/reel/CxhXv-gO6C7/.

6. Sarah Blahovec, "Your Unsolicited Health Advice Isn't Just Irritating. It's Damaging," *Huffington Post*, June 29, 2017, https://www.huffpost.com/entry/your-unsolicited-health-advice-isnt-just-irritating_b_59554111e4b0326c0a8d0eaf.

7. Russell Lehmann, @russl.co, Instagram, December 14, 2023, https://www.instagram.com/p/C01wzUVRiRW/.

8. Graham, "Dealing with Unsolicited Advice."

Chapter 18: Support People with Non-Apparent Disabilities

1. Meryl K. Evans, email interview with the author, January 18, 2024.

2. Elena Keates, email interview with the author, January 29, 2024.

3. Puneet Singh Singhal, email interview with the author, January 24, 2024.

4. Christine Miserandino, "The Spoon Theory," But You Don't Look Sick, https://but youdontlooksick.com/articles/written-by-christine/the-spoon-theory/.

5. Miserandino.

6. Miserandino.

7. Thea Touchton, email interview with the author, January 23, 2024.

8. "Living with Non-Visible Disabilities," The Disability Unit, December 17, 2020, https://disabilityunit.blog.gov.uk/2020/12/17/living-with-non-visible-disabilities/.

9. Touchton, email interview.

10. Tiffany Yu, @ImTiffanyYu, Instagram, July 13, 2023, https://www.instagram.com /reel/CuqHUhaJoRJ/.

11. "Endometriosis: The Condition That Can Take over Seven Years to Diagnose," BBC, October 6, 2019, https://www.bbc.com/news/av/stories-49925760.

12. Made of Millions Team, "Made of Millions Tackles Youth Mental Health Treatment Gap with New Campaign, 'No One Told Me,'" Yahoo Life, May 3, 2020, https://www.yahoo .com/lifestyle/made-millions-tackles-youth-mental-003041084.html.

13. "7 Ways to Be More Inclusive of People with Invisible Disabilities," Hive Learning, https://www.hivelearning.com/resource/diversity-inclusion/invisible-disabilities/.

14. "Did You Know? Invisible Disabilities," Center for Disability Rights, https://cdrnys .org/blog/development/did-you-know-invisible-disabilities/.

15. "Hidden Disabilities: What Do the Sunflower Lanyards Mean?," Healthwatch: Wigan and Leigh, September 15, 2020, https://healthwatchwiganandleigh.co.uk/advice-and -information/2020-09-15/hidden-disabilities-what-do-sunflower-lanyards-mean.

16. Karen Schwartz, "Sunflowers Have a Hidden Meaning for Travelers with Disabilities," Washington Post, March 9, 2023, https://www.washingtonpost.com/travel/2023/03/09 /hidden-disabilities-sunflower-airports/.

17. "7 Ways to Be More Inclusive of People with Invisible Disabilities."

18. Chronicon—a Chronic Illness Community, @ChroniconOfficial, and TiffanyYu, @ImTiffanyYu, Instagram, October 23, 2022, https://www.instagram.com/reel/CkE_3ICpNg9/.

Chapter 19: Don't Treat Disabled People as Your Inspiration

1. Stella Young, "I'm Not Your Inspiration, Thank You Very Much," TED, April 2014, https://www.ted.com/talks/stella_young_i_m_not_your_inspiration_thank_you_very_much.

2. Young.

3. Emily Rapp, "Adventures of a Super Crip," The Alcalde, March 2, 2015, https:// medium.com/the-alcalde/adventures-of-a-super-crip-d94a17081df1.

4. Katherine Coble, "Your Excuse Is Invalid," Just Another Pretty Face, January 27, 2012, https://mycropht.wordpress.com/2012/01/27/your-excuse-is-invalid/.

5. Young, "I'm Not Your Inspiration, Thank You Very Much."

6. Scott Hamilton, @ScottHamilton84, Twitter, August 16, 2019, https://twitter.com/ScottHamilton84/status/1162414993805107200.

7. Young, "I'm Not Your Inspiration, Thank You Very Much."

8. "Beyoncé & the 'Beyhive' Help Fan with Cerebral Palsy Attend Concert," *Today*, September 24, 2023, https://www.today.com/video/beyonce-the-beyhive-help-fan-with-cerebal-palsy-attend-concert-193660485636.

9. Remy Tumin, "When He Missed a Beyoncé Concert, the Hive Went to Work," *New York Times*, September 22, 2023, https://www.nytimes.com/2023/09/21/us/beyonce-concert-wheelchair-plane.html.

10. Gil Kaufman, "Beyoncé Fan in Wheelchair Will 'Treasure' Kind Words, Hugs from Singer After Long Odyssey to Attend Houston Gig," *Billboard*, September 22, 2023, https://www.billboard.com/music/rb-hip-hop/beyonce-fan-wheelchair-airline-texas-concert-beyhive-help-1235418880/.

11. Lolo Spencer, @LiveSoloNow, Instagram, September 25, 2023, https://www.instagram.com/p/CxnxSLdR68o/.

12. Misfit Media, @MisfitMediaAgency, and Kelsey Lindell, @Kelsey_Lindell, Instagram, September 25, 2023, https://www.instagram.com/p/CxoSVMmJdWq/.

13. Tiffany Yu, @ImTiffanyYu, Instagram, January 7, 2021, https://www.instagram.com/reel/CJvsbd2J02_/.

14. Tiffany Yu, LinkedIn, 2023, https://www.linkedin.com/posts/tiffanyayu_ghc23-disabilityinclusion-accessibility-activity-7113557880515035136-rJrP/.

15. Katherine Harmon, "How Has Stephen Hawking Lived Past 70 with ALS?," *Scientific American*, January 7, 2012, https://www.scientificamerican.com/article stephen-hawking-als/.

Chapter 20: Be in Community with Disabled People

1. "Constitution," World Health Organization, https://www.who.int/about/accountability/governance/constitution.

2. ASH Media, "New Surgeon General Advisory Raises Alarm About the Devastating Impact of the Epidemic of Loneliness and Isolation in the United States," US Department of Health and Human Services, May 3, 2023, https://www.hhs.gov/about/news/2023/05/03/new-surgeon-general-advisory-raises-alarm-about-devastating-impact-epidemic-loneliness-isolation-united-states.html.

3. "'Nobody Likes Me': Understanding Loneliness and Self-shame," PsychAlive, https://www.psychalive.org/nobody-likes-me/.

4. Eric Emerson, Nicola Fortune, Gwynnyth Llewellyn, and Roger Stancliffe, "Loneliness, Social Support, Social Isolation and Wellbeing Among Working Age Adults with and Without Disability: Cross-Sectional Study," *Disability and Health Journal* 14, no. 1 (2021): 100965, https://doi.org/10.1016%2Fj.dhjo.2020.100965.

5. Erin Tatum, "Diversability Founder Tiffany Yu Launches a New Era of Disability Advocacy," *Cliché Mag*, February 7, 2023, https://clichemag.com/celebrity-news/interviews-celebrity-news/diversability-founder-tiffany-yu-launches-a-new-era-of-disability-advocacy/.

6. Maddie Crowley, "Disability History: The 1977 504 Sit-In," Disability Rights Florida, https://disabilityrightsflorida.org/blog/entry/504-sit-in-history.

7. Nitika Chopra, email interview with the author, January 29, 2024.

8. Marc Schulz and Robert Waldinger, "An 85-Year Harvard Study Found the No. 1 Thing That Makes Us Happy in Life: It Helps Us 'Live Longer,'" CNBC, February 10, 2023, https://www.cnbc.com/2023/02/10/85-year-harvard-study-found-the-secret-to-a-long -happy-and-successful-life.html.

9. Tatiana Figueiredo, "5 Tips for Turning Your Social Media Following into a Paid Membership Community," Buffer, November 14, 2023, https://buffer.com/resources /paid-membership-community/.

10. "Dr. Vivienne Ming: Unleashing the Potential of a Diverse Workforce," Domino, March 15, 2018, https://dominodatalab.wistia.com/medias/rjrdlfu6bh.

11. Yema Yang, email interview with the author, January 26, 2024.

12. Yang.

Chapter 21: Ask Better Questions

1. "Can an Employer Ask for Proof of Disability?," Mizrahi Kroub, September 9, 2022, https://www.mizrahikroub.com/blog/can-an-employer-ask-for-proof-of-disability.

2. Tiffany Yu, @ImTiffanyYu, "Day 89," Instagram, April 27, 2021, https://www.insta gram.com/reel/COLqfdqJLK_/.

3. Tiffany Yu, @ImTiffanyYu, "Day 159," Instagram, January 10, 2022, https://www .instagram.com/reel/CYj45ljJ5OH/.

4. Keely Cat-Wells, LinkedIn, 2022, https://www.linkedin.com/posts/keelycatwells _accessibility-mentalhealth-licreatoraccelerator-activity-6884248852304547841-zUmx.

5. Tiffany Yu, @ImTiffanyYu, "Day 160," January 12, 2022, https://www.instagram.com /reel/CYpVRoyJZ5s/.

6. "Raising an Ally to the Disability Community: A Guide to Building an Inclusive World," Save the Children, https://www.savethechildren.org/content/dam/usa/reports/cg 1840886-toolkit-international-day-persons-disabilities-2023updatev1.pdf.

7. Nancy DeVault, "How to Be a Disability Ally During Disability Pride Month," Ameridisability, July 12, 2023, https://www.ameridisability.com/how-to-be-a-disability -ally-during-disability-pride-month/.

8. Kelley Coleman, email interview with the author, January 28, 2024.

9. Tiffany Yu, @ImTiffanyYu, "Day 72," Instagram, March 30, 2021, https://www.instagram .com/reel/CNEZSebpVmV/.

10. Andrew Gurza, @AndrewGurza6, Instagram, February 20, 2021, https://www.insta gram.com/p/CLhXFuKjxf_/.

11. Gurza.

12. Tiffany Yu, @ImTiffanyYu, "Day 58," Instagram, March 10, 2021, https://www.insta gram.com/reel/CMP3QW6JBW9/.

13. Andrew Gurza, Instagram.

Chapter 22: Treat Disabled People with Respect and Dignity

1. "Protecting the Rights and Dignity of the Disabled and Mentally Ill," North Coast Community Homes, August 21, 2019, https://www.ncch.org/blog/2019/08/21/protecting-the-rights-and-dignity-of-the-disabled-and-mentally-ill.

2. Danielle Connolly, email interview with the author, January 25, 2024.

3. Kofi Annan, "In Larger Freedom: Towards Development, Security and Human Rights for All," United Nations, 2005, https://press.un.org/en/2005/ga10334.doc.htm.

4. "Universal Declaration of Human Rights," United Nations, December 10, 1948, https://www.un.org/en/about-us/universal-declaration-of-human-rights.

5. "Convention on the Rights of Persons with Disabilities," United Nations, https://www.un.org/development/desa/disabilities/convention-on-the-rights-of-persons-with-disabilities/convention-on-the-rights-of-persons-with-disabilities-2.html.

6. "Personal Outcome Measures: Measuring Personal Quality of Life," Council on Quality and Leadership, 2017, https://www.c-q-l.org/wp-content/uploads/2020/03/2017-CQL-POM-Manual-Adults.pdf.

7. Carli Friedman, "Being Respected Improves People with Disabilities' Quality of Life," The Council on Quality and Leadership, June 5, 2018, https://www.c-q-l.org/resources/articles/being-respected-improves-people-with-disabilities-quality-of-life/.

8. Friedman.

9. Catarina Rivera, email interview with the author, January 22, 2024.

10. Friedman, "Being Respected Improves People with Disabilities' Quality of Life."

11. "Protecting the Rights and Dignity of the Disabled and Mentally Ill."

12. "Protecting the Rights and Dignity of the Disabled and Mentally Ill."

13. Bella Webb, "Tommy Hilfiger Ramps Up Adaptive Fashion. Who's Next?," *Vogue Business*, March 22, 2021, https://www.voguebusiness.com/fashion/tommy-hilfiger-ramps-up-adaptive-fashion-whos-next.

14. Alden Habacon, "6 Ways You Can Support People with Disabilities," *Vancity*, September 21, 2017, https://blog.vancity.com/6-ways-can-support-people-disabilities/.

15. "Disability Etiquette: Treat Everyone with Respect," New York State Department of Health, https://www.health.ny.gov/publications/0951.pdf.

Chapter 23: Exist in the Contradictions

1. Thomas Lu and Sylvie Douglis, "Don't Be Scared to Talk About Disabilities. Here's What to Know and What to Say," NPR, February 22, 2022, https://www.npr.org/2022/02/18/1081713756/disability-disabled-people-offensive-better-word.

2. Amy Purdy, December 2, 2020, Facebook, https://www.facebook.com/AmyPurdyGurl/photos/a.10151978306490132/10158745643525132/.

3. Aubrey Blanche-Sarellano, LinkedIn, 2023, https://www.linkedin.com/posts/adblanche_disability-activity-7018304156331360256-Ta3B.

4. Link 20: Act Up for Inclusion, Facebook, February 6, 2018, https://www.facebook.com/Link20usa/photos/a.320496798361142/367368153674006.

5. Mia Mingus, "Access Intimacy: The Missing Link," *Leaving Evidence*, May 5, 2011, https://leavingevidence.wordpress.com/2011/05/05/access-intimacy-the-missing-link/.

6. Denise Hamilton, @OfficialDHam, Threads, 2024, https://www.threads.net/@officialdham/post/Cz4b1X0PKyG.

7. Mia Mingus, "How Our Communities Can Move Beyond Access to Wholeness," *Leaving Evidence*, February 12, 2011, https://leavingevidence.wordpress.com/2011/02/12/changing-the-framework-disability-justice/.

8. "6 Elements of Friendships in Online Communities," Business of Community, November 8, 2023, https://businessofcommunity.co/blog/6-elements-friendship.

Chapter 24: Take Accountability for Ableist Harm

1. Francisco Pallarés-Santiago, "6 Ways to Respectfully Be a Better LGBTQ Ally," *Oprah Daily*, June 27, 2019, https://www.oprahdaily.com/life/relationships-love/a28159555/how-to-be-lgbtq-ally/.

2. Soogia, @Soogia1, and Tiffany Yu, @ImTiffanyYu, TikTok, March 11, 2022, https://www.tiktok.com/@imtiffanyyu/video/7074019514114903338.

3. Spencer West, @Spencer2TheWest, TikTok, April 28, 2023, https://www.tiktok.com/@spencer2thewest/video/7227141182801923334.

4. Mia Mingus, "The Four Parts of Accountability & How to Give a Genuine Apology," *Leaving Evidence*, December 18, 2019, https://leavingevidence.wordpress.com/2019/12/18/how-to-give-a-good-apology-part-1-the-four-parts-of-accountability/.

5. Mingus.

6. Mingus.

Chapter 25: Lower the Disability Tax

1. "ETAC One-Handed Cutting Board 1 Hand Food Preparation with Rocker Knife," Walmart, https://www.walmart.com/ip/ETAC-One-Handed-Cutting-Board-1-Hand-Food-Preparation-With-Rocker-Knife/514784963.

2. Nanette Goodman, Zachary Morris, Michael Morris, and Stephen McGarity, "The Extra Costs of Living with a Disability in the U.S.—Resetting the Policy Table," National Disability Institute, October 2020, https://www.nationaldisabilityinstitute.org/wp-content/uploads/2020/10/extra-costs-living-with-disability-brief.pdf.

3. Eric Lauer, Sarah Boege, and Andrew Houtenville, "2019: Annual Disability Statistics Compendium," Institute on Disability, University of New Hampshire, 2020, https://files.eric.ed.gov/fulltext/ED605680.pdf.

4. Meredith Lilly, Audrey Laporte, and Peter Coyte, "Labor Market Work and Home Care's Unpaid Caregivers: A Systematic Review of Labor Force Participation Rates, Predictors of Labor Market Withdrawal, and Hours of Work," *Milbank Quarterly* 85, no. 4 (2007), https://doi.org/10.1111/j.1468-0009.2007.00504.x.

5. Becca Lory Hector, LinkedIn, 2023, https://www.linkedin.com/posts/beccaloryhector _disabilityinclusion-disabilityawareness-companyculture-activity-7054425083481657344--BOQ.

6. Hector.

7. Sara-Louise Ackrill, LinkedIn, 2023, https://www.linkedin.com/posts/sara-louise-ackrill -frsa-9490871b3_actuallyautistic-adhder-emotionalregulation-activity-708596240841378 2016-bdOh.

8. Jae Kennedy, Elizabeth Geneva Wood, and Lex Frieden, "Disparities in Insurance Coverage, Health Services Use, and Access Following Implementation of the Affordable Care Act: A Comparison of Disabled and Nondisabled Working-Age Adults," *Inquiry: The Journal of Health Care Organization, Provision, and Financing* 54 (November 2017), https://doi .org/10.1177/0046958017734031.

9. Goodman et al., "The Extra Costs of Living with a Disability in the U.S."

10. Goodman et al.

11. "Who Can Get SSI," Social Security Administration, https://www.ssa.gov/ssi /eligibility.

12. "Working While Disabled: How We Can Help," Social Security Administration, 2024, https://www.ssa.gov/pubs/EN-05-10095.pdf.

13. Neil Hughes, email interview with the author, January 23, 2024.

14. Goodman et al., "The Extra Costs of Living with a Disability in the U.S."

15. Rachel Litchman, "Navigation Anxiety: The Administrative Burdens of Being Poor and Disabled," Century Foundation, July 26, 2023, https://tcf.org/content/commentary /navigation-anxiety-the-administrative-burdens-of-being-poor-and-disabled/.

16. Litchman.

17. "Plan Benefits," CalABLE, https://calable.ca.gov/benefits.

18. Deepa Fernandes and Ashley Locke, "Asset Limits Are Just One Economic Hurdle People with Disabilities Face," WBUR, November 27, 2023, https://www.wbur.org /hereandnow/2023/11/27/disability-ssi-senate-bill.

19. Fernandes and Locke.

20. Hector, LinkedIn.

Chapter 26: Inclusive Design Benefits Everyone

1. Frank Greve, "Curb Ramps Liberate Americans with Disabilities—and Everyone Else," McClatchy, June 11, 2007, https://www.mcclatchydc.com/news/article24460762.html.

2. Angela Glover Blackwell, "The Curb-Cut Effect," *Stanford Social Innovation Review*, 2017, https://ssir.org/articles/entry/the_curb_cut_effect.

3. Liz Jackson, "We Are the Original Lifehackers," *New York Times*, May 30, 2018, https://www.nytimes.com/2018/05/30/opinion/disability-design-lifehacks.html.

4. Brandon Leip, "Journey Through Typewriter Evolution: From Inception to Modern Designs," Typewriters.com, October 13, 2022, https://typewriters.com/blogs/journey -through-typewriter-evolution-from-inception-to-modern-designs/.

5. "Jacuzzi Heritage," Jacuzzi, https://www.jacuzzi.com/en-gb/our-brand/heritage.html.

6. Valerie Liston, "Behind the Design: OXO's Iconic Good Grips Handles," OXO, January 31, 2017, https://www.oxo.com/blog/behind-the-scenes/behind-design -oxos-iconic-good-grips-handles.

7. Dr. Amy Kenny, email interview with the author, January 24, 2024.

8. Polly Trottenberg, "Protected Bicycle Lanes in NYC," New York City Department of Transportation, September 2014, https://www.nyc.gov/html/dot/downloads/pdf/2014-09 -03-bicycle-path-data-analysis.pdf.

9. "The Economic Benefits of Sustainable Streets," New York City Department of Trans-portation, January 13, 2014, https://www.nyc.gov/html/dot/downloads/pdf/dot-economic -benefits-of-sustainable-streets.pdf.

10. "WITH Workshops: Our 2020 Universal Design Symposium Goes Virtual," Side-bench, 2020, https://sidebench.com/universal-design-symposium-recap/.

11. David Gibson, "Why Website Accessibility Overlay Toolbars, Widgets & Plugins Fail Compliance," Accessibility.Works, updated January 19, 2024, https://www.accessibility .works/blog/avoid-accessibility-overlay-tools-toolbar-plugins/.

12. Michelle Putnam and Christine Bigby, eds., *Handbook on Ageing with Disability* (New York: Routledge, 2021), https://doi.org/10.4324/9780429465352.

13. Julio Madeira, "Microsoft Inclusive Design," Microsoft, July 17, 2020, https:// devblogs.microsoft.com/premier-developer/microsoft-inclusive-design/.

14. Jutta Treviranus, "The Three Dimensions of Inclusive Design: Part One," FWD50 on Medium, March 28, 2018, https://medium.com/fwd50/the-three-dimensions-of-inclu sive-design-part-one-103cad1ffdc2.

Chapter 27: Make Public Spaces Accessible (in Person and Digitally)

1. Keely Cat-Wells, LinkedIn, 2023, https://www.linkedin.com/posts/keelycatwells _representationmatters-accessibility-activity-7074370519206100994-eqR6/.

2. Alice Wong, Mia Mingus, and Sandy Ho, "Access Is Love: Suggested Actions: A Place to Start," Disability Intersectionality Summit, https://www.disabilityintersectionality summit.com/places-to-start/.

3. Wong, Mingus, and Ho.

4. Wong, Mingus, and Ho.

5. Mia Mingus, "Access Intimacy: The Missing Link," *Leaving Evidence*, May 5, 2011, https://leavingevidence.wordpress.com/2011/05/05/access-intimacy-the-missing-link/.

6. Sheri Byrne-Haber, LinkedIn, 2023, https://www.linkedin.com/posts/sheribyrneha ber_sheribyrnehaberquotes-accessibility-disability-activity-7143637409186959360-tkf8/.

7. Arielle Dance, "Making Your Events More Accessible," August 11, 2022, Diversabil-ity, https://mydiversability.com/blog/2022/8/10/making-your-events-more-accessible.

8. Dance.

9. "Access Suggestions for Public Events," Sins Invalid, June 8, 2020, https://www.sinsin valid.org/news-1/2020/6/8/access-suggestions-for-public-events.

10. Wong, Mingus, and Ho, "Access Is Love."

11. Wong, Mingus, and Ho.

12. Wong, Mingus, and Ho.

13. "Access Suggestions for Public Events."

14. "Access Suggestions for Public Events."

15. 1IN4 Coalition, @1in4coalition, Instagram, July 18, 2023, https://www.instagram.com/p/Cu21BpTpPHW/.

16. "Sensory Advisory Guide for How to Dance in Ohio," How to Dance in Ohio, December 6, 2023, https://howtodanceinohiomusical.com/wp-content/uploads/2023/12/Ohio-SAG-12.6.23.pdf.

17. Higher Priestess, @Higher_Priestess, Instagram, August 24, 2021, https://www.instagram.com/p/CS9U5IXrijY/.

18. Emma Grey Ellis, "The Problem with YouTube's Terrible Closed 'Craptions,'" *Wired*, October 1, 2019, https://www.wired.com/story/problem-with-youtubes-terrible-closed-craptions/.

19. Dance, "Making Your Events More Accessible."

20. Wong, Mingus, and Ho, "Access Is Love."

21. Meryl Evans, CPACC (deaf), LinkedIn, 2023, https://www.linkedin.com/posts/meryl_merylmots-gaad-accessibility-activity-7065008140747997184-AARD/.

22. Wong, Mingus, and Ho, "Access Is Love."

23. "Access Suggestions for Public Events."

Chapter 28: Hire Disabled People

1. "Article: Increasing Employment for People with Disabilities," Harkin Institute, 2018, https://harkininstitute.drake.edu/2020/01/27/article-increasing-employment-for-people-with-disabilities/.

2. Bureau of Labor Statistics, "News Release," US Department of Labor, February 23, 2023, https://www.bls.gov/news.release/pdf/disabl.pdf.

3. Mason Ameri, Lisa Schur, and Douglas Kruse, "As ADA Turns 30, People with Disabilities Still Last Hired, First Fired," *New York Daily News*, July 25, 2020, https://www.nydailynews.com/2020/07/25/as-ada-turns-30-people-with-disabilities-still-last-hired-first-fired/.

4. Rob Wile, "Employment Among People with Disabilities Hits Post-Pandemic High," NBC News, July 7, 2023, https://www.nbcnews.com/business/economy/jobs-for-people-with-disabilities-hit-new-post-pandemic-high-rcna93084.

5. Wile.

6. Brian Cheung and J. J. McCorvey, "Disabled Workforce Expands Thanks to the Job Boom—and Long Covid," NBC News, March 10, 2023, https://www.nbcnews.com/business/economy/disabled-workforce-expands-thanks-job-boom-long-covid-rcna72803.

7. Jolie Lee, "Fear Hinders Hiring People with Disabilities," Federal News Network, July 26, 2012, https://federalnewsnetwork.com/workforce/2012/07/fear-hinders-hiring-people-with-disabilities/.

8. Vegar Bjørnshagen and Elisabeth Ugreninov, "Disability Disadvantage: Experimental Evidence of Hiring Discrimination Against Wheelchair Users," *European Sociological Review* 37 (March 2021), http://dx.doi.org/10.1093/esr/jcab004.

9. "Persons with a Disability: Barriers to Employment and Other Labor-Related Issues News Release," US Bureau of Labor Statistics, March 30, 2022, https://www.bls.gov/news.release/archives/dissup_03302022.htm.

10. "Companies Leading in Disability Inclusion Have Outperformed Peers, Accenture Research Finds," Accenture, October 29, 2018, https://newsroom.accenture.com/news/2018/companies-leading-in-disability-inclusion-have-outperformed-peers-accenture-research-finds.

11. "Companies That Lead in Disability Inclusion Outperform Peers Financially, Reveals New Research from Accenture," Accenture, November 27, 2023, https://newsroom.accenture.com/news/2023/companies-that-lead-in-disability-inclusion-outperform-peers-financially-reveals-new-research-from-accenture.

12. "Companies That Lead in Disability Inclusion Outperform Peers Financially."

13. Laura Sherbin and Julia Taylor Kennedy, "Disabilities and Inclusion: US Findings," Center for Talent Innovation, 2017, https://www.talentinnovation.org/_private/assets/DisabilitiesInclusion_KeyFindings-CTI.pdf.

14. Luisa Alemany and Freek Vermeulen, "Disability as a Source of Competitive Advantage," *Harvard Business Review* (July 2023), https://hbr.org/2023/07/disability-as-a-source-of-competitive-advantage.

15. Thomas Aichner, "The Economic Argument for Hiring People with Disabilities," *Humanities and Social Sciences Communications* 8, no. 22 (2021), https://doi.org/10.1057/s41599-021-00707-y.

16. James P. Kaletta, Douglas J. Binks, and Richard Robinson, "Creating an Inclusive Workplace: Integrating Employees with Disabilities into a Distribution Center Environment," *Professional Safety* 57, no. 6 (2012), https://www.letsgettoworkwi.org/wp-content/uploads/2012/09/LGTW-resource-safety-worksite.pdf.

17. "Companies That Lead in Disability Inclusion Outperform Peers Financially."

18. Alemany and Vermeulen, "Disability as a Source of Competitive Advantage."

19. Alemany and Vermeulen.

20. Team Disclo, "ADA Accommodations Readiness Checklist," Disclo, October 10, 2023, https://www.disclo.com/resources/ada-accommodations-readiness-checklist.

21. Jamie Shields, LinkedIn, 2023, https://www.linkedin.com/posts/shieldsjamie_tuesdaythoughts-diversityandinclusion-activity-7132638807291498496-ISNV.

22. Shields.

23. Tara Sophia Mohr, "Why Women Don't Apply for Jobs Unless They're 100% Qualified," *Harvard Business Review*, August 25, 2014, https://hbr.org/2014/08/why-women-dont-apply-for-jobs-unless-theyre-100-qualified.

24. Team Disclo, "ADA Accommodations Readiness Checklist."

25. "Job Listings," Row House Publishing, https://www.rowhousepublishing.com/jobs.

26. Chang Liu, LinkedIn, 2020, https://www.linkedin.com/posts/changliule _neurodiversity-codeswitch-diversity-activity-6712470496803467264-DCAA.

27. Gili Malinsky, "Just 21% of People with Disabilities Were Employed in 2022— How Employers Can Reduce Hiring Bias," CNBC, July 28, 2023, https://www.cnbc .com/2023/07/28/21-percent-of-people-with-disabilities-were-employed-in-2022.html.

28. "Careers," Chani, https://chaninicholas.com/careers/.

Chapter 29: Rethink Accommodations

1. Aubrey Blanche-Sarellano, email interview with the author, January 28, 2024.

2. Rebekah Taussig, "The Disempowering Experience of Flying as a Disabled Person," *Time*, November 1, 2021, https://time.com/6111731/flying-disabled/.

3. Brian Cheung and J. J. McCorvey, "Disabled Workforce Expands Thanks to the Job Boom—and Long Covid," NBC News, March 10, 2023, https://www.nbcnews.com /business/economy/disabled-workforce-expands-thanks-job-boom-long-covid-rcna72803.

4. Kim Samuel, "Remote Jobs Gave People with Disabilities More Opportunities. In-Office Mandates Take Them Away," *USA Today*, October 2, 2023, https://www.usatoday .com/story/opinion/2023/10/02/return-office-work-mandates-accommodate-ada-people -disabilities/70963365007/.

5. "The ADA Accommodations Toolkit for Employers," Disclo, https://www.disclo.com /toolkit.

6. "Costs and Benefits of Accommodation," Job Accommodation Network, updated April 5, 2024, https://askjan.org/topics/costs.cfm.

7. "The ADA Accommodations Toolkit for Employers."

8. "A to Z of Disabilities and Accommodations," Job Accommodation Network, https:// askjan.org/a-to-z.cfm.

9. "Post-Traumatic Stress Disorder (PTSD)," Job Accommodation Network, https://askjan .org/disabilities/Post-Traumatic-Stress-Disorder-PTSD.cfm.

10. Katie Rose Guest Pryal, "Accommodations and Accessibility: What's the Difference?," *Psychology Today*, November 6, 2023, https://www.psychologytoday.com/us/blog /living-neurodivergence/202310/accommodations-and-accessibility-whats-the-difference.

11. "Understanding Accommodations," IRIS Center, Peabody College, Vanderbilt University, https://iris.peabody.vanderbilt.edu/micro-credential/micro-accommodations/p01/.

12. Eric Garcia, email interview with the author, January 17, 2024.

13. Becca Lory Hector, LinkedIn, 2023, https://www.linkedin.com/posts/becca loryhector_disabilityinclusion-deib-inclusive-activity-7135976207401041920-Yggh/.

14. Pryal, "Accommodations and Accessibility."

15. Pryal.

16. Marisa Hamamoto, LinkedIn, 2023, https://www.linkedin.com/posts/marisa hamamoto_autism-ndeam-disability-activity-7123281503563776000-n7Je.

Chapter 30: Build a Disability-Inclusive Work Culture

1. "2023 Disability Equality Index Report," Disability:IN, 2023, https://disabilityin.org/2023-dei-report/.

2. Laurie Henneborn and Chad Jerdee, "Enabling Change," Accenture, 2020, https://www.accenture.com/content/dam/accenture/final/a-com-migration/pdf/pdf-142/Accenture-Enabling-Change-Getting-Equal-2020-Disability-Inclusion-Report-1.pdf.

3. Courtney Connley, "1 in 4 U.S. Adults Have a Disability—and It's Past Time to Make Space for Them," Chief, May 17, 2022, https://chief.com/articles/disability-workplace-inclusion.

4. Connley.

5. Vanessa Ho, "Leaders Who Revealed Their Disabilities Found Unexpected Rewards—and So Did Their Teams," Microsoft, October 1, 2019, https://news.microsoft.com/source/features/diversity-inclusion-leaders-who-revealed-disabilities-found-unexpected-rewards/.

6. Henneborn and Jerdee, "Enabling Change."

7. Yarelbys Túa, email interview with the author, January 29, 2024.

8. Henneborn and Jerdee, "Enabling Change."

9. "ESG and Disability Data," Valuable 500, 2023, https://content.knowledgevision.com/account/9dc0b952-1010-4206-805c-7e1a61f9a960/content/assets/attachment/ESG_and_Disability_Data_white_paper_pdf_1684237211919/ESG_and_Disability_Data_white_paper_02763821-5b88-4cd6-bcc9-8cc2f828bdfe.pdf.

10. Vanessa Ho, "'I Have Dyslexia': A Chief Engineer Spoke Up to Help Others with Learning Disabilities," Microsoft, October 1, 2019, https://news.microsoft.com/source/features/diversity-inclusion/i-have-dyslexia-chief-engineer-spoke-up-help-others-learning-disabilities/.

11. Vanessa Ho, "'This Is Who I Am': How a Top Manager Opened Up About His Mental Illness and Found Compassion," Microsoft, October 1, 2019, https://news.microsoft.com/source/features/diversity-inclusion/who-i-am-top-manager-opened-up-mental-illness-found-compassion/.

12. Samantha Masunaga, "Remote Work Gave Them a Reprieve from Racism. They Don't Want to Go Back," *Los Angeles Times*, August 8, 2023, https://www.latimes.com/business/story/2023-08-08/remote-work-racism-reprieve-return-to-office.

13. Arthur Gwynne, email interview with the author, January 29, 2024.

14. Gwynne.

15. Gabrielle Sinacola, "Salary Transparency Laws by State in 2023," Mosey, June 13, 2023, https://mosey.com/blog/salary-transparency-laws-by-state-best-practices/.

16. Marianne Wilson, "In a First, Walgreens Annual Bonus Plan to Include Disability Rep Metric," *Chain Store Age*, November 10, 2022, https://chainstoreage.com/first-walgreens-annual-bonus-plan-include-disability-rep-metric.

17. Henneborn and Jerdee, "Enabling Change."

18. Vanessa Ho, "'By the Way, I'm Visually Impaired': Sharing Her Disability Helped Others Feel More Welcome at Work," Microsoft, October 1, 2019, https://news.microsoft.com/source/features/diversity-inclusion/im-visually-impaired-sharing-disability-helped-others-feel-more-welcome/.

19. Laura Sherbin and Julia Taylor Kennedy, "Disabilities and Inclusion: US Findings," Center for Talent Innovation, 2017, https://www.talentinnovation.org/_private/assets/DisabilitiesInclusion_KeyFindings-CTI.pdf.

20. "Building a Career at Bloomberg: Department Changers," Bloomberg, September 29, 2023, https://www.bloomberg.com/company/stories/building-a-career-at-bloomberg-department-changers/.

21. "The Mental Health of People with Disabilities," Centers for Disease Control and Prevention, last reviewed November 20, 2023, https://www.cdc.gov/ncbddd/disabilityandhealth/features/mental-health-for-all.html.

22. Henneborn and Jerdee, "Enabling Change."

23. Henneborn and Jerdee.

24. Jessica Lopez, LinkedIn, 2022, https://www.linkedin.com/posts/realjessl_today-is-my-last-day-at-diversability-a-activity-6932808643662819328-lwUT/.

Chapter 31: Cater to Disabled Customers

1. "Annual Report 2020," Return on Disability, 2020, https://www.rod-group.com/research-insights/annual-report-2020/.

2. Michelle Yin, Dahlia Shaewitz, Cynthia Overton, and Deeza-Mae Smith, "A Hidden Market: The Purchasing Power of Working-Age Adults with Disabilities," American Institutes for Research, April 17, 2018, https://www.air.org/resource/report/hidden-market-purchasing-power-working-age-adults-disabilities.

3. Taylor Lindsay-Noel, @AccessByTay, TikTok, December 12, 2023, https://www.tiktok.com/@accessbytay/video/7311863607703244037.

4. Taylor Lindsay-Noel, @AccessByTay, TikTok, December 28, 2023, https://www.tiktok.com/@accessbytay/video/7317751664595848454.

5. Lindsay-Noel, December 12, 2023.

6. Denise Malloy Deaderick, Cedric Clark, and Alvis Washington, "Small Changes, Big Impact: Sensory-Friendly Hours Return," Walmart, November 7, 2023, https://corporate.walmart.com/news/2023/11/07/small-changes-big-impact-sensory-friendly-hours-return.

7. Andrew Pulrang, "5 Simple Ways to Make Your Business More Welcoming to Disabled Customers," Forbes, July 22, 2022, https://www.forbes.com/sites/andrewpulrang/2022/07/22/5-simple-ways-to-make-your-business-more-welcoming-to-disabled-customers/.

8. Pulrang.

9. Sonia Thompson, "What Walmart's New Sensory-Friendly Hours Mean for Your Brand," Forbes, November 30, 2023, https://www.forbes.com/sites/soniathompson/2023/11/30/what-walmarts-new-sensory-friendly-hours-means-for-your-brand/.

10. Thompson.

11. Meryl K. Evans, email interview with the author, January 19, 2024.

12. Karina Boycheva, "Customer Service for People with Disabilities," Deque, June 30, 2020, https://www.deque.com/blog/customer-service-for-people-with-disabilities/.

13. "Diverse Perspectives: People with Disabilities Fulfilling Your Business Goals," US Department of Labor, https://www.dol.gov/agencies/odep/publications/fact-sheets/diverse-perspectives-people-with-disabilities-fulfilling-your-business-goals.

Chapter 32: Support Disability Entrepreneurship

1. Keely Cat-Wells, LinkedIn, 2023, https://www.linkedin.com/posts/keelycatwells_disabilityrights-enterpreneurship-activity-7139976226344980480-7Yn8/.

2. Keely Cat-Wells, LinkedIn, 2022, https://www.linkedin.com/posts/keelycatwells_inclusionmatters-disability-business-activity-6759827645246111744-R-Bz.

3. Diego Mariscal, email interview with the author, January 29, 2024.

4. "The Economic Impact of Certified Disability-Owned Business Enterprises," Disability:IN, July 12, 2022, https://disabilityin.org/resource/the-economic-impact-of-certified-disability-owned-business-enterprises/.

5. Andrew Gurza, @AndrewGurza6, Twitter, September 8, 2021, https://twitter.com/andrewgurza6/status/1435606415247388673.

6. Cory Lee, email interview with the author, January 24, 2024.

7. Lee.

8. Gus Alexiou, "Disabled Founders 400 Times Less Likely to Receive VC Funding, Says New Report," Forbes, August 15, 2023, https://www.forbes.com/sites/gusalexiou/2023/08/15/disabled-founders-400-times-less-likely-to-receive-vc-funding-says-new-report/.

9. "Transforming Opportunities & Outcomes for Disabled Entrepreneurs," Access-2Funding, 2023, https://static1.squarespace.com/staic/619e1d7a522f9748f55d6a17/t/638b7007b3b4ae3a0159b28e/1670082578331/Access2Funding.pdf.

10. "Transforming Opportunities & Outcomes for Disabled Entrepreneurs."

11. Alexiou, "Disabled Founders 400 Times Less Likely to Receive VC Funding."

12. Alexiou.

13. "Transforming Opportunities & Outcomes for Disabled Entrepreneurs."

14. "The Economic Impact of Certified Disability-Owned Business Enterprises."

15. Diego Mariscal, "Entrepreneurship Is a Pathway for Founders with Disabilities to Address Wealth and Employment Gaps," Ewing Marion Kauffman Foundation, October 26, 2022, https://www.kauffman.org/currents/2gether-international-entrepreneurs-with-disabilities/.

16. Mariscal, "Entrepreneurship Is a Pathway."

17. Christine Hall, "Wheel the World Grabs $6M to Offer Guaranteed Accessibility, Price Match for Hotel Rooms," March 9, 2023, Tech Crunch, https://techcrunch.com/2023/03/09/wheel-the-world-travel-disabilities/.

18. "Empowering People with Disabilities to Become Entrepreneurs," Viscardi Center, May 17, 2023, https://www.viscardicenter.org/empowering-people-with-disabilities-to-become-entrepreneurs/.

19. "Entrepreneurship," Job Accommodation Network, https://askjan.org/topics/Entrepreneurship.cfm.

20. "Helping Small Business Is Our Job," Small Business Hub, https://www.disabilitysmallbusiness.org/.

21. "Plan to Achieve Self-Support (PASS)," Social Security Administration, https://www.ssa.gov/disabilityresearch/wi/pass.htm.

22. Ingrid Lunden, "Airbnb Buys 'Airbnb for Disabled People' Startup Accomable in Accessibility Upgrade," TechCrunch, November 16, 2017, https://techcrunch.com/2017/11/16/airbnb-buys-accomable-a-specialist-in-travel-listings-for-disabled-people/.

23. "Keely Cat-Wells," Forbes, https://www.forbes.com/sites/keelycatwells/.

24. Emily Ladau and Kate Caldwell, "2023 Disability Holiday Gift Guide," EmilyLadau.com, November 24, 2023, https://emilyladau.com/2023/11/2023-disability-holiday-gift-guide/.

25. Diversability, @Diversability, Instagram, November 25, 2023, https://www.instagram.com/p/C0FkT_Evzxp/.

26. Jessica Lopez, LinkedIn, January 2, 2024, https://www.linkedin.com/posts/realjessl_disability-disabilityinclusion-accessibility-activity-7147759879649206273-s-Ws.

27. John Kitching, "Entrepreneurship and Self-Employment by People with Disabilities," OECD, 2014, https://www.oecd.org/cfe/leed/background-report-people-disabilities.pdf; "Self-Employment for People with Disabilities," Office of Disability Employment Policy, US Department of Labor, December 15, 2013, https://www.dol.gov/sites/dolgov/files/odep/pdf/2014startup.pdf.

28. "Small Business Ownership by People with Disabilities: Challenges and Opportunities," National Disability Institute, April 2022, https://www.nationaldisabilityinstitute.org/wp-content/uploads/2022/07/ndi-small-business-research-report-executive-summary.pdf.

Chapter 33: Advocate with Disabled People

1. Amy Gaeta, "Introducing the Radical Disability Allyship Issue," Invisible Disability Project, May 1, 2020, https://www.invisibledisabilityproject.org/new-blog/2020/5/1/vud3upelofww0hjc92i3fy8ty9r0ez.

2. "Allyship and Advocacy: What Is the Best Way to Offer Active Support in the Workplace?," Mursion, March 21, 2023, https://www.mursion.com/articles/allyship-and-advocacy/.

3. "Allyship and Advocacy."

4. Nina Overdorff, "Nothing About Us Without Us: Input from People with Disabilities," Equidox, April 8, 2020, https://equidox.co/blog/nothing-about-us-without-us-input-from-people-with-disabilities/.

5. Stephanie Watson, "How Much Do Cochlear Implants Cost?," Forbes Health, August 31, 2023, https://www.forbes.com/health/hearing-aids/cochlear-implants-cost/.

6. Overdorff, "Nothing About Us Without Us."

7. Marc Maurer, "Opportunity, Danger, and the Balance of Risk," National Federation of the Blind, July 8, 2011, https://nfb.org/sites/www.nfb.org/files/images/nfb/publications /convent/banque2011.htm.

8. Amanda Morris, "For Blind Internet Users, the Fix Can Be Worse Than the Flaws," *New York Times*, July 13, 2022, https://www.nytimes.com/2022/07/13/technology /ai-web-accessibility.html.

9. David Gibson, "Why Website Accessibility Overlay Toolbars, Widgets & Plugins Fail Compliance," Accessibility.Works, updated January 19, 2024, https://www.accessibility .works/blog/avoid-accessibility-overlay-tools-toolbar-plugins/.

10. Overlay Fact Sheet, https://overlayfactsheet.com/.

11. Gibson, "Why Website Accessibility Overlay Toolbars, Widgets & Plugins Fail Compliance."

12. Imani Barbarin, "Disabled People Have an Ally Problem: They Need to Stop Talking for Us," *Crutches & Spice*, May 15, 2018, https://crutchesandspice.com/2018/05/15 /disabled-people-have-an-ally-problem-they-need-to-stop-talking-for-us/.

13. Barbarin.

14. Holly Tuke, "How to Be a Good Disability Ally," *Life of a Blind Girl*, July 17, 2022, https://lifeofablindgirl.com/2022/07/17/how-to-be-a-good-disability-ally/.

15. Andrew Pulrang, "3 Ways Disability Allyship Can Go Off Track," *Forbes*, April 14, 2021, https://www.forbes.com/sites/andrewpulrang/2021/04/14/3-ways-disability -allyship-can-go-off-track/.

16. Ryan Prior, email interview with the author, January 19, 2024.

17. Drew Dakessian, "How to Be a Good Ally to Disabled People," World Institute on Disability, https://wid.org/how-to-be-a-good-ally-to-disabled-people/.

18. Joseline Raja Vora, "Amplifying Their Voice by Lowering Ours: What It Means to Be a Disability Ally," NACCHO, May 14, 2021, https://www.naccho.org/blog/articles /amplifying-their-voice-by-lowering-ours-what-it-means-to-be-a-disability-ally.

19. Andrew Pulrang, "5 Simple Ways to Support Disability Activism," *Forbes*, May 15, 2021, https://www.forbes.com/sites/andrewpulrang/2021/05/15/5-simple-ways-to -support-disability-activism/.

20. Jess Cochran, "How to Be a Disability Ally," Forward, July 21, 2022, https://fas.org.au /how-to-be-a-disability-ally/.

Chapter 34: Get Civically Engaged

1. Tiffany Yu, LinkedIn, 2022, https://www.linkedin.com/posts/tiffanyayu_antiableism -disability-ada32-activity-6948379752646803456-wpX8.

2. Tiffany Yu, @ImTiffanyYu, TikTok, March 24, 2023, https://www.tiktok.com/@im tiffanyyu/video/7214184493958319406.

3. Aliya Schneider, "Philly Voters Approve Ballot Question Making Office for the People with Disabilities Permanent," *Philadelphia Inquirer*, November 7, 2023, https://www.inquirer.com/politics/election/office-people-disabilities-ballot-question-2023-20231107.html.

4. Nico Meyering, @NameStartsWithN, Instagram, December 16, 2023, https://www.instagram.com/p/C060BRkrbKX/.

5. Nico Meyering, email interview with the author, January 28, 2024.

6. Dominique Sighoko, Anne Marie Murphy, Bethliz Irizarry, Garth Rauscher, Carol Ferrans, and David Ansell, "Changes in the Racial Disparity in Breast Cancer Mortality in the Ten US Cities with the Largest African American Populations from 1999 to 2013: The Reduction in Breast Cancer Mortality Disparity in Chicago," *Cancer Causes & Control* 28, no. 6 (2017): 563–568, https://doi.org/10.1007/s10552-017-0878-y.

7. Tiffany Yu, @ImTiffanyYu, Instagram, December 13, 2021, https://www.instagram.com/p/CXbh1gzJyMs/.

8. Isabel Mavrides-Calderón, email interview with the author, January 30, 2024.

9. Mavrides-Calderón.

10. Talia Lakritz, "US Paralympic Athletes Will Receive Equal Pay for the First Time at the Tokyo Olympics," *Business Insider*, July 21, 2021, https://www.businessinsider.com/tokyo-olympics-paralympic-athletes-equal-pay-2021-7.

11. Michael Wittner, "Ruderman Foundation Helps Secure Equal Pay for Paralympians," *Jewish Journal*, October 4, 2018, https://jewishjournal.org/2018/10/04/ruderman-foundation-helps-secure-equal-pay-for-paralympians/.

12. US Paralympics and IPC, "Paralympians to Earn Equal Payouts as Olympians in the USA," International Paralympic Committee, September 24, 2018, https://www.paralympic.org/news/paralympians-earn-equal-payouts-olympians-usa.

13. Keely Cat-Wells, @Keely_Cat_Wells, Instagram, December 15, 2023, https://www.instagram.com/p/C04xYoGODqZ/.

14. Ned S. Levi, "Airlines Damage Passenger Wheelchairs—More Than 200 a Week," Travelers United, August 7, 2023, https://www.travelersunited.org/the-time-is-now-for-the-airlines-to-stop-damaging-so-many-passenger-wheelchairs/.

15. "Take Action for Accessible Air Travel," Paralyzed Veterans of America, 2023, https://pva.org/research-resources/tips-tools-resources/.

16. "Supplemental Security Income (SSI) and the 'Spousal Deeming' Marriage Penalty," Disability Rights Education & Defense Fund, August 22, 2022, https://dredf.org/2022/08/22/supplemental-security-income-ssi-and-the-spousal-deeming-marriage-penalty/.

17. "Brown, Cassidy Announce First Bipartisan, Bicameral Bill in Decades to Update Supplemental Security Income Program," Sherrod Brown, US Senator for Ohio, September 12, 2023, https://www.brown.senate.gov/newsroom/press/release/brown-cassidy-announce-first-bipartisan-bicameral-bill-in-decades-to-update-supplemental-security-income-program.

18. Cat-Wells, Instagram.

19. Alonzo Plough, "How Can We Further Progress on Disability Rights?," Robert Wood Johnson Foundation, July 19, 2023, https://www.rwjf.org/en/insights/blog/2023/07/how-can-we-further-progress-on-disability-rights.html.

20. Tiffany Yu, "018: Disability Pride, ADA30 & Diversability's D-30 Disability Impact List ft. Alex Locust (Glamputee)," *Tiffany & Yu*, July 21, 2021, https://www.tiffanyyu.com/podcast/018.

21. "Take Action to Stop Care Rationing," #NoBodyIsDisposable, https://nobodyisdisposable.org/stop-care-rationing/.

22. "Part 3: Advocacy! Taking Action for the Human Rights of People with Disabilities," Human Rights Library, University of Minnesota, http://hrlibrary.umn.edu/edumat/hreduseries/TB6/html/Part3.html.

23. "Taking Action: How to Be an Effective Advocate for Disability Rights," Keri Gray Consulting Group, October 4, 2023, https://withkeri.com/how-to-be-an-effective-advocate-for-disability-rights/.

Conclusion: The Anti-Ableist Manifesto

1. Michael F. Leonen, "Etiquette for Activists," *Yes!* magazine, May 21, 2004, https://www.yesmagazine.org/issue/hope-conspiracy/2004/05/21/etiquette-for-activists.